Modes of Viewing in
Hellenistic Poetry and Art

Publication of this volume has been made possible
in large part through the generous support and
enduring vision of Warren G. Moon.

Modes of Viewing in Hellenistic Poetry and Art

Graham Zanker

THE UNIVERSITY OF WISCONSIN PRESS

The University of Wisconsin Press
1930 Monroe Street
Madison, Wisconsin 53711

www.wisc.edu/wisconsinpress/

3 Henrietta Street
London WC2E 8LU, England

5   4   3   2   1

Library of Congress Cataloging-in-Publication Data
Zanker, G. (Graham), 1947–
    Modes of viewing in Hellenistic poetry and art / Graham Zanker.
    p.   cm. — (Wisconsin studies in classics)
  Includes bibliographical references and index.
  ISBN 0-299-19450-7 (cloth : alk. paper)
    1. Greek poetry, Hellenistic — History and criticism.   2. Visual perception
in literature.   3. Art and literature — Greece.   4. Point of view (Literature)
5. Description (Rhetoric)   6. Rhetoric, Ancient.   7. Art, Hellenistic.   I. Title.
II. Series.
PA3083 .Z36   2003
881'.0109 — dc21   2003005678

For Tom and Hugo

Contents

Illustrations

Acknowledgments

In this book I explore the ways in which the visual arts and the poetry of the Hellenistic age direct the viewer and the reader to look at the subjects that they portray in their respective media. I therefore hope that what I have to say will be of interest to two audiences: on the one hand, students of Hellenistic art and archaeology, and, on the other, students of Hellenistic poetry. The mindsets, presuppositions, and approaches of these two groups are often very different, and if I have made my arguments and findings clear to both, I will be very happy. It seems to me that students in the two fields have a lot to learn from pooling their resources.

Many institutions and friends helped me in the course of research and writing. The German Academic Exchange Service, with its characteristic generosity, supported two study-visits to Tübingen's unstintingly hospitable Philologisches Seminar at the beginning and the end of the project (1998 and 2002). This support also led to two stays at the German Archaeological Institute in Rome, where the directors, Paul Zanker and Dieter Mertens, made me welcome and put the Institute's uniquely comprehensive photograph collection at my disposal. I am especially indebted to Giorgia Migatta, who gave much kind and practical help in securing the photographs. A Summer Fellowship at the Harvard Center for Hellenic Studies in Washington, D.C., in 2002 allowed me to prepare the final manuscript for the press in the most congenial and helpful circumstances. Two eight-month periods of study-leave granted by the University of Canterbury gave me vital time for uninterrupted research and writing. The Department

of Classics at Canterbury gave a generous contribution toward
the costs I incurred in purchasing the illustrations and permis-
sions.

Paul Zanker helped shape my thinking at its initial stages.
Richard Kannicht was a critical and constructive listener on many
occasions and supported the whole undertaking from beginning
to end. Peter Parsons always gave encouragement and support
when it counted. Alan Shapiro, Bettina Bergmann, and Andrew
Stewart read the whole manuscript; their generosity and colle-
giality were phenomenal, and their contribution was fundamen-
tal to the presentation of the archaeological side of my argument.
Marco Fantuzzi kindly directed me to crucial discussions of Hel-
lenistic epigram that appeared just after I submitted the final
manuscript. The readers for the University of Wisconsin Press
gave extensive and welcome advice, all of which I have gratefully
adopted. Patrick O'Sullivan provided a judicious second opinion
on specific points. My students at the University of Canterbury
patiently listened as I picked at my doubts. They also commented
helpfully and put a human face on my readers.

My final debt is to my family: to my wife, Ruth, whose enthu-
siasm for things visual and written enlivened proceedings enor-
mously, and to my sons, Tom and Hugo, whose intelligent curio-
sity about my work added agreeably to my sense that I was on to
something interesting. I affectionately dedicate this book to these
fine young men.

All translations are my own.

Abbreviations

Standard reference works and collections or editions of ancient authors are cited as follows. Journals and monograph series are cited in full in the Bibliography.

Bastianini-Gallazzi	Bastianini, G., and Gallazzi, C., with the collaboration of C. Austin. *Posidippo di Pella: Epigrammi (P. Mil. Vogl. VIII 309). Papiri dell' Università degli Studi di Milano* 8. Milan, 2001.
Campbell	Campbell, D. A. *Greek Lyric.* Vol. 3. Cambridge, Mass., 1991.
DAI	Deutsches Archäologisches Institut, Rome.
FGE	Page, D. L. *Further Greek Epigrams: Epigrams before A.D. 50 from the Greek Anthology and Other Sources, Not Included in "Hellenistic Epigrams" or "The Garland of Philip."* Cambridge, 1981.
HE	Gow, A. S. F., and Page, D. L. *The Greek Anthology: Hellenistic Epigrams.* Cambridge, 1965.
Hollis	Hollis, A. S. *Callimachus: Hecale.* Oxford, 1990.
LIMC	*Lexicon Iconographicum Mythologiae Classicae.* 8 vols., with 2 index vols. Zurich 1981–99.
Pfeiffer	Pfeiffer, R. *Callimachus.* Vol. 1. Oxford, 1949.

Powell Powell, J. U. *Collectanea Alexandrina: Reliquiae Minores Poetarum Graecorum Aetatis Ptolemaicae 323–146 A.C. Epicorum, Elegiacorum, Lyricorum, Ethicorum.* Oxford, 1925.

Schmidt Schmidt, W. *Herons von Alexandria Druckwerke und Automatentheater.* Leipzig, 1899.

SH Lloyd-Jones, H., and Parsons, P. J. *Supplementum Hellenisticum.* Berlin and New York, 1983.

Spengel Spengel, L. *Rhetores Graeci.* 3 vols. Leipzig, 1853–56.

Usher Usher, S. *Dionysius of Halicarnassus: The Critical Essays.* Vol. 1. Cambridge, Mass., 1974.

Modes of Viewing in
Hellenistic Poetry and Art

1

Aims, Approaches, and Samples

What processes were at work when hearers or readers of poetry in the Hellenistic period envisaged the scenes presented by the poets of their day? How did people in that period view contemporary works of art? And to what extent are we entitled to talk in terms of analogies between the two types of viewing — the one based on words which create a picture in the mind's eye, the other centering on images which one can view directly and move around spatially? This book aims to examine certain aspects of these questions. If it transpires that there is indeed a common process of constructing mental images or relating to actual *objets d'art* which can be differentiated from the habits current in the fifth or fourth centuries B.C., we shall have learned some important lessons about the function of poetry and art in the Hellenistic age and about the period's poetic and artistic strategies. Quite apart from that, there is the considerable intrinsic interest involved in discovering more about how an age and a culture as sophisticated as the Hellenistic advanced the experience of viewing in Western poetry and art.

In pursuing this aim, I will often use the sister arts of the Hellenistic period, by which I mean its poetry and visual art, to see what light they may shed on one another in the matter of viewing. Often, too, the results of modern research in one field will be applied to the other. New analyses by the art historians of the period will enable us to see the images of its poets from unexpected new angles, and, conversely, some of the poetic techniques characteristic of the age will be tested for their applicability to the reconstruction of the Hellenistic way of viewing painting and

3

sculpture. In essence, the poetry of the period and some of its strategies will help us to place the tone of certain works of art, while art and some of its strategies will literally open our eyes to the poets' unprecedented techniques of visual description and narrative.

Framed in these terms, the aim of this book is not as narrow as that of the chapter in T. B. L. Webster's *Hellenistic Poetry and Art* which was concerned with the influences of the one art on the other in that period.[1] Admittedly, this question will have to be addressed on occasion, but of greater general significance is a much broader issue: the common modes of viewing that I think can be detected in the sister arts in the period. Nor do I intend such a wide overview of the Hellenistic aesthetic as attempted more recently by B. H. Fowler,[2] who in practice offers not so much a definition of the Hellenistic aesthetic as a description of the shared subject matter, genres, styles, and modes of Hellenistic art and literature. The object of my undertaking is more specialized, with the emphasis placed firmly on modes of viewing in Hellenistic poetry and art. To a coverage of Hellenistic taste in general as offered by John Onians' *Art and Thought in the Hellenistic World*[3] I have likewise no pretension, stimulating though I have found it many times. I have, by contrast, found a highly sympathetic approach in an essay by Andrew Stewart[4] which forcefully and illuminatingly pursues the analogy of Asianism in Hellenistic rhetorical theory and the "Hellenistic Baroque." Stewart's literary criteria and terminology are strikingly helpful in our understanding of this much misunderstood and unquestionably vital facet of Hellenistic art. In the present study, the rhetorical treatises on (or, more often, fulminations against) Asianism have their counterparts in the abundant pictorially descriptive poetic texts of the early third century, from which we can infer what was valued in viewing, although comparatively little in the way of direct formulation has survived.

The underlying contention here is that if a Hellenistic poetic description of a person, an animal, the weather, a scene, or an *objet d'art* adopts a particular way of viewing, we have independent evidence for the habits of viewing that Hellenistic people would have brought to their contemplation of representational art. The Hellenistic poets have set down in words the ways in which their contemporaries observed works of art — or rather, perhaps, their "putative" contemporaries, since we are forced to deal with generalities when talking about the "viewership" or "audience" of any age. Whether or not the putative viewers verbalized what they saw, their words are available to us only when Quintilian, for example, gives us his direct opinions of the periods and artists of Greek sculpture.

These observations feed into the modern debate over "visuality" and "vision." "Visuality" denotes the way of seeing in a particular historical period; "vision," the way of seeing which essentializes and universalizes. For the control that the written response or way of viewing provides will guide our reconstruction of how Hellenistic people viewed things in a way which, even if imperfectly, can lift us out of the solipsism of "our vision" into the "visuality" of another age, and perhaps even alert us to modes of viewing far more exacting than modern vision theory might lead us to suppose.[5]

In my use of the term "Hellenistic," I have adopted the now generally accepted parameters, the death of Alexander and the battle of Actium. More problematic is the question of contact versus discontinuity between the Hellenistic and earlier periods in poetry and art. Here my rationale will be to compare Hellenistic texts and art objects with their antecedents in order to identify what is specifically Hellenistic about Hellenistic viewing. Theocritus' commentary on the boxing match between Polydeuces and Amycus in *Idyll* 22 will be compared with the Polyphemus episode in *Odyssey* 9; the figure of Aphrodite in Hellenistic poetry will be compared with the late Classical Cnidia of Praxiteles; the Suicidal Gaul will be set in relation to its predecessors as a victory monument; and so on.

A special question concerns the relationship between viewing in what we would call "pre-Hellenistic" poets and artists and in their Hellenistic successors. It is well known, for example, that Hellenistic poets saw "pre-Hellenistic" poets like Antimachus or Erinna as stylistic precursors; and clearly the Melian Venus gains particular meaning if we know that her sculptor consciously located her in the tradition of the Cnidia. (To that extent, both Hellenistic poetry and art are "intertextual.") Poets like Antimachus and Erinna survive in fragmentary state and are of little value to a study of viewing. On the other hand, what are we to say of Lysippus' statue of Heracles resting from the labor of the Augean stables and the depiction of a similar off-moment from the same episode in the pseudo-Theocritean *Idyll* 25? Some forty to fifty years must have separated the statue from the poem.

Here I think it will emerge that the Hellenistic poets and artists may have consciously or unconsciously taken up cues in the imaging of their more immediate predecessors and developed their modes of viewing to a greater—even an unprecedented—degree. And this matter of degree will be found vital in defining what is Hellenistic about Hellenistic viewing. In short, in the Hellenistic poetic and artistic modes of viewing as in so much else, there is contact with the Hellenic past in that its motifs and techniques are self-consciously developed and extended; but there is self-definition and discontinuity precisely in the degree of that development and extension.

This point can now be graphically illustrated by a series of poems from the papyrus called the New Posidippus. Entitled ἀνδριαντοποιικά (*andriantopoiika*, "epigrams on statues"), it features one epigram of particular interest in this connection—a piece on a self-portrait of the sixth-century B.C. sculptor Theodorus of Samos (X 38–XI 5 Bastianini-Gallazzi). According to Pliny at *Natural History* 34.83, the artist depicted himself holding a miniature chariot in his left hand and a file in his right. Posidippus praises Theodorus' painstaking precision in rendering the chariot and its parts, just as Pliny was later to praise Theodorus' verisimilitude (*similitudo*) and fineness (*subtilitas*). Posidippus clearly sees Theodorus as a forerunner of the realism particularly associated in these poems with Lysippus, while presenting the latter and other sculptors active just before or at the dawn of the Hellenistic age, Myron and Hecataeus, as novel in their outstanding capacity for the lifelike quality.[6]

Having thus outlined the limits and main thrust of my inquiry, I offer as an obvious entrée into it an examination of Hellenistic poetry's practice of describing works of art, actual, imaginary, or situated at some point in between.[7] Later Greek rhetoric knew of such passages as ἐκφράσεις ἀγαλμάτων (*ekphraseis agalmatôn*, "descriptions of works of art"). These *ekphraseis agalmatôn* were a subcategory of ἔκφρασις (*ekphrasis*), or vividly pictorial literary description, whose domain was felt to be primarily historiography and poetry. The fifth-century A.D. Greek rhetor Nicolaus is the first author attested to have discussed such descriptions as a separate category of *ekphrasis*.[8] However, the term is now conventionally limited to this kind of description, sometimes with undesirable effects. *Ekphrasis* in the original, broader sense—the ocular presentation in literature of any phenomenon in nature and culture—is obviously of greater general significance for a study like the present one.[9]

We may, however, for the moment allow that poetic descriptions of works of art occupy a special place in an inquiry into modes of viewing. That a study of *ekphraseis* of works of art can tell us an enormous amount about how a society views things is demonstrated by Jaś Elsner in his use of Philostratus and Cebes to illustrate the parameters for Roman viewers.[10] It is significant and useful to be reminded, for example, that *ekphraseis* may well be bad guides for reconstructing paintings and so forth because they emulate, rather than merely reproducing in words, the objects of art which they describe, but that in the hands of a Philostratus the literary form taught the viewer how to look at art. It provided a context from the viewer's own experience (of Homer, for instance) and tested the boundaries of illusionism by exposing its ultimate failure to generate a relationship between the observer and the observed, however willing the observer may have been to maintain it. It is also valuable to know that at the same period in time Cebes presented his *Tabula* as a rejection of common-sense expectations about the world of the beholder's physical experience, in accordance with an allegorical system whereby the act of correct viewing itself entails a truth and salvation. And all this was being thought while Pliny was enthusiastically gathering anecdotes like the one about Zeuxis' grapes (*NH* 35.65).

What precise advantages may we hope to gain by considering *ekphraseis agalmatôn* in the context of this study? They may, first, be expected to show an explicit, verbally expressed response to viewing which we cannot hope to have in the artistic monuments themselves or the copies by which we know them, though, if the aims of objects of visual art can be reconstructed with any security, and if they dovetail with what we explicitly learn from a poet's description, the evidence of art will corroborate what we learn about viewing from poetic descriptions. And if the testimony of poetic descriptions coincides with perceived aims of *objets d'art*, it will help corroborate our interpretations of painting and sculpture where the aims are not verbally expressed.

Second, the Greek rhetors regarded *ekphrasis agalmatôn* as a means of teaching their students how to view art.[11] This didactic aim is not present in the descriptions of works of art in the poetry of the Hellenistic period, but the dual process which Elsner observed can be found there: the object of art is fitted into the viewer's knowledge and experience and thereby changes both the sum of the viewer's knowledge and the meaning of the art object.[12] This process, inherent in the viewing of visual art, is paralleled in the theory of *ekphrasis*, for *ekphrasis* depicts material objects, but, by invoking the audience's *phantasia*, it can also go beyond the surface to a deeper reality which the audience is invited to impose, thus changing the meaning of the description.[13] With Philostratus, moreover, the audience is presented with the ecphrast's "reading in," designed precisely in order to channel the audience's perception and the work's meaning in new directions.[14]

Third, in Hellenistic poetry there is — particularly in the case of *ekphraseis agalmatôn* — an assumption that the describing poet expects his reading viewer to put in some of the work. It will be interesting to see what kind of work is meant. Supplementation and the audience engagement it engendered were well understood and actively commended in Hellenistic literary criticism, and later criticism came to expect them in both poetry and art. We have it on the authority of the second- or first-century B.C. rhetorical treatise attributed to Demetrius of Phalerum[15] that Theophrastus himself advised orators not to tell all the details at great length and with minute precision, but leave some for the hearer to comprehend and supplement for himself (λογίζεσθαι ἐξ αὐτοῦ); the listener will in this way be disposed to act as a witness (*On Style* 222). Earlier in the same treatise, the author recommends indirect and allegorical expression, for a modicum of latitude means that "each person makes his own conjecture" (ἄλλος εἰκάζει ἄλλο τι: 100). In this context it is interesting to note that Lucian at *How to Write History* 57 criticizes precisely the poets of the Alexandrian movement like Callimachus, Euphorion, and Parthenius for descriptive prolixity: "If Parthenius, Euphorion, or Callimachus were speaking, how many words would it take them to bring the water up to Tantalus' lips or to set Ixion's wheel spinning?" In Lucian's judgment these Hellenistic poets cannot leave anything to the reader's imagination. It will be useful to examine to what extent he had a point.

Be that as it may, in later criticism of poetry and art, as Fritz Graf points out, Dio Chrysostom (12.55–83) prized ἐνάργεια (*enargeia*, "visual vividness") as a means whereby poetry could outstrip art, since it allows the mind to tolerate an unreal subject like the figure of Eris described by Homer at *Iliad* 4.442–43, in a way in which an artist could never hope to succeed.[16] Similarly, Peter von Blanckenhagen[17] argues that the mimesis of Classical art, limited to the seen, gives way to the *phantasia* of Philostratus' *Life of Apollonius* 2.19, whereby the unseen can be pictured, with Hellenistic art providing the link because of the demands it makes on the viewer to supplement material. Of course, Erika Simon[18] is right to point out that Homer's description of Achilles' shield and Aeschylus' description of the shields in the *Seven against Thebes* presuppose that their audiences will exercise their powers of imagination, so that the activity is attested far earlier in literature than in fine art. On the other hand, in the Hellenistic period which is the subject of this book, there is perhaps surprisingly little evidence of the conscious thought that literary descriptions of the visual, especially explicit descriptions of art objects, might compete with representational art's creation of visual images. An index of this is provided by the so-called ecphrastic epigrams, which by and large offer only minimal description of the works of art they celebrate, preferring instead to interpret them. We do not encounter a self-conscious program of emulation in such explicit form until the Second Sophistic and beyond.[19] But it is the very explicitness of the discussions of *ekphrasis agalmatôn* which particularly brings to a head considerations on the matter of audience participation which are vital to any attempt to reconstruct Hellenistic approaches to the acts of viewing and imaging in both poetry and art.

Fourth, the theme of admiring illusionism in the visual arts is obviously a commonplace in Hellenistic *ekphraseis agalmatôn*, but it is permeated by the consideration that *ekphrasis agalmatôn* is the crucial area in which the limits of illusionism are challenged and exposed: the gaps between the object, its image, and the observer are unbridgeable.[20] This rider makes the analysis of poetic description of art and the art in which the lifelike quality can be descried more interesting than the traditional understanding of them allows.

To illustrate how poetry may enhance our understanding of how Hellenistic readers of poetry and observers of visual art actually viewed mental or plastic images, and to give a specimen of how strikingly analogous were the processes of viewing in the sister arts, I have chosen a well-known passage, the description of the Goatherd's cup in Theocritus' first *Idyll* (27–56). As an *ekphrasis agalmatôn,* the cup description is a potentially valuable source of verbally articulated evidence for Hellenistic viewing: apart from descriptions in poetry like it we have no other contemporary verbal evidence whatsoever. The questions of the disposition of the scenes on the cup and its (probable) inspiration from actual art works[21] mercifully do not concern us here as much as the individual images and how they are presented to the mind's eye. I shall therefore concentrate exclusively on the lines describing the three scenes on the cup (32–54). If the description of a work of art, even if it were to be proved indisputably fictive, can give us insights into Hellenistic habits of imaging and viewing, we may widen our inquiry to include poetic *ekphraseis* in general, and we would incidentally have some lead into how the painters and sculptors of the period expected their viewers to experience their products.

ἔντοσθεν δὲ γυνά, τι θεῶν δαίδαλμα, τέτυκται,
ἀσκητὰ πέπλῳ τε καὶ ἄμπυκι· πὰρ δέ οἱ ἄνδρες
καλὸν ἐθειράζοντες ἀμοιβαδὶς ἄλλοθεν ἄλλος
νεικείουσ' ἐπέεσσι· τὰ δ' οὐ φρενὸς ἅπτεται αὐτᾶς·   35
ἀλλ' ὅκα μὲν τῆνον ποτιδέρκεται ἄνδρα γέλαισα,
ἄλλοκα δ' αὖ ποτὶ τὸν ῥιπτεῖ νόον· οἳ δ' ὑπ' ἔρωτος
δηθὰ κυλοιδιόωντες ἐτώσια μοχθίζοντι.
τοῖς δὲ μετὰ γριπεύς τε γέρων πέτρα τε τέτυκται
λεπράς, ἐφ' ᾇ σπεύδων μέγα δίκτυον ἐς βόλον ἕλκει   40
ὁ πρέσβυς, κάμνοντι τὸ κάρτερον ἀνδρὶ ἐοικώς.
φαίης κεν γυίων νιν ὅσον σθένος ἐλλοπιεύειν,
ὧδέ οἱ ᾠδήκαντι κατ' αὐχένα πάντοθεν ἶνες
καὶ πολιῷ ἐόντι· τὸ δὲ σθένος ἄξιον ἄβας.
τυτθὸν δ' ὅσσον ἄπωθεν ἀλιτρύτοιο γέροντος   45
περκναῖσι σταφυλαῖσι καλὸν βέβριθεν ἀλωά,
τὰν ὀλίγος τις κῶρος ἐφ' αἱμασιαῖσι φυλάσσει
ἥμενος· ἀμφὶ δέ νιν δύ' ἀλώπεκες, ἃ μὲν ἀν' ὄρχως

φοιτῆ σινομένα τὰν τρώξιμον, ἃ δ᾽ ἐπὶ πήρᾳ
πάντα δόλον τεύχοισα τὸ παιδίον οὐ πρὶν ἀνησεῖν   50
φατὶ πρὶν ἢ ἀκράτιστον ἐπὶ ξηροῖσι καθίξῃ.
αὐτὰρ ὅγ᾽ ἀνθερίκοισι καλὰν πλέκει ἀκριδοθήραν
σχοίνῳ ἐφαρμόσδων· μέλεται δέ οἱ οὔτε τι πήρας
οὔτε φυτῶν τοσσῆνον ὅσον περὶ πλέγματι γαθεῖ.

Within [i.e. between the upper and lower rim patterns],[22]
  a woman is incised, art the gods would create,
Adorned with cloak and circlet. Next to her, two men
With beautiful locks argue from either side one after the other
With their ripostes. Yet she is not touched by any of this,   35
But with a smile now looks at one of them,
While the next moment she turns her thoughts to the other.
  Hollow-eyed
With love as they are, their efforts are in vain.
Beside these, an old fisherman and a rock are carved,
A rugged one on which the old man hastily drags a great net
  in for a cast,   40
Looking like a man laboring hard.
You would think he was fishing with all the strength of his limbs,
So swollen are the sinews all around his neck,
Gray-haired though he is, but his strength is worthy of
  a young man's.
Just a little way from the sea-worn old man   45
Is a vineyard weighed down with a beautiful yield
  of reddening clusters;
A little boy guards it sitting on the dry-stone wall.
On either side of him are two foxes, the one going to and fro
  along the vine rows
Devouring the ripe grapes, while the other, her mind on
  the boy's food bag,
Tries every trick to get it and swears she won't let the
  child alone   50
Until he sits on the dry stones robbed of his breakfast (?).
But the boy is plaiting a pretty grasshopper cage, asphodel
Woven with rush. Neither the food bag nor the vines
  interest him
As much as the pleasure of his weaving.
Idyll 1.32–54

The first scene on the cup, as opposed to the cup's decoration,
is the courtship of a young woman by two handsome men. The

description introduces sufficient "filling in" detail for the audience to provide a setting for the scene. The high quality of the execution of the woman's image is conveyed by the Goatherd's comment that she is an artistic achievement such as the gods might manufacture (32). She wears a cloak and a circlet (33). The men have beautiful long hair (34), and are hollow-eyed with love (37–38). The details here are selective and, as we shall see, pertinent, but allow ample play for the imagination.

Narrative too is included, in a number of ways. First, motion is implied as the woman is said to look with a favoring smile and attention at each man in turn (36–37), an achievement attested for real art in both antiquity and the modern period.[23] The moment when the proceedings are captured also leaves room for a denouement. The woman, who as we are explicitly told (35) is not at all concerned with the rivals' claims and counterclaims (34–35), is rather enjoying herself and her suitors' discomfiture: the smile with which she graces the men at various times is ambiguous. Her game-plan is indeed to appear come-hitherish, but any encouragement that her smile might give the men is illusory, since, as we are told, their lovelorn efforts are "in vain" (38). Through his commentary on the outcome of the episode, which would, like the alternation of the woman's gaze, have been entirely within the competence of a Hellenistic artist, the Goatherd has effectively told the whole story. In these ways, the audience has been invited to supplement a narrative, teasing it out of the moment of depiction.[24]

Together with this subtle means of implying events beyond the scene comes a remarkable interest in the psychology of love and its symptoms. The scene may provide a formal *ABA* structure which is perfectly credible within a Hellenistic work of art, but it also presents the audience with a triad in the psychological sense, and indeed the evidence is that the woman is indulging in a little more or less harmless coquetry, while the men's hollow eyes demonstrate some deeper currents of emotion. The contrast of emotional states is typical of Hellenistic poetry and art alike.

The fisherman scene is described with a considerably greater amount of "flat" detail. The fisherman's age is emphasized (39, 41, 45); he is "gray-haired" (44) and "sea-worn" (45); and we have the closely observed detail of the sinews which stand out from his neck as he hauls in his net (43). The activity in which he is engaged — his eager hauling-in of his large net in preparation for his cast (40) — is precisely caught at a particular moment. The scenery is filled in sufficiently both to situate him in space — a rugged rock (39-40) is obviously the ideal place from which to make an effective cast — and to emphasize his solitariness, as contrasted with the three-figure groups which flank him on the cup.

But the element of interpretation is also striking. The Goatherd is made to remark, in his own person and as his own reaction, that the old man looks like "a man laboring hard" (41), and, admiringly, that "his strength is worthy of a young man's" (44). More particularly, the interpretation takes on the form of an address to Thyrsis and from Thyrsis to the reader, when the Goatherd comments that "you would think that [the fisherman] was fishing with all the strength of his limbs, so swollen are the sinews all around his neck, gray-haired though he is" (42-44). In this way, the Goatherd involves Thyrsis and the reader in the "flat" description, having shown his own involvement in it. Furthermore, the moment at which the artist has captured the old man, while allowing the describer to expatiate on the details of the fisherman's musculature and indirectly to express admiration for the artist's realism, is anticipatory to the culminating act of the net-cast. The artist and, through him, the Goatherd thus invite the audiences to do some work and supply the climactic moment in their imagination. As in the wooing scene, narrative can be, and is meant to be, extrapolated from the visual clues, in a manner wholly consonant with what we know of the actual representational art of the period. The scene of the fisherman also illustrates Theocritus' deft and subtle handling of the motif of admiration for realism in the visual arts, which becomes a commonplace in all branches of Hellenistic poetry.

The third scene, the longest in the series, presents in abundance all the features noted in the other two. The *ABA* framing device of the little boy with the two foxes corresponds with the lovers' triad and together with it forms part of an overall *ABA* plan, sandwiching between them the solitary figure of the fisherman. The flat, descriptive elements include the scene-setting details of the vineyard with its beautiful yield of reddening clusters of grapes and the dry-stone wall on which the boy sits as he guards the harvest (46-48). The one fox's depredations amid the ripe grapes are described as a matter of fact (48-49), but the activity of the other,

as she awaits her opportunity to steal the little boy's food bag, is
to a large degree defined by the Goatherd's reading of her mo-
tives: bringing all her cunning to bear on the project, he com-
ments, she "swears" that she won't give up until her purpose has
been fulfilled (49–51). Likewise, the little boy, who is plaiting his
grasshopper cage (52–53), is interpreted from the visual clues
as being more preoccupied and delighted with his work on the
cage than with watchfulness over his food bag or the vines (53–
54). Here again, the Goatherd's activity as an interpreter of the
scene invites his audiences to become similarly involved. This
they must do in order to appreciate the narrative that can be thus
reconstructed from the moment of representation which antici-
pates the inevitable outcome: the one fox will continue eating the
grapes to her heart's content, while the other will have her way
with the little boy's food, such is his absorption in his play.

   It is instructive to remember the context of the scenes as part of
a cup which is styled as a "goatherd's marvel" (αἰπολικὸν θάημα:
56). The phrase itself is consciously modeled on the Homeric tag
"outstanding marvel," describing the grand shield of Achilles (τὸ
δὴ περὶ θαῦμα τέτυκτο: *Il.*18.549). The description as a whole is re-
garded as consciously standing in the tradition of the Iliadic pas-
sage. In terms of mere materials, the precious metals of the shield
have given way to the carved wood of the cup, wood being a de-
cidedly lowly material for a drinking vessel. If we survey what re-
mains of contemporary Hellenistic metal cups, we do indeed find
thematic connections,[25] and the discrepancy of the wood of the
cup and the precious metals of the cups in polite currency is there-
fore the more likely to have been clear and telling to Theocritus'
immediate audiences. In a very real sense, therefore, the motif of
the description of a work of art has come down in the world.

   This feeling is further reflected in the personnel of the three
scenes. The young woman and her two suitors are not easily
placed on any specific social level at all: the woman's circlet need
not denote luxury, and may be as much a part of the idealizing
tendency of the description as the men's graceful long hair. But
they are probably to be seen as young country people, given the
cup's stated overall designation. They would then fit in with the
fisherman and the country boy in the other scenes, for these
would have been unhesitatingly placed low on the social scale in
Hellenistic times. We therefore have the depiction of lowly objects

and people placed by allusion in a grand form and tradition — those of epic, to be precise. This is a procedure I examined in *Realism in Alexandrian Poetry*,[26] but we may now add that the procedure is precisely paralleled in the art of the period.

There is general agreement among archaeologists and art historians that a defined *Rangordnung* addressed the subjects appropriate for depiction in major statuary, materials, and styles, and that major statuary in the Hellenistic period was starting to experiment with subjects which would previously have been regarded as inappropriately low on the social and aesthetic scale. There are also signs that the art historians are beginning to perceive this experimentation specifically in terms of the strategy that I have described for poetry.[27] The Spinario in the Palazzo dei Conservatori (see Ill. 30), for example, is marked as belonging to an elevated iconographical tradition not only by its materials, but also by "citations" of its ancestry in Classical statuary such as the motif of Hermes resting or the way the hairdo, rendered in the severe style, cites the tradition of the Classical ephebe. This analogy, I would argue in a way in which neither art historians nor literary scholars have done so far, helps us to place the tone of the period's art and poetry dealing with such subjects. We may posit a sense of pleasant incongruity and friction involving effects ranging from deflation to elevation, or, as in the case of the cup and the Spinario, a gently amusing play-off between traditional expectations and novel experimentation with them. With gentle irony this strategy elevated the previously "inappropriate," even comic, subject matter, or indeed idealized it to a level where one could see, with new eyes, its unexpected charm. So the incongruity of the Spinario can be viewed in a positive light, far from being devalued because of the merely derivative type of eclecticism for which the statue is often dismissed.[28]

What has the cup description taught us about the act of viewing in Hellenistic poetry and art? It has shown clearly that the eye was provided with background-setting detail in which images could be placed spatially. It has shown an interest in precise, visually accurate, even clinically accurate, physiological detail, and an appreciation of realism in artistic representations. It demonstrates a fascination with presenting a moment in a narrative, which can in turn be supplemented to include events before and after the moment depicted. Here the audience's or viewer's imagination is shown at work in the interpretative commentary offered by the describer, who is made to see to it that the person for whom he is describing the art object becomes integrally involved not only in the object but also in the process of its interpretation. It shows a distinct interest in the emotional or psychological states of humans at all stages of life. It shows that humble subject matter and people were regarded as viable for depiction in surprisingly high-flown media, and totally worthy of serious poetic and artistic representation, and that in fact such subjects were essential for the creation of novel tonal effects.

All these tastes can be discerned in the painting and sculpture of the period. In a sense, since the cup description at least purports to be a description of a work of art, this perhaps comes as no great surprise. What is so enormously valuable about looking at the Goatherd's verbal account from this perspective is precisely that his description puts into words modes of viewing, expectations, and responses which cannot be expressed anywhere near so directly in actual representational art, and thus helps us define certain Hellenistic viewing practices with a precision that is not otherwise open to us. Nor is the Goatherd's description alone in helping us in this way. By the same token, what we can learn from descriptions of works of art like this can shed light on how audiences may have responded to descriptions, within poetry itself, of other things, from people in poor physical shape to athletes, from herdsmen to heroes and deities, from "stills" to narratives, a range of subjects and modes of representing them as wide as that of Hellenistic art itself.

Calling on contemporary Hellenistic poetry to help us define responses to the period's painting and sculpture is especially useful in the notoriously difficult problem of placing the tone of certain themes and motifs in Hellenistic art, a subject which forms the second part of this book. For example, critics like J. J. Pollitt have wondered about the originally perceived mood and meaning of artistic groups like the Barberini Faun (see Ill. 10), the Sleeping Eros in New York (Ill. 1), and the Erotes imitating human activities like hunting or wearing armor, as in Aëtion's painting of the marriage of Alexander and Roxane as described by Lucian (*Herodotus or Aëtion* 4-6). Pollitt finds it hard to class as "rococo" the New York Sleeping Eros, since we do not know its original purpose; the piece "may look 'cute' to us, but the Greeks may

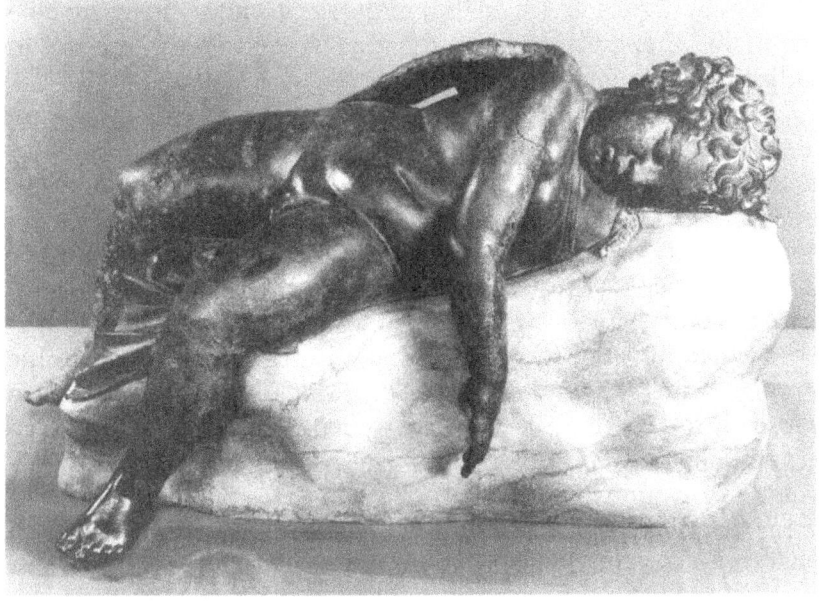

1. Sleeping Eros. Metropolitan Museum of Art, New York. All rights reserved, The Metropolitan Museum of Art, Rogers Fund, 1943 (43.11.4)

have looked upon him as a formidable, even dangerous, being." On the other hand, though the hunting Erotes may have been inspired by royal iconography, their "playfulness . . . seems fairly described as 'rococo'."[29]

These are legitimate misgivings. But, for one thing, literature can help place the tone of the Eros imagery of visual art. I have elsewhere attempted to plot the tonal progress of Eros in the third book of Apollonius' *Argonautica* (3.111-65, 275-87).[30] It begins with Eros as the mischievous "problem child" of Olympus, in the famous scene in which he is depicted as beating Ganymedes at knucklebones (114-28). Though I consider it to be misleading to suggest that the scene is modeled on a specific work of plastic art, the Astragalizontes of Polyclitus,[31] the temptation to do so is in itself significant. The poetic pictorialism of the image of the children of Olympus at play is, as I have argued, to be seen in the context of aims within poetry itself, notably *enargeia*, rather than in the possible influence of the artistic group; yet the representation of the moment in both media inclines us to conclude that, at this stage in Apollonius' narrative, the emphasis is on the everyday

element in the scene. Given that in the *Argonautica* the figure pos-
ing in this ambience is a deity, the tone here is indeed "rococo" in
Pollitt's "limited use of the term."

Yet there are already hints of the little god's more disturbing
aspect. The fact that Eros' playmate is Ganymedes is in itself no-
table, since Ganymedes' mere presence on Olympus is the result
of Zeus's erotic involvement with the boy (115–17), and Eros can
consequently be considered at least an indirect agent in getting
Ganymedes to Olympus in the first place. Here, then, is the god,
tauntingly beating (Aphrodite suggests that her son has in fact
been cheating: 129–30) a personage who is to some degree his
protégé. And is the reward that Aphrodite offers for Eros' future
services, the toy ball that the baby Zeus played with (132–41),
a symbolic recognition of Eros' possession of the whole uni-
verse?[32] Certainly the description of the god's descent to earth to
carry out his mission more emphatically presents the notion of
Eros as master of all he surveys, an increasing tonal progression
as the motif of his interference gains in tension. Moreover, the
word with which Apollonius expresses Eros' delight at beating
Ganymedes, "with a laugh," καγχαλόωντι (124), is the same one
used to describe his pleasure in wreaking havoc with human
lives, καγχαλόων (286), when he pierces Medea's heart with his
arrow and love for Jason. Pleasure at play, it seems, is on a par
with malicious meddling in the lives of mortals who have no
means of resisting such external forces. The full import of this is
brought out when the narrator, in his own voice, pronounces his
conclusion about Eros' involvement in driving Medea to murder
her brother Apsyrtus: "Cruel Eros, great cause of misery, great
object of hatred among mortals, from you proceed accursed
quarrels, groans, and lamentations, while countless other griefs
arise beside these; may you rise up, deity, and arm yourself
against the sons of my enemies as you were when you hurled
hateful madness upon Medea."

Σχέτλι' Ἔρως, μέγα πῆμα, μέγα στύγος ἀνθρώποισιν,
ἐκ σέθεν οὐλόμεναί τ' ἔριδες στοναχαί τε γόοι τε,
ἄλγεά τ' ἄλλ' ἐπὶ τοῖσιν ἀπείρονα τετρήχασιν·
δυσμενέων ἐπὶ παισὶ κορύσσεο δαῖμον ἀερθείς
οἷος Μηδείῃ στυγερὴν φρεσὶν ἔμβαλες ἄτην.
(4.445–49)

Later, when Medea and Jason are forced to marry in an atmosphere of terrified apprehension, wondering whether Alcinous will abide by his decision to defend them against the avenging Colchians, the author again intrudes by commenting: "We tribes of suffering mortals never tread the path of happiness with the whole of our foot, but some bitter pain always accompanies our joy."

ἀλλὰ γὰρ οὔποτε φῦλα δυηπαθέων ἀνθρώπων
τερπωλῆς ἐπέβημεν ὅλῳ ποδί, σὺν δέ τις αἰεί
πικρὴ παρμέμβλωκεν ἐυφροσύνῃσιν ἀνίη.
(4.1165–67)

This remark again graphically captures the ambiguity of the power of love as understood in Hellenistic thinking.

The tonal range of the Hellenistic perception of Eros, then, was, to judge by Apollonius, remarkably wide.[33] It therefore seems perfectly justified to take the Eros riding on a tiger as a motif in which Hellenistic viewers would indeed have seen what we would call "rococo" elements. The Sleeping Eros and the Barberini Faun, together with groups like the Pan and Shepherd Boy and the Aphrodite aiming a slipper at Pan (Ill. 2),[34] would probably have been perceived as ambivalent, or marginally disturbing. In the group of the Centaur taunted by Eros (Ill. 3),[35] the Hellenistic viewer would, on the other hand, certainly have sensed real pathos. The Eros-type in which Eros holds a torch downward has clear funerary connotations, and we have the absolute reverse side of the god's playful aspect,[36] which highlights just how serious a significance these amusing figures could have. Artists, in other words, could avail themselves of the tonal flexibility of the image of Eros exactly as the poets could, and in this case we have the narrator of the *Argonautica* feeding us more tangible and, ultimately, explicit clues to tonal placement.

Pollitt also engages with the current controversy over the Hellenistic reception of the statues of drunken old women (see Ill. 34), herdsmen, fishermen with varicose veins (see Ill. 29), or the famous Terme Boxer (see Ill. 8). Is the taste for this sort of thing, he asks, motivated by what he calls "social realism" or an "aristocratic contempt for the ugliness of the low-born"?[37] Study of the physiognomy of these statues led H.-P. Laubscher to conclude that their verism does not mean that their subjects were admired—

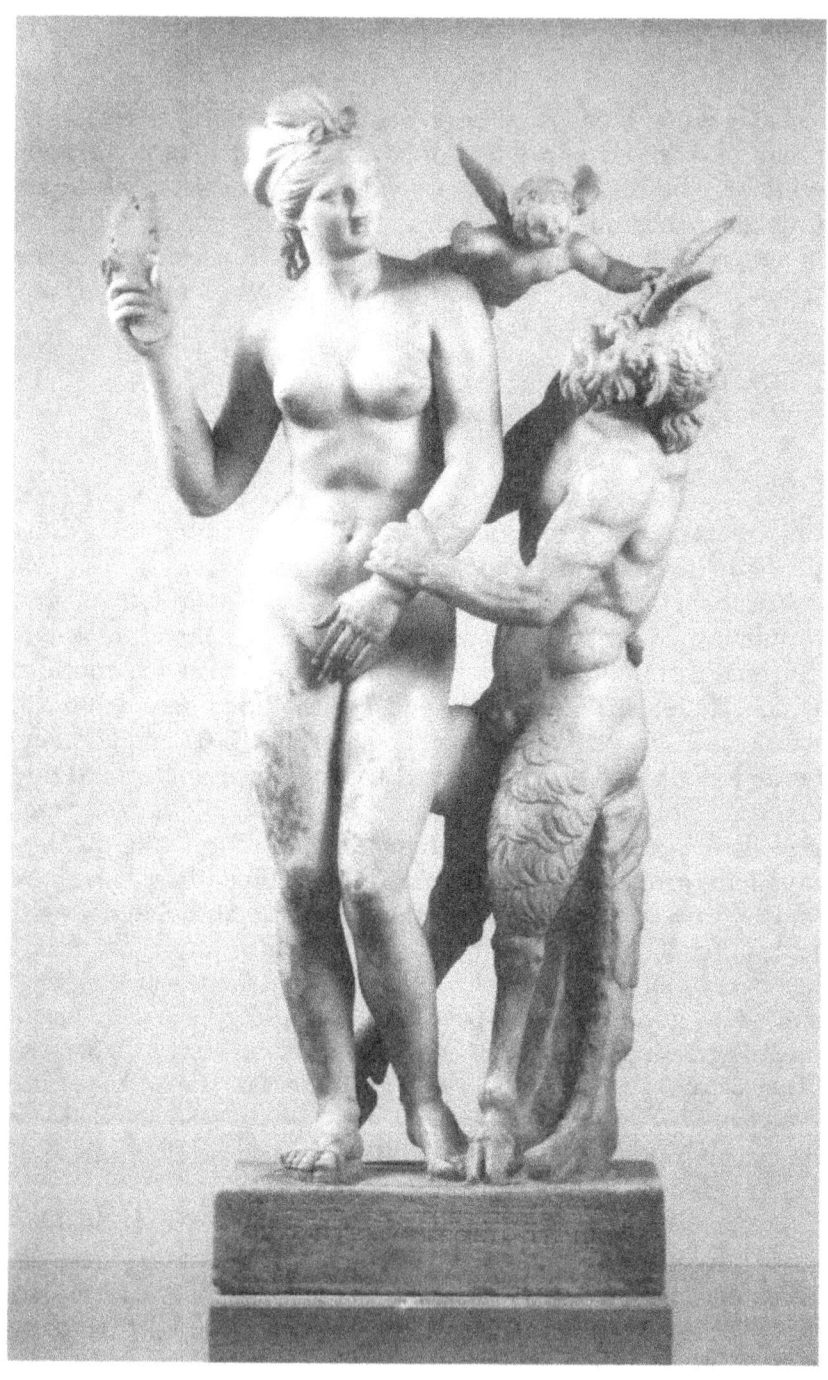

2. Slipper Slapper group. National Museum, Athens. Dr. Klaus Valtin von Eickstedt.

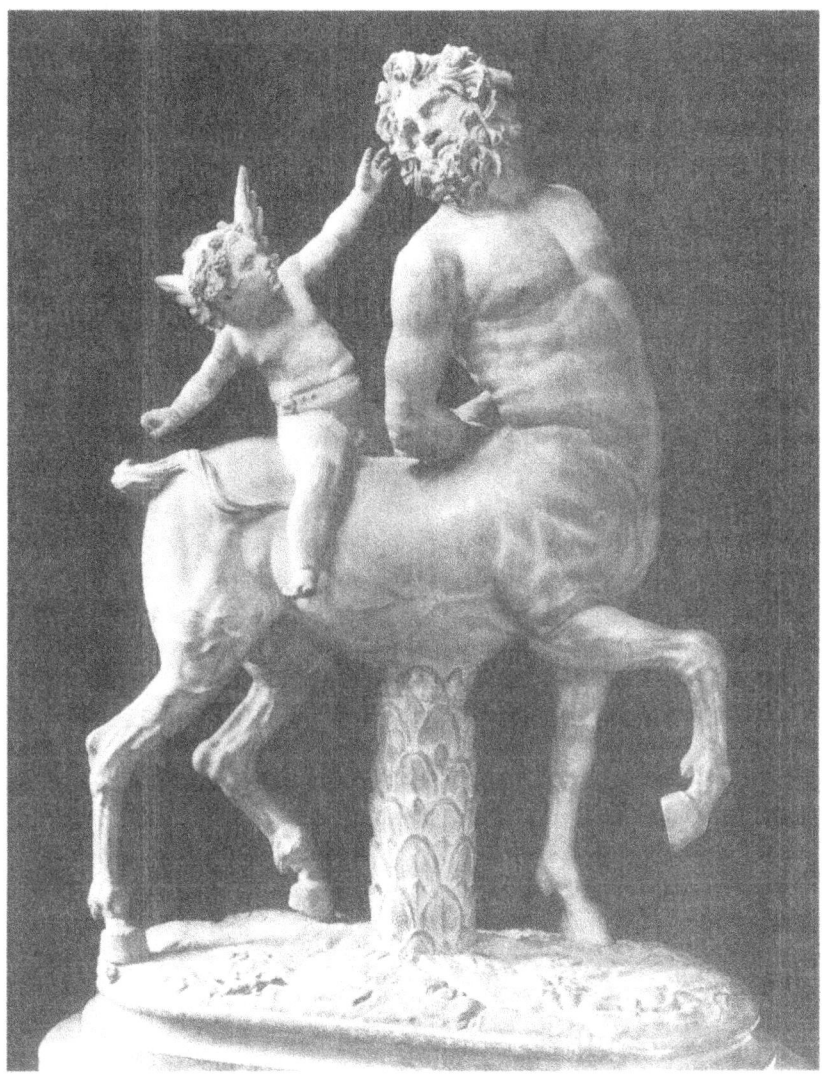

3. Eros and Centaur. Musée du Louvre, Paris. Alinari 22573

quite the reverse (Simon's review of his book raised strong objections to this reading).[38] Pollitt himself wonders whether the artists, as artisans, might not have felt more pathos in them than their patrons' *hauteur* might have inclined them to appreciate.

It is a notorious fact that we know next to nothing about the contexts of the fisherman and rustic statues, though Paul Zanker has convincingly argued that the setting for the Drunken Old Woman was the Lagynophoria at Alexandria.[39] Here again literature can aid us in defining the possible parameters of response. Admittedly, literary genres like epigram seem to put the motif of the drunken old woman well and truly in the context of comedy (where, of course, such figures were common).[40] But, within statuary, the example of the drunken old woman in the Munich Glyptothek appears to break down such blanket categorization, especially on Zanker's interpretation of her as an image reminding the more fortunate viewer that a fall is always a possibility.[41] On the other hand, it is hard to find outright contempt for shepherds and country people in, for instance, Theocritus' pastorals. *Idyll* 3 may elicit laughter at a country yokel's capacity for self-deception, but also sympathy for his all-too-familiar plight. This is also true, *mutatis mutandis,* of the portrayal of the rusticated Polyphemus of *Idylls* 6 and 11. *Idyll* 4 provokes our amusement at the platitudes and banalities associated with country conversation; *Idyll* 5 abounds in humor at the unbridled "rustic bawdiness" of country life. All are ironically couched in the high literary form of the hexameter, a literary Doric dialect, and at times highfalutin diction. But there is the moment of "pastoral tragedy" in the fate of the legendary Daphnis in *Idyll* 1, and *Idyll* 7 celebrates the beauty of a farm festival and does not hesitate to present a goatherd as a pre-eminent poet.[42]

The artistic representations of shepherds, like the old shepherdess (Ill. 4) featured by Pollitt,[43] may accordingly be seen in an analogous way: high formal aspects—material and style—juxtaposed with low subject matter, evincing various degrees of irony while at the same time expressing a painfully accurate observation of subjects previously ignored.[44] For the statue of the fisherman, we have the picture of the old fisherman about to cast his net which forms part of the cup description of *Idyll* 1, examined above. The point to notice here is that the old man's neck sinews stand out from the physical effort, and yet his strength is said to be like a young man's, an observation which, as we have concluded, surely betokens at least a degree of admiration.[45] On the other hand, the fisherman of the pseudo-Theocritean *Idyll* 21, whose hopeless dream of fortune and naïve fear of an oath (made during the dream) never to fish again are cut short by the gruff voice of harsh reality, conveys a pathos born of sentimentalization

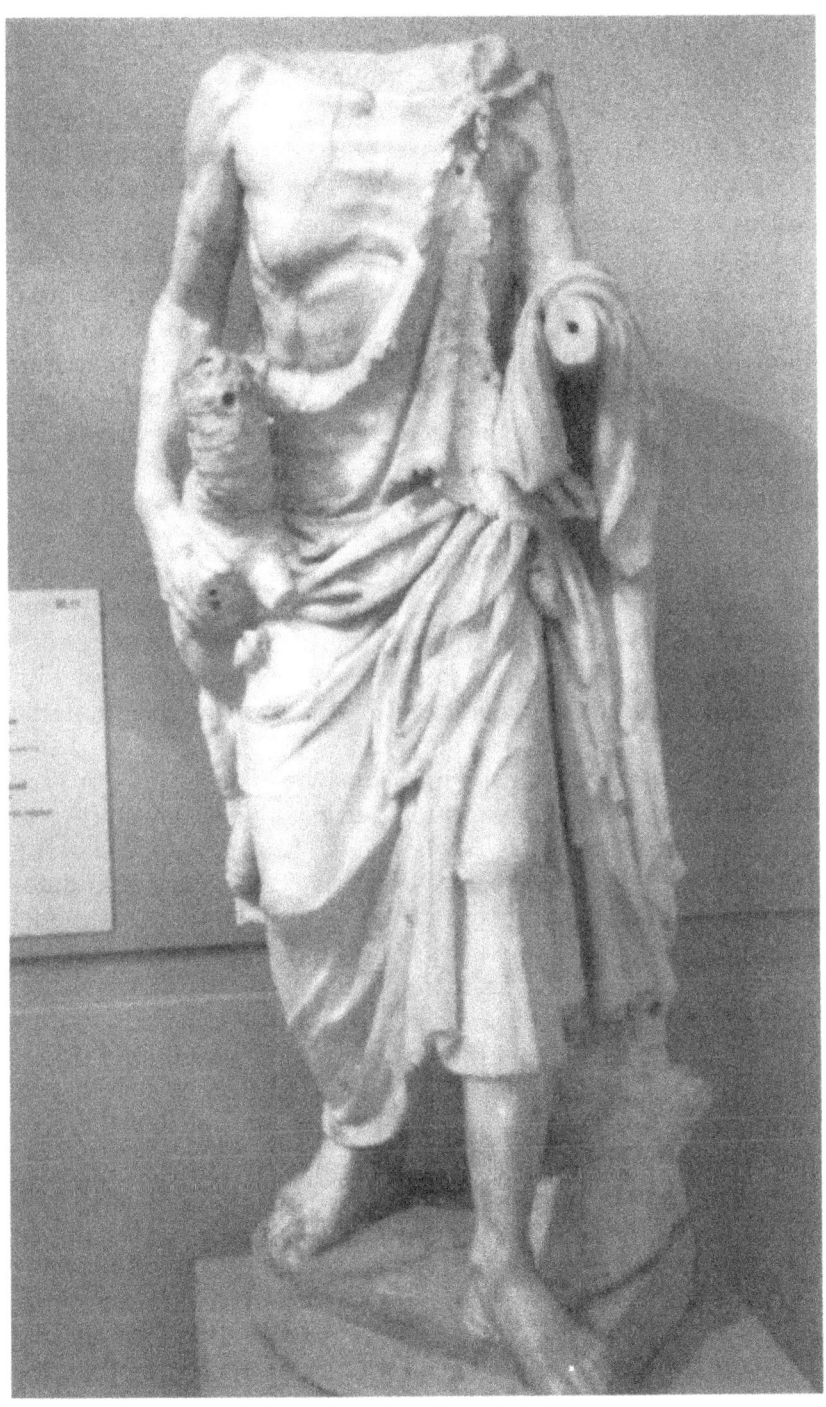

4. Old Shepherdess. Palazzo dei Conservatori, Rome (currently housed in the Centrale Montemartini). Author

which may indeed have catered to the smug tastes traditionally associated with the well-off. But it remains poignant pathos none the less, though Pollitt, I think, misreads the evidence of *Idyll* 21 in placing the emphasis the other way around.[46]

Perhaps this literary evidence also acts as a corrective to Laubscher's reconstruction of Hellenistic receptions of the fisherman statues, and perhaps a Hellenistic viewer's response to such figures was a good deal more sympathetic, even if a degree of humor was involved.[47] Pollitt proposes the hypothetical case that in Roman times these figures of aged people were disseminated to cater to tastes informed by the spirit of Virgil and Horace.[48] Close to the spirit hypothesized by Pollitt are works from the early Imperial period like the Munich Farmer relief, which Henner von Hesberg places within the tonal range of *pax* and *pietas,* not bucolic utopianism: the ideal of the simple life is realizable.[49] Thus we can detect a change of emphasis in the mode of viewing such material, and this is another area where a close engagement with the literature of the Hellenistic period can shed some light on the location of tone and intention in art.

As for the Terme Boxer, comparisons with Theocritus' Amycus in *Idyll* 22 are often made, though perhaps the Amycus of Apollonius in Book 2 of the *Argonautica* (1–97) has been undeservedly neglected. We should note, however, that Theocritus' account of the boxing match of Amycus and Polydeuces involves elements of humor that are not present in Apollonius' version. Moreover, in Amycus we are of course dealing with a king, who is portrayed in both poetic versions as a discourteous, bullying, and evil ruffian, by no means a sympathetic figure. It is these differences, in fact, which help in placing the tone of the bronze statue with some reliability, and we can have no real quarrel with Pollitt's conclusion that the Terme Boxer "becomes a nobly battered figure who elicits sympathy, rather like Lysippos's images of the weary Herakles."[50]

In his chapter on pictorial illusion and narration, Pollitt also addresses the fiercely controversial question of the origins of the "Odyssey landscapes," where, for the first time in Western art, man is dominated by the immensity of nature. But the taste for landscape detail was already well established in poetry by the time of the Telephus frieze and other artefacts mentioned by Pollitt.[51] A good example is present in Theocritus' account of Amycus and Polydeuces' boxing match itself, where, in contrast with the hideous picture of Amycus, Theocritus describes the landscape which forms the backdrop of the main narrative: beneath a smooth overarching rock a spring in whose clear waters gleaming pebbles can be seen and around which grow tall trees and scented flowers (Id. 22.37–43). This penchant is particularly well exemplified in the *Argonautica* of Apollonius. In Book 2, for instance, we have the extensive and atmospheric rendering of the Acherousian Headland, believed to be an entry to Hades (728–51). The description is inspired by scientific observation, and the site has actually been identified.[52] In Book 3, there is the eerie Plain of Circe, through which Jason and his followers must make their way to the palace of Aeëtes (200–209). Book 4 has the Syrtes of Libya, where the Argo runs hopelessly aground (1232–49). Later rhetorical treatises were to call this kind of passage ἔκφρασις τόπων (*ekphrasis topôn*, "description of places") and were to see the chief quality in *ekphrasis* in general as being *enargeia*.[53] In fact, *enargeia* is an older term by far than *ekphrasis*; it was current in its aesthetic sense in the third century B.C., as we now know from the new Posidippus papyrus.[54] The quality denoted by the word was certainly highly prized in the period's literary criticism.[55]

In their turn, of course, these moments in the poetry associated with Alexandria are pre-dated by the late fourth-century Vergina tomb-paintings, especially by the hunt scene. In contrast to the quite traditional anthropocentrism of the Vergina landscapes, however, the eye of the Alexandrian poets of the following century was directed at nature far more for its own sake, as is evidenced particularly well by Apollonius' passage on the Acherousian Headland. Therefore, whether or not Alexandrian art was as concerned with landscape as Achille Adriani's famous third-century cup suggests[56]—and Stewart has claimed that "late fourth-century Vergina has produced a painted landscape that casts anything from Egypt into the shade"[57]—the Alexandrian poetry of the period certainly was. That poetry shows that quite early in the Hellenistic age there was a sensitivity to natural scenery that was unprecedented in Greek culture. Shouldn't such evidence be considered in our thinking about Hellenistic and Roman landscape art? Clearly it should (though this is not the forum in which to pursue the matter further), and therefore we have another instructive analogy between the sister arts of the period.

The approach adopted here to the relationship of poetry and art in the Hellenistic period is, as I hope to have shown already, more useful than the attempts (by Webster and others)[58] to find subjects, styles, and motifs directly "inspired" by one or the other medium. At the same time, as I remarked at the outset, my focus is much narrower than that of more general books on Hellenistic culture and aesthetics like Onians' and Fowler's. Instead, my contention here is that the close parallelism between the different periods of the Hellenistic age and their poets' and artists' choices of modes, matter, and ethos and the analogues between Hellenistic poetry and art are striking enough to encourage us by all means to use the sister arts to orientate and enrich our interpretation of both arts' aims and methods in visual representation. In pursuit of this proposition I shall explore first the poetic and artistic techniques of visualization and their impact on the Hellenistic audiences' or spectators' viewing, particularly in terms of their spatial involvement with the image they are presented with. Second, I shall consider some of the ways in which the Hellenistic viewing of the period's new visual themes and material in both poetry and art is likely to have been manipulated in order to provoke more specifically emotional responses, whether laughter, surprise, erotic arousal, or pity.

2

Full Presentation of the Image

Hellenistic visual art and poetry created modes of viewing in order to involve viewers and readers visually and spatially. This chapter and the two which follow examine this process. Here recent findings by art historians are particularly worth transferring to our approaches to poetry, for they serve as a model for defining some of the period's techniques with a clarity that has not been adequately appreciated.

By what means do Hellenistic artists and poets put their viewers and readers *in* the picture? I suggest that for the Hellenistic period we can identify three main methods, all in some way involving the act of supplementation, all common to both art and poetry. The first is obvious enough. The visual artist fills in all the details of both the main subject and its background, with the result that the viewer can place the main subject within a spatial context. An example in architectural relief-sculpture is the Telephus frieze in the Pergamon Altar, where the tortuous story of Telephus is retold visually in great detail, including trees as setting details and scene-dividers in the foreground, and registering the responses of other characters in the background of the scene. The Gigantomachy itself, of course, provides overwhelming visual detail. Particularly fascinating are the moments when, for example, the foot of a virtually free-standing giant (Ill. 5) is placed on one of the stairs—outside the monument's space and into the viewer's space. The viewer is confused by the trespass on his reality and is at least momentarily drawn into the image by the blurring of the boundary. In statuary on the small scale it has been shown how the Conservatori Satyr and Maenad group of the first century B.C.

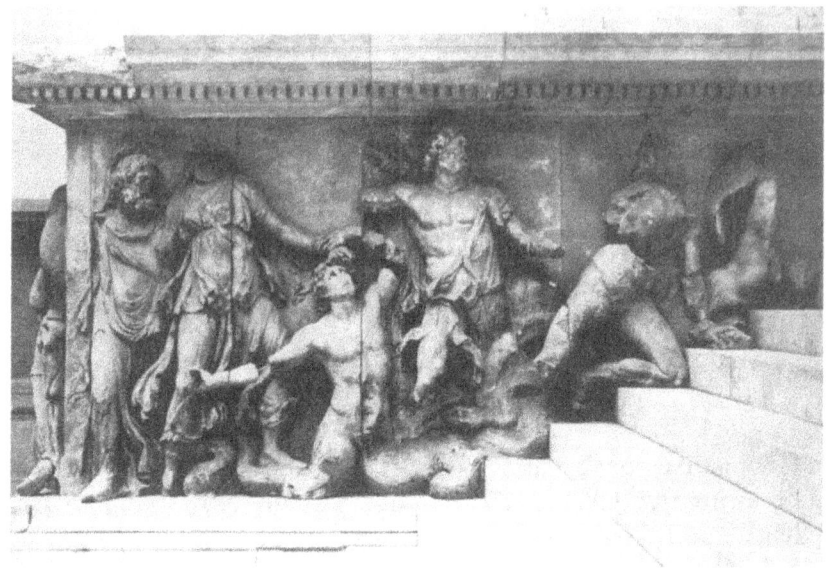

5. Giant on step of Pergamon Altar. Pergamon-Museum, Berlin. DAI, negative number 55.71

(Ill. 6) is designed to tell an actual narrative through its visual detail.[1] Depending on the viewer's position, the satyr first appears to smile in triumph at an impending sexual conquest; then, once the precariousness of his carefully detailed hold on the maenad has been noticed, the viewer realizes that nothing is going to happen and observes the satyr's grin turning into a grimace of defeat and frustration.

In poetry there are abundant examples; I adduced and discussed many of them (from a different perspective from the one which interests us here) in my book on the realism of Alexandrian poetry. The boxing matches described in Theocritus' twenty-second *Idyll* and the beginning of the second book of Apollonius' *Argonautica* are especially striking in this connection, given the evocation of the physical appearance of King Amycus, the predominantly visual narrative of the fights themselves, and the way in which the two poets dwell upon the natural ambience and the human onlookers. All this happens in precisely the way the Greek rhetors, writing from the first century B.C. onward, commend *enargeia* and *ekphrasis*, which "bring the subject before our eyes." A striking formulation of this quality can be seen in the manner in

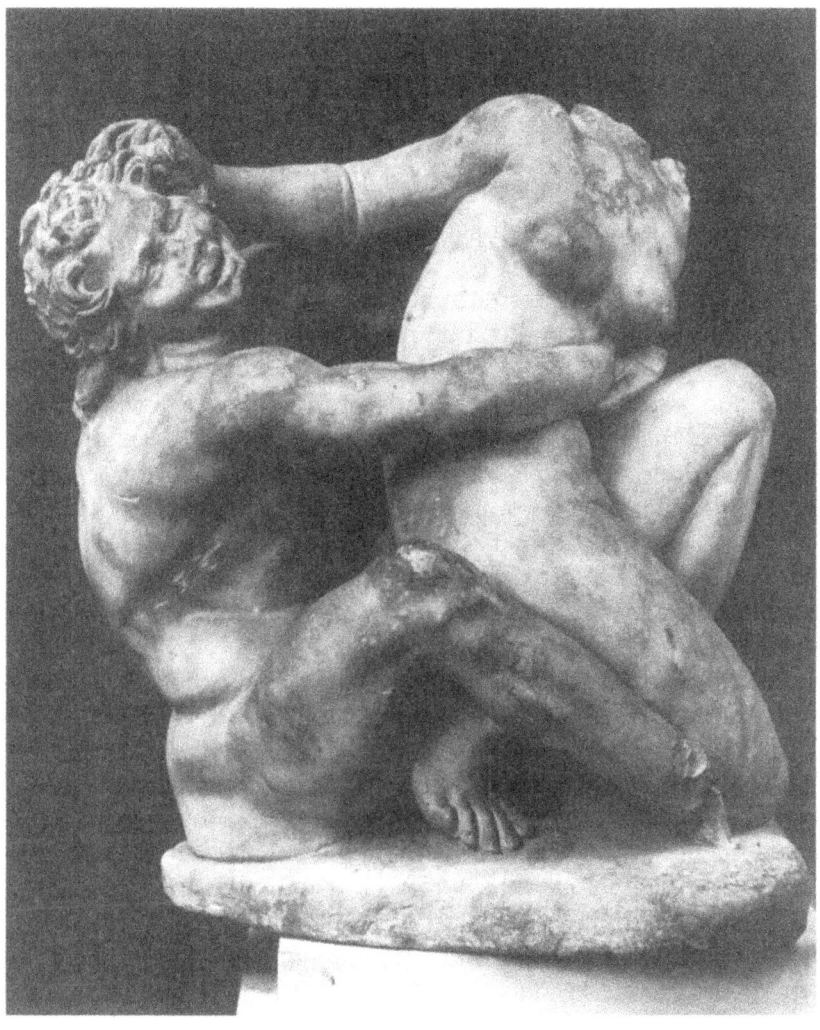

6. Conservatori Satyr and Maenad. Palazzo dei Conservatori, Rome (currently housed in the Centrale Montemartini). Faraglia, DAI negative number 33.424

which Dionysius of Halicarnassus expresses his admiration for the Classical Athenian orator Lysias, whose recreations of the scene of the crime cause the audience to feel as if they were present: "The style of Lysias is full of *enargeia*. This is a capacity for bringing subjects within our senses, and is effected when we can apprehend the attendant details. Nobody who pays real attention to the speeches of Lysias could be so gauche, hard to please, or dull-witted as not to imagine that he is witnessing (ὁρᾶν) what is being described as if it were actually happening and that he is in the very presence of any characters the orator may introduce" (*Lysias* 7 Usher).[2]

Nor should we feel that because Dionysius is talking about a stylistic quality exhibited in a writer from the Classical period we are wrong to regard this kind of evocativeness as peculiarly Hellenistic, for the Greek rhetors quote Homer or Herodotus as illustrating *enargeia*.[3] Dionysius and the rhetors liked to find and cite parallels in early literature to illustrate (and perhaps legitimize) their contemporary Hellenistic tastes, much as Aristotle draws upon Homer for examples illustrating his precepts about effective oratory in his day and age. In other words, in Hellenistic literature and theory the enthusiasm for qualities like *enargeia* intensifies to an unprecedented degree, as we shall see when we compare Theocritus' boxing-match commentary in *Idyll* 22 with the fights in Homer. In the case of the first technique for involving the reader or viewer, therefore, it is the artists or poets who do all the supplementation: both supply every conceivable detail to draw their viewers and readers into the scene.

For the second method whereby the age's artists and poets engage their viewers and readers through visual means, we are fortunate to have recourse to the fascinating studies by art historians like Peter von Blanckenhagen, Hugo Meyer, and Henner von Hesberg.[4] These scholars, with von Blanckenhagen as the pioneer, have demonstrated how Hellenistic representative art often expected its viewers to perform the act of supplementation. Meyer, for example, discusses the so-called white and red Marsyas groups. He argues that the "white" Marsyas statue (Ill. 7a)— but not the "red" Marsyas (Ill. 7b)—was accompanied by the Scythian executioner playing his gruesome role. Apollo, however, was not present and had to be supplemented by the viewer. Caution should be exercised here, for Brunilde Ridgway now concludes that "it is unclear which type was accompanied by additional statues," though she thereby leaves open the possibility that one type was unaccompanied.[5] If Meyer's reconstruction is still accepted, the "white" Marsyas would have required the observer who knows his mythology to supplement the group by adding the god, just as von Blanckenhagen holds that we have to supply a fleeing Theseus or an arriving Dionysus to supplement

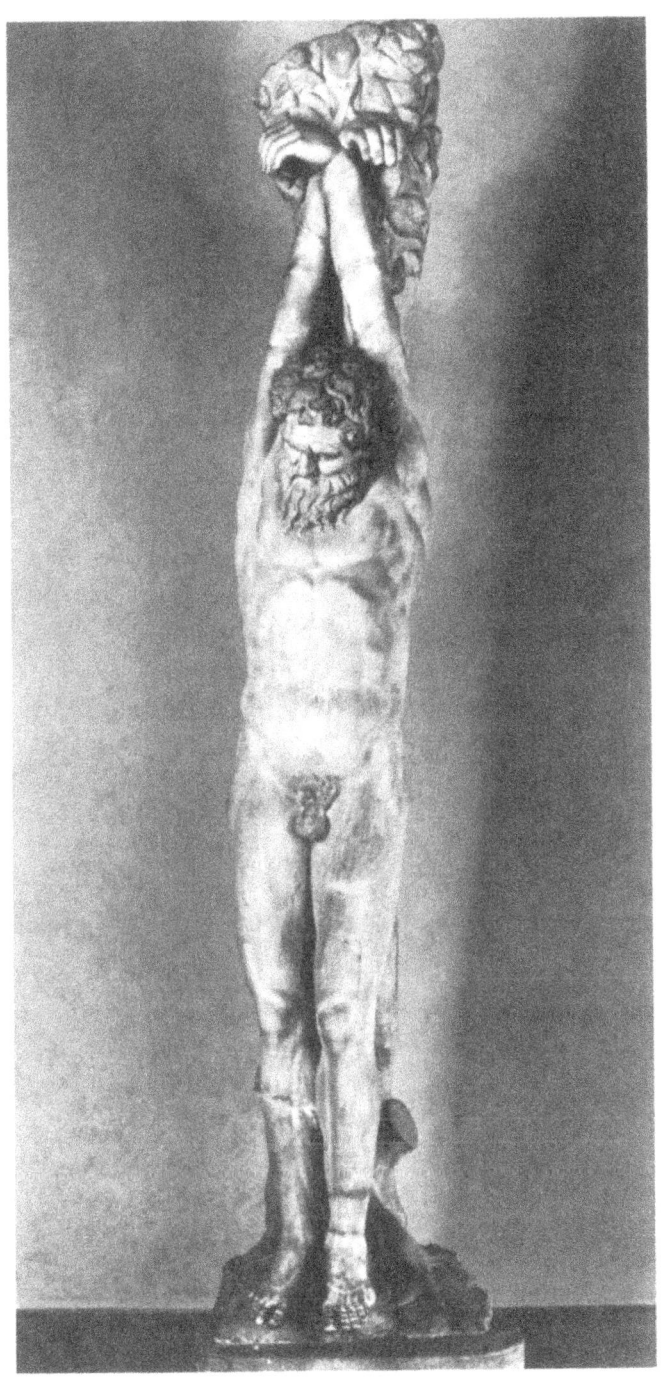

7a. "White" Marsyas. Uffizi, Florence. Rossa, DAI negative
number 77.379

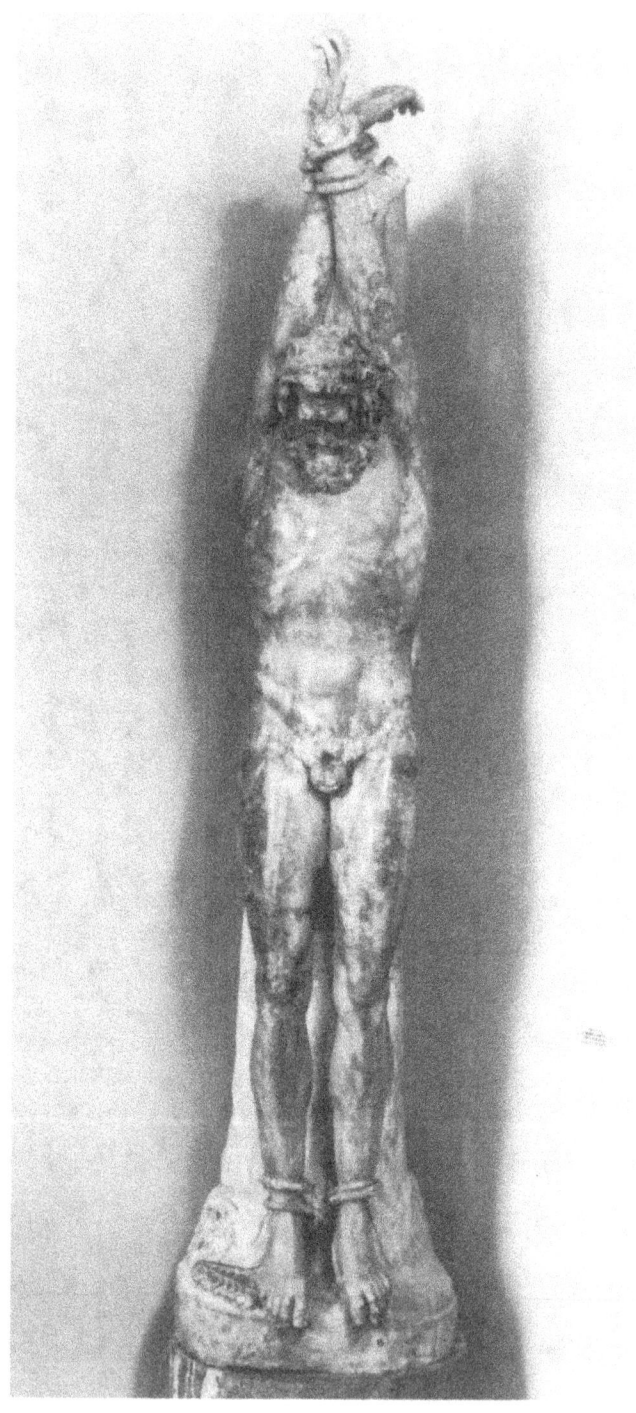

7b. "Red" Marsyas. Palazzo dei Conservatori, Rome. Rossa,
DAI negative number 74.2741

the Sleeping Ariadne.[6] The viewer's personal visual input would, so to speak, commit him or her to entering into the images.

An analogue for this approach in contemporary poetry is to be found in the pseudo-Theocritean twenty-fifth *Idyll*, as I shall argue in detail below. Suffice it to note here that the actual occasion of the poem, the cleaning of Augeas' stables, is cleverly sketched in by means of many "adventitious" visual clues that the poet has left. Like the viewer of the statues, the reader of *Idyll* 25 is committed to entering into the fiction by his or her efforts to visualize the untold labor. Here, then, the artist or poet "makes" the observer or the reader do the supplementation, though they have in fact done all the spade-work in strategically placing the visual clues.

The studies of these scholars direct us naturally to the third technique that I see as a striking Hellenistic innovation in involving viewers and readers. Here the viewer or reader is, to use von Hesberg's term, actually "integrated" into the image. If, as Meyer contends, the Scythian flayer did not figure in the "red" Marsyas group (see Ill. 7b), the viewer is to some extent put in the executioner's place.[7] We also have the uncontentious example of the statues of Aphrodite naked, surprised before or after her bath, or as she crouches; the viewer feels discomfort at being caught in the act of looking at the goddess at such intimate junctures. Analogous "integration" can be discerned in certain funerary epigrams — even fictional ones — where the reader is directly addressed or subsumed in a question-and-answer sequence between an imaginary reader and the monument itself. It can also be observed in poems like Callimachus' mimetic hymns. The second *Hymn* is a good example: the master of ceremonies addresses the imaginary worshipers, but the hymn's readers must be included in this audience — the envoi on Callimachus' and contemporary poetry makes that a certainty. The reader of the hymn is thus integrated into its action. To put it in other terms relevant to our inquiry, the readers themselves at least partially supplement the worshipers in the ritual presented by the hymn.[8]

Theocritus' description of the boxing match between Polydeuces and Amycus in *Idyll* 22 (75–134) impressively illustrates one of the ways a poet of the period saw and then set down in writing what he had "seen." In this case, what we shall be observing is the poet's determination to give the fullest visual representation possible, so that the reader is turned into an eyewitness and can view the proceedings in all their detail, as if at first hand. And, as will I hope become apparent, the way of seeing and imaging has striking analogues in the art of the age.

It is remarkable to note, first of all, how much care Theocritus spends on locating the figures and the action in a spatial framework and context. Against the backdrop of the rest of the Argonauts making themselves comfortable on the sheltered beach (30–33), we have the motif of the more adventurous Castor and Polydeuces venturing forth to explore the "wild wood" on the hill inland (34–36). The contrast already helps us to contextualize what is in store. The *locus amoenus* in which Amycus is first met is in heightening contrast with the grim figure he cuts.[9] Theocritus calls the reader's particular attention to the clarity of the spring's water, and the way pebbles can be seen shining on the bottom (37–40).

εὗρον δ' ἀέναον κρήνην ὑπὸ λισσάδι πέτρῃ,
ὕδατι πεπληθυῖαν ἀκηράτῳ· αἱ δ' ὑπένερθε
λάλλαι κρυστάλλῳ ἠδ' ἀργύρῳ ἰνδάλλοντο
ἐκ βυθοῦ.

Beneath a smooth rock [Castor and Polydeuces] found
    an ever-flowing spring,
Full of clear water. From the depths below
The stones appeared, like crystal or silver.

The visual contrast of human brawn and natural beauty was later to be exploited on the Telephus frieze. On the third panel, in which Heracles sees Auge, his physical power contrasts with the soft and luxuriant foliage of a tree. The contrast is even stronger on the twelfth panel, where Heracles sees Telephus feeding from a lioness's teat; here the hero's bulky musculature is even more emphasized, and his rather terrifying lion-skin is hanging down and "looking" at the live lioness—all set against the background tree and leaves, as well as the tender suckling scene. In *Idyll* 22, the lovely visual detail of the countryside setting, especially the description of the spring water, makes it all the more understandable that the Argonauts should want to drink here, as Polydeuces asks the king of the region for permission to do (62–63). The "landscape-painting" thus has a narrative as well as a more narrowly aesthetic function.

It also provides an instructive control on the fundamental distinctness of the Hellenistic mode of viewing. The model for the passage is the sight Odysseus and his men first have of Polyphemus in *Odyssey* 9.182–86. There they see the Cyclops in his domain, a high cave near the sea, overarched with laurels, where sheep and goats would spend the night, and a lofty courtyard with stones embedded in the earth, tall pines, and leafy oaks. Homer has economically sketched in just enough detail to convey the crudeness of the abode, and to set the scene for the heroes' quick getaway from the cave to the ship. Theocritus, however, introduces, in addition to the spring and its pellucid water, tall pines, poplars, plane trees, and cypresses, with all kinds of spring flowers being harvested by shaggy bees. The Hellenistic poet's pictorialism is, first, noticeably more extensive, largely in order to emphasize the contrast with the "monstrous" figure of Amycus, "terrifying to look upon." It is, second, strikingly more intense and penetratingly observed, as the detail of the pebbles demonstrates. The Hellenistic poet is thus concerned with a far more precisely imagined and lingering evocation of a mental scene; it goes well beyond the exigencies of narrative and is unprecedentedly concerned with making an aesthetic impression on the mind's eye.

After the dialogue, we find Amycus calling his subjects and Castor gathering his fellow Argonauts to watch his brother during the boxing match (75–84). This detail is important because through it Theocritus supplies his readers with responses from onlookers with which the readers can identify, and which will amplify their own reactions in the manner of reaction shots in modern film — a close-up of a person or persons reacting to something that is said or done in a previous shot or off-scene.[10] This happens when the Bebrycians cheer as Amycus makes a confused and angry attack and the Argonauts grow afraid that Polydeuces will be hemmed in within the constricted space (91–94), and when the Argonauts cheer when they see that Polydeuces has evaded the danger and the king is severely cut around the face and spitting blood, his eyes bruised into slits (98–101). We can easily reconstruct the scene of the match as surrounded by the two groups of supporters. The Bebrycians occupy the area beneath the plane trees (76) near the spring (40–41); between the groups is the "narrow space" of the "ring" (94). Even the sun has a part to play. It is toward evening — the other Argonauts are preparing beds and

fires on the beach (33)—so the sun is in the west, and each con-
testant initially tries to make his opponent face in that direction in
order to dazzle him.[11]

The protagonists thus play out their roles against a precisely
conceived and described backdrop. But their physical appear-
ances, especially that of Amycus, are drawn in strikingly graphic
detail. Amycus, with his cauliflower ears, huge chest muscula-
ture, broad back, and upper-arm muscles like stones rounded
smooth by a river's winter current, is all boxer (44–52).

> ἔνθα δ᾽ ἀνὴρ ὑπέροπλος ἐνήμενος ἐνδιάασκε,
> δεινὸς ἰδεῖν, σκληρῆσι τεθλασμένος οὔατα πυγμαῖς·   45
> στήθεα δ᾽ ἐσφαίρωτο πελώρια καὶ πλατὺ νῶτον
> σαρκὶ σιδηρείῃ, σφυρήλατος οἷα κολοσσός·
> ἐν δὲ μύες στερεοῖσι βραχίοσιν ἄκρον ὑπ᾽ ὤμου
> ἔστασαν ἠύτε πέτροι ὀλοίτροχοι οὔστε κυλίνδων
> χειμάρρους ποταμὸς μεγάλαις περιέξεσε δίναις·   50
> αὐτὰρ ὑπὲρ νώτοιο καὶ αὐχένος ἠωρεῖτο
> ἄκρων δέρμα λέοντος ἀφημμένον ἐκ ποδεώνων.

Here a monstrous man sat in the sun,
Terrifying to look upon, his ears crushed by harsh blows.   45
His massive chest and broad back were rounded out
With flesh of iron, like a statue of forged metal.
Beneath the tips of his shoulders the muscles in his hard arms
Stood out like rounded stones which a river in winter has rolled
And smoothed in its mighty eddies.   50
From his back and neck was hanging
A lion-skin fastened by the paws.

Though we are impressed primarily by the frontal view of the
king, the detail of the broad back gives us a feeling that we have
him to some extent in the round. And, as we have just seen, he is
set against the background of the *locus amoenus* of which he is
king. The descriptive phraseology at one point suggests that we
are looking at a statue. His skin and flesh are said to be "iron, like
a statue (*kolossos*) of forged metal" (47), giving us a very compel-
ling sense of the appearance and texture of Amycus' skin. The fact
that we have the Boxer in the Terme Museum (Ill. 8) has led schol-
ars to postulate a direct influence from the one work of art to the
other, though the statue is dated to the third or the first century.[12]
On either dating we may ask: is the possibility of direct influence

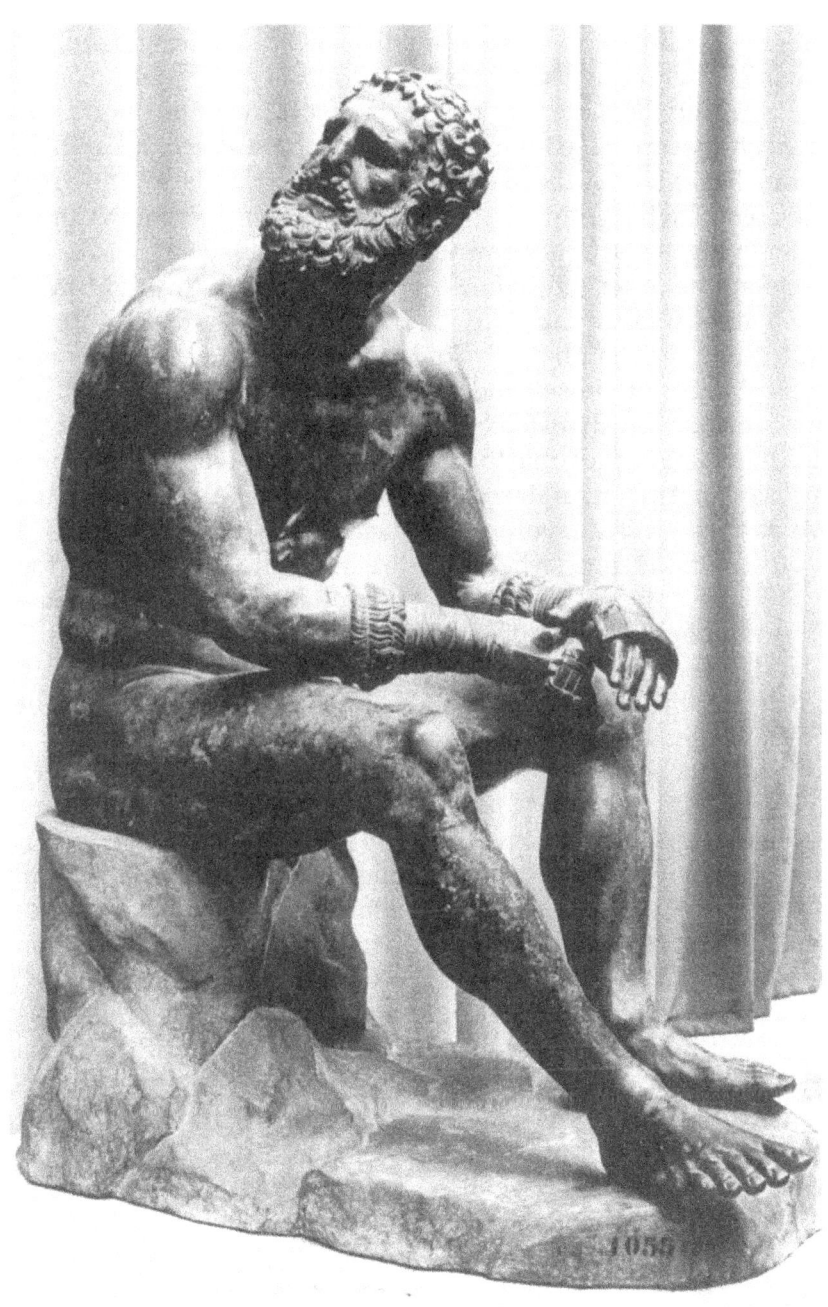

8. Terme Boxer. Museo Nazionale Romano (Terme), Rome. Koppermann, DAI negative number 66.1689

present, or did the two artists go their independent ways in de-
picting common subject matter?

I suggest the latter as the more likely scenario. First, the
wounds to Amycus' ears are not recent (45, *tethlasmenos*),[13] but the
Terme Boxer has just been fighting, and his wounds are still drip-
ping blood, which the artist has marked with copper inlay. Corre-
spondingly, Amycus is wearing a lion-skin, which hangs over his
back and neck (51–52), while the Boxer is naked, his fight over.
The two boxers are thus at two separate stages in their contests.
At the end of the fight with Polydeuces, moreover, Amycus is a
mere shadow of himself and vanquished, while the Terme Boxer
appears indeed exhausted but quite unbowed and still defiant.[14]
It is therefore improbable that the sculptor wanted to give an im-
pression of Amycus after the contest to counterbalance the image
which the poet created of Amycus before the event. What the two
representations show, whether the earlier or the later dating of the
Boxer is accepted, is that the sculptor and poet depicted the same
subject independently but analogously: we see both boxers in the
round, depicted with a fascination for the effects of ancient Greek
boxing on the human body and for the accurate rendering of
physical detail.[15] Comparing the two images in itself tells us a
lot about the analogous modes of viewing in Hellenistic poetry
and art.

Here again comparison with the Homeric passage on which
the description of Amycus is modeled helps us calibrate the
distinctiveness of Hellenistic pictorialism. Homer makes Odys-
seus recount his and his comrades' first viewing of Polyphemus
at *Odyssey* 9.187–92 by calling the Cyclops "terrifyingly huge"
(πελώριος) as he sits in the courtyard. The hero tells how Poly-
phemus routinely herded his flocks separately from the other
Cyclopes in his utter disregard for social institutions and civiliza-
tion; Odysseus remarks that Polyphemus was truly monstrous in
resembling not so much a human being as a wooded mountain
peak that stands apart from the other peaks. Alfred Heubeck
notes that the description is "concentrated more on the sociologi-
cal side" than on the fantastic elements,[16] but the "sociological"
outweighs the visual component as well: Polyphemus' appear-
ance is indicated indirectly, through his resemblance to a moun-
tain peak. This strategy contrasts dramatically with Theocritus'
direct preoccupation with the physiology of Amycus' ears and

musculature, reinforced by means of the indirect description in the simile of the boulders rounded and smoothed by a river's winter torrent.

The boxing match itself (80–134) is presented in such a way as to give the reader a ring-side seat. The spatial location is defined; we have the reactions from the crowd. The stichomythia has enabled us to watch the preceding direct interchange as if the parties were preparing for a brawl before our eyes. So the fight begins, and the strengths and weaknesses of both men are conveyed by the visual depiction of their moves. Polydeuces demonstrates his skill in maneuvering Amycus so that he looks into the sun, and he drives home his advantage by flustering the king with a punch to his chin, which causes Amycus to show a tendency to lose his cool as he puts his head down and barges into his opponent in frustration (83–91). Amycus' unscientific approach is picturesquely parodied when he has his forehead skinned and falls backward among the leaves and flowers of the area outside the "ring." Amycus tires dramatically and visibly, to judge from his muscle shrinkage,[17] while, as Polydeuces warms up, his color looks even better (107–14). The description of Polydeuces' *coup de grâce* is brilliantly precise and immediately picturable. Amycus, desperate, grabs Polydeuces' left hand in his own,[18] thus bringing his body weight forward. He throws a right uppercut at the left side of Polydeuces' head, but Polydeuces weaves out of danger and hits Amycus' left temple with his own right, causing a severe cut. He finishes off the fight with a further weltering around Amycus' face (118–30).

> ἤτοι ὅγε ῥέξαι τι λιλαιόμενος μέγα ἔργον
> σκαιῇ μὲν σκαιὴν Πολυδεύκεος ἔλλαβε χεῖρα,
> δοχμὸς ἀπὸ προβολῆς κλινθείς, ἑτέρῳ δ’ ἐπιβαίνων   120
> δεξιτερῆς ἤνεγκεν ἀπὸ λαγόνος πλατὺ γυῖον.
> καί κε τυχὼν ἔβλαψεν Ἀμυκλαίων βασιλῆα·
> ἀλλ’ ὅγ’ ὑπεξανέδυ κεφαλῇ, στιβαρῇ δ’ ἅμα χειρὶ
> πλῆξεν ὑπὸ σκαιὸν κρόταφον καὶ ἐπέμπεσεν ὤμῳ·
> ἐκ δ’ ἐχύθη μέλαν αἷμα θοῶς κροτάφοιο χανόντος·   125
> λαιῇ δὲ στόμα κόψε, πυκνοὶ δ’ ἀράβησαν ὀδόντες·
> αἰεὶ δ’ ὀξυτέρῳ πιτύλῳ δηλεῖτο πρόσωπον,
> μέχρι συνηλοίησε παρήϊα. πᾶς δ’ ἐπὶ γαίῃ
> κεῖτ’ ἀλλοφρονέων καὶ ἀνέσχεθε νεῖκος ἀπαυδῶν
> ἀμφοτέρας ἅμα χεῖρας, ἐπεὶ θανάτου σχεδὸν ἦεν.   130

Amycus, longing to perform a great deed,
Grabbed Polydeuces' left hand in his own left,
Leaning sideways from his guard, and, stepping forward
    with his right foot.   120
He brought his broad fist up from his right flank.
He would have harmed the king of Amyclae if he had
    landed his punch,
But Polydeuces ducked his head, and with his stout hand
He struck Amycus below the left temple, throwing
    his shoulder into the blow.
Dark blood quickly poured from Amycus' gaping temple.   125
Polydeuces struck his mouth with his left, and
    the closely set teeth clattered.
He beat his face with an increasingly fast welter
Until his cheeks were crushed. Amycus was totally
Laid out on the ground, dazed, and he held up both his hands
    calling off the fight,
For he was near death.   130

The precise observation of body positioning and weight distribution is, again, a feature of contemporary sculpture. A superb example of this is the Boy with a Goose (see Ill. 23). The baby boy, who cannot be more than a year old and is clearly not yet able to walk, has a considerable head weight. When he reaches up with his right hand, imploring the viewer to pick him up, he has to counterbalance by leaning to his left, which has the unfortunate effect of squashing his poor pet.

All this illustrates perfectly the process described in Hellenistic and Imperial *enargeia* theory. The audience is made to feel as if they are included in the scene, primarily because of the visual clarity of Theocritus' presentation, which is unparalleled in earlier descriptions of boxing matches like those at *Iliad* 23.685–99 and *Odyssey* 18.89–99, and is a precious index of the eye for detail of which the Hellenistic mode of viewing was capable in poetry. The description of Epeius and Euryalus' match in the *Iliad* is quite brief: mention is made of details like sweat and teeth-clattering, Epeius' lunging and landing his punch, and Euryalus' spitting blood and being dragged off by his friends. In the ten-and-a-half-line depiction of the contest between Irus and Odysseus, five lines are devoted to the nonpictorial motif of Odysseus' mental decision not to kill Irus outright, and five and a half lines have Irus striking Odysseus on the right shoulder while Odysseus delivers a bone-crushing blow to Irus' neck beneath the ear (whether the right or left ear is unspecified), causing Irus to fall, grinding his teeth and kicking the ground. Nothing in either passage matches Theocritus' graphic commentary on the multiple trading of punches or on the body movements of each contestant, and it is in such pictorialism that the Hellenistic poet outbids his ancient literary model.[19]

Theocritus' technique of following through a minutely observed sequence of events with extensive pictorialism is thrown into even deeper relief by a comparison with the Polyphemus episode of *Odyssey* 9 as a whole. If Heubeck is right in claiming that "the adventure with Polyphemus is among the most elaborately developed" in the *Odyssey*,[20] Homer's narrative will provide another control on the essentially Hellenistic pictorialism of Theocritus' narrative of the boxing match. The stone with which Polyphemus seals the entrance to his cave provides a useful detail for comparison. Of course it is huge: while the Cyclops can lift it high, not even twenty-two wagons would have been able to lift it off the ground (*Od.* 9.240–43), and Odysseus quickly realizes that he cannot kill Polyphemus while he is in his defenseless, drunken sleep without consigning himself and his comrades to death immured in the cave (299–305). So when the blinded giant opens the door, he spreads his arms out to stop Odysseus and his men from escaping (416). This forms an elaborate build-up to Odysseus' display of *mêtis* over and above the blinding and the Nobody trick: the countermove with the rams.

Homer's approach is in fact supremely judicious and economical: just enough detail is provided to set the scene for the next step in the sequence. Nor is it anywhere near so dependent on minute pictorial precision and detail as Theocritus' boxing commentary, nor does it dwell on the pictorial as much as Theocritus' narrative, though the culminating moment of Polyphemus' blinding is certainly tactile, with its similes of the shipwright's smoking drill and the blacksmith's curing of the iron for an axe or an adze (382–94). Theocritus' scene-setting and sequencing strive for plausibility in visual detail where they do not strive for pictorial appeal alone.

But the boxing match of *Idyll* 22 introduces us to fascinating features of Hellenistic poetry and art other than brilliance in vi-

sual realism, and these features merit closer inspection. The first
is the interest in in-the-round portrayal; the second is the desire to
fill in the background of the main scene; the third is the fascina-
tion with optical effects; and the fourth is the concern to present
the ethos and essence of human subjects.

The impression that we can see Amycus from all angles is re-
flected in a well-known aspect of third- and second-century artis-
tic taste. Perhaps the most illustrious forebear of this means of
presentation is the Cnidian Aphrodite of Praxiteles (Ill. 9), prob-
ably to be dated to 350–340. The statue certainly has a focal angle:
the goddess's body, which twists to the left, has an optimal view-
ing angle of 45 degrees, according to Stewart.[21] Given the variety
of the extant copies, we have no means of telling whether her
glance met the observer's gaze at the same angle; if anything, the
point at which she is looking will have been even further to her
left. Be that as it may, the successive settings in which the Cnidia
was displayed in the Hellenistic period are particularly signifi-
cant for gauging the increase in appreciation of all-round view-
ability and display of statues during that period, and possibly
during the lifetime of Theocritus himself. When the statue was
originally made in the late Classical period, it was most probably
housed in a small, rectangular shrine, a *naiskos,* open only at the
front.[22] Circumambulation of the Cnidia was thereby hindered.
But Pliny mentions a rotunda as her setting,[23] and this was ap-
parently a third- or second-century construction.[24] In this context,
Pliny says, the statue was "equally admirable from every angle."
The Hellenistic temple curators and architects therefore both re-
cognized and realized the potential for all-round display, and thus
went further than their Classical counterparts.

As testimony to an apparently even later stage in the framing
of the Cnidia, we have the elaborate and enthusiastic response to
her rear view in Pseudo-Lucian, who describes a visit to the statue
when it was situated in a *naiskos* with two doors. One led to a rear
view of the goddess, the other to her front, "so that no part of her
was left unadmired."[25] (Of course, the visitors' entry through the
back door is a set-up for a joke on the gay Athenian Callicratides,
who is enflamed by what he sees.) This makes it plain that the
builders of the *naiskos* mentioned by Pseudo-Lucian felt that she
was to be viewed in the round. The door behind the goddess
would have led the viewer's gaze first to what was evidently a

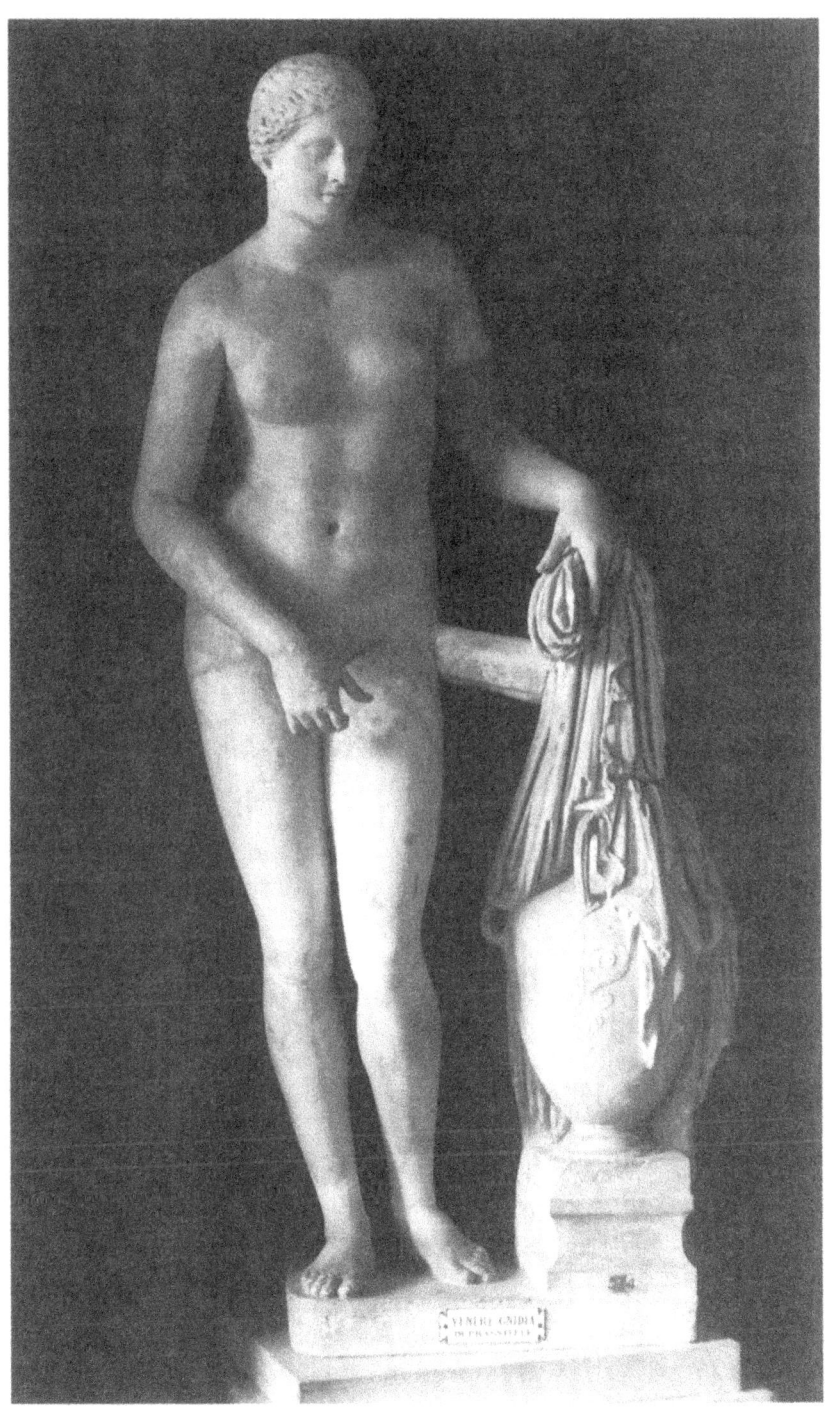

9. Cnidian Aphrodite by Praxiteles. Vatican, Rome. Faraglia, DAI negative number 28.26

prize feature, then around the goddess. Moving to the right would have afforded a view first of her genitals behind her covering hands and then of her amused, knowing, and superior (this is the implication of Pseudo-Lucian's description) smile at the engrossed viewer. Moving around her to the left, the viewer would have been confronted with her "little haughty smile" and then the beauty of her body, an equally powerful and subtle psychological stroke. Pseudo-Lucian's *naiskos* perhaps represents a successive stage in the history of the shrine and was erected after the rotunda Pliny reported on, possibly in order to construct a means of viewing the Cnidia's rear through the agency of a priestess who unlocked the back door (apparently on demand), while conserving the frontal display more characteristic of a traditional *naiskos*.

Stewart has now offered a fresh examination of the multiangle viewability of the Cnidia and a persuasive reconstruction of how the (male) viewer of Pseudo-Lucian's period was manipulated if he entered through the front door. He would have seen the statue frontally, and Aphrodite's efforts to conceal her genitalia would have been felt to have been triggered by his approach, but her smile is directed to his right, as if to another viewer, whose perspective the original viewer would have been enticed to share. In this way the statue's ambiguous focus, hand gestures versus smile, would have kept the viewer changing his viewing position in a kind of love triangle—even if we need not go so far as to say that "his ocular gropings turn into physical frustration."[26] This is the second major way in which the Cnidia's all-round viewability involves the spectator.

It is thus possible that the visual meaning of the Cnidia literally changed as her setting changed, and that, in any case, our vision of the goddess is largely Roman. Early in the statue's life, and certainly in the Hellenistic period, it was felt that the Cnidia's all-round viewability was a major asset, and one to be capitalized upon. The Hadrianic Cnidia in her round building at Tivoli may in fact illustrate how the statue was to be viewed in her rotunda at Cnidus, or at least how the Hellenistic Greeks and Romans saw her.[27] The upshot of all this is, however, that in the Hellenistic period the Cnidia was housed in two different settings so that it could be viewed in a way which, whether it was intended by Praxiteles or not, spoke to a Hellenistic taste for portrayal in the round. That taste was clearly developed beyond the limits of the Classical period.

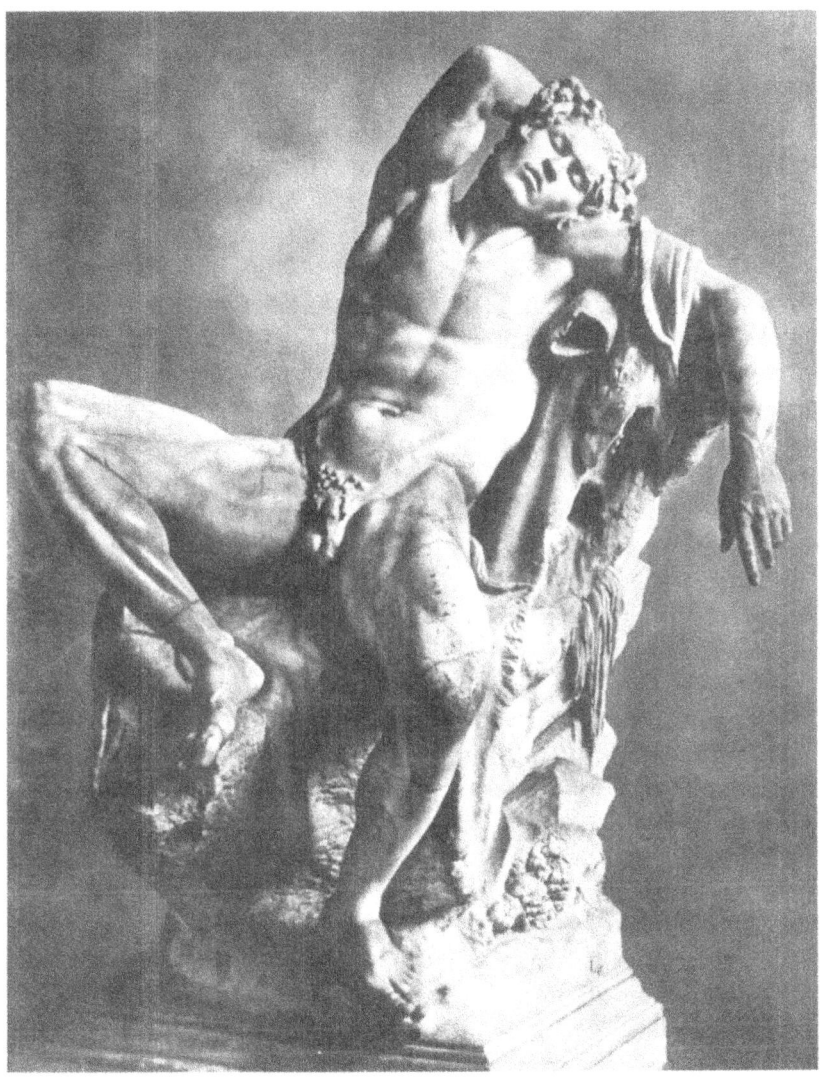

10. Barberini Faun. Glyptothek, Munich. DAI negative number 54.357

Closer to Amycus in both subject and (probably) time of original execution is the Barberini Faun (Ill. 10).[28] The sculptor has not conceived the statue to be viewed from all sides, but the axis of the lower body is markedly different from that of the head, which rests uneasily on the creature's left shoulder. There is an optimal viewing angle, but one must move to take in both the major focal point, the genitals between the provocatively spread legs, and the minor viewing angle, the axis of the head. In this respect, there is perhaps an ambiguity comparable to that which Stewart sees in the Cnidia. From all angles, however, there are the developed muscles and arteries, the latter dilated by the Faun's inebriated state. The viewer is invited to become involved in the realism of the statue, and thus to examine it from multiple if not all angles. In three important essays Ridgway has shown how the original settings of sculptures like the Barberini Faun, including the Invitation to the Dance (Ill. 11) and the Farnese Heracles (see Ill. 21), can be differentiated from those of Classical sculpture by the movement away from display in religious and civic locations to private gardens, gymnasia, schools, and parks. Sculpture and reliefs projected into their setting, she demonstrates, so that an even greater illusionism was achievable, as would definitely have been the case with the Faun.[29] The analogy with Theocritus' strategy in his description of Amycus is plain.[30]

Both the art and the poetry of the Hellenistic period show an interest in giving main subjects an in-the-round, three-dimensional depth. Added to this is a desire to place the main subject in a background setting invested with three-dimensionality and depth of field. The latter interest is in fact evidenced earlier for poetry than for painting and sculpture, as we shall see. Here again, the Amycus and Polydeuces episode has provided us with an excellent starting point, with its location of Amycus in his countryside setting, its positioning of the boxing match within a mentally picturable locale, and its deployment of reaction shots from the boxers' respective supporters.

Theocritus' keen eye for the details of the local setting of his narrative is demonstrated by a comparison with a work of art whose original he may actually have seen. This is the engraving on the Ficoroni cista from the late fourth century, which has been presumed to go back to a painting or a painter's sketch from the second half of the fourth century.[31] Its depiction of Polydeuces tying Amycus to a tree involves onlooking Argonauts, a picture of the beached Argo with one Argonaut climbing down the ship's ladder with two pitchers, another Argonaut lighting a fire on the beach, and a picture of the spring restored to general access, with a silen sitting on a nearby rock while an Argonaut practices boxing on a punching-bag suspended from a tree and another silen peacefully drinks the spring's water out of a cup. The motifs

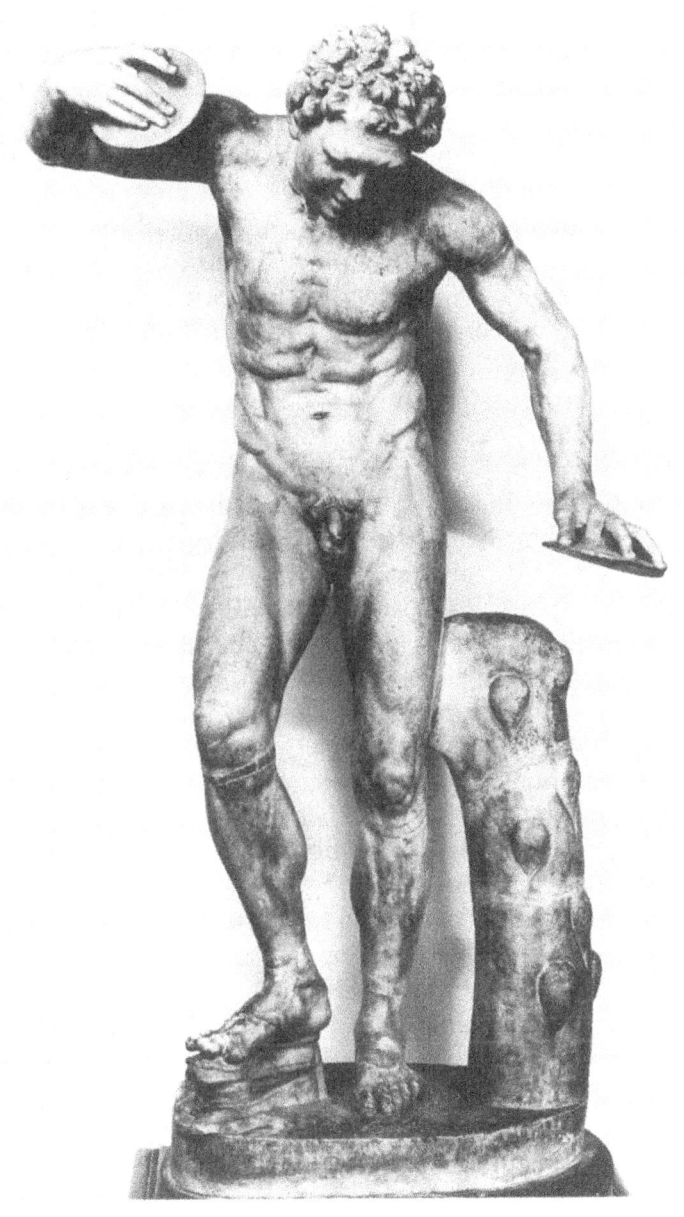

11. Invitation to the Dance. Uffizi, Florence. Koppermann, DAI negative number 65.2134

of scenery and onlookers are indeed present, but Theocritus' de-
tailed observation of the spring's water, the natural setting in gen-
eral, and the onlookers is far more developed than that on the re-
markable cista, whose two trees, beach, rocks, and spring are
largely necessitated by the plot, though the spring is individual-
ized by being given the form of a lion's head, from whose mouth
the spring emanates. The cista certainly tries within the limits of
its medium to give a full evocation of the epic moment and thus
provides an analogy with Theocritus' pictorial narrative, but the
analogue in fact merely highlights the poet's infinitely more thor-
ough image-making.

We would expect this strategy to be followed through particu-
larly in Theocritus' pastoral *Idylls.* As modern readers have long
noticed, however, provision for the rustics' background setting is
surprisingly scant. The only really extended example is, of course,
the scene of the harvest festival described by Simichidas in *Idyll*
7, lines 131-57. The scene, with its rush couches for the guests,
the elms and poplars overhead, the babbling stream of water, the
sound of the cicadas, birds, and bees, the autumn smells of the
fruit falling near the reclining guests, is admittedly a *tour de force,*
and certainly succeeds in helping us place the party in a visual
context (though all five senses are appealed to). At one remove,
we have the emphasis on the sweetness of the setting described
by Thyrsis and the Goatherd in *Idyll* 1, lines 1-14, though this is
tone-setting, establishing the harmonious relationship of the two
herdsmen, rather than scene-setting for the scene's sake.

Apart from that, we really only have the moments where The-
ocritus makes his rustics describe the respective merits of the
places they have chosen to sing in, as Lacon and Comatas do in
their aggressive interchange at *Idyll* 5, lines 31-34 and 45-61. Here
the scenes, as bargaining points, are again primarily intended to
color in the characters of the contestants, not the setting. In the
pastoral poetry of the first half of the third century, therefore,
landscape plays a surprisingly circumscribed role as a means of
giving depth of field to our mental picture of the increasingly
popular theme of rustic life. Nonetheless, the fact that extensive
visualization is by and large reserved for more heightened, "po-
etic" contexts actually strengthens our findings about the impor-
tance of Hellenistic poetry's novel techniques of engaging and
manipulating the viewing reader.

In one perhaps unexpected way, however, the countryside does provide a kind of perspective — when the natural world reacts to human suffering, in adumbration of the "pathetic fallacy." In other words, landscape itself provides a reaction shot. This is first evidenced for pastoral in the first *Idyll*, when jackals, wolves, and lions, and then Daphnis' own oxen, bulls, heifers, and calves mourn his death (71–75). Later Daphnis takes leave of them (115–21), calling for his bucolic world's reversal: "may you brambles, may you thistles bear violets, may the beautiful narcissus wave on junipers, may all things turn into their opposite, may the pine tree bear pears, since Daphnis is dying, and may the deer harry the hounds and the owls from the mountains sing against nightingales" (132–36). The motif is expanded in the pseudo-Moschan *Epitaph of Bion* (1–35) and Bion's *Lament for Adonis* (32–39), dated to the late second or early first century B.C.[32]

The idea of the countryside as actively sympathetic to its inhabitants' suffering may be related to the traditional view of it as an index of peace and order as maintained by its masters.[33] Callimachus provides an example when he describes the ravaged condition of Molorchus' property in the *Victoria Berenices*.[34] As Peter Parsons translates the fragments, Molorchus says, "May the lion perish . . . so that . . . again fuel for the fire, with no miserable lack of wood . . . for the young trees have no knowledge of the pruning-hook . . . the she-goat, though eager to bite at the clover, bleats, shut up within the gates."[35] Here the landscape illustrates the disorder into which the area has fallen as a result of the Nemean lion's depredations, a theme also found in the pseudo-Theocritean account of the same story, where Heracles cannot ask questions concerning the lion's whereabouts since the country people have all fled from their work in the fields in fear of it (168, 201–3, 218–20, 280–81). Here the countryside itself is the sufferer (in contrast to the pathetic fallacy, where nature responds to human pain), but it sets the scene in a significant way.

For the motif of human onlookers providing depth and perspective, we have, first, Apollonius' companion piece to Theocritus' account of the boxing match between Amycus and Polydeuces (*Argonautica* 2.1–97). Interestingly, this is an area in which Apollonius' version is more jejune than Theocritus' and demonstrates the latter's far greater attention to visual detail in his description of the event: we are told only that Amycus and

Polydeuces "looked around for a venue which pleased them, and seated all their men in two separate groups on the sand" (35–36), and that, at the fatal defeat of Amycus, the Argonauts "gave a roar" (96–97). As Jason undergoes Aeëtes' contest in *Argonautica* 3.1278–407, we are merely told that the Argonauts are afraid when they see Aeëtes' bronze bulls (1293), that Aeëtes is amazed at Jason's strength (1314), that Jason's companions encourage him while he waits for the Earthborn men to sprout up, that the Colchians give a cheer when they see Jason's superhuman stonecast, while Aeëtes is struck dumb at the feat (1370, 1372–73), and, finally, that Aeëtes is downcast at the sight of his massacred Earthborn men, like a gardener whose saplings have been flattened by rain, the simile conveying Aeëtes' reaction indirectly, however effectively (1399–404).[36] More extensive in its treatment of the motif is the moment when the Nereids guide the Argo past the Planctae off Sicily, and Hephaestus "looks on in awe at them from the smooth top of a peak, leaning his mighty shoulder against the handle (?) of his hammer," while Hera, "standing over the scene in radiant heaven, throws her arms around Athene, such is her fear as she looks on" (4.956–60). This interesting variation on the theme of the divine audience incorporates genre elements, especially when the terrified Hera hugs her ally, and in the process gives a female perspective on the epic moment; Hephaestus, too, admires the females involved in the heroic adventure.

Of greater interest is the detail of the men looking at Io in the description of Europa's basket in Moschus' *Europa* (48–49): "men stood in a group on the brows of each coastal height [i.e. of the Bosporus] and gazed in amazement at the sea-going heifer." First, the reaction is implied in the words "gazed in amazement" and in the paradoxical description of the heifer as "sea-going," emphasizing how remarkable the sight is. Second, the detail occurs in a description of a work of art and probably owes something to actual visual art: since the date of the *Europa* is the mid-second century B.C., the poem is probably separated by only a few years from the Telephus frieze, on which two panels show the two maids of Auge looking on in grief as craftsmen construct the boat that will expose their mistress at sea (see Ill. 20).[37] It is true that the maids do more than just provide reaction shots, for they are typical mourning onlooker-slaves, quoted from three generations of Attic fourth-century gravestones,[38] and are thus also a Classical allusion. More directly comparable are the Apulian vases with Europa observed by figures viewing from a higher level.[39] We are reminded also of the two shepherds who look on as representatives of country peace invaded by the events of myth while the Laestrygonians attack Odysseus' men on the Odyssey landscape-murals of the next century.[40] Moschus thus shows us fascinatingly how sculpture and painting have trained his eye in the selection of detail, here simultaneously giving spatial depth of field, providing an emotional perspective, and directing the reader's eye toward the central figure.[41]

There is, finally, the passage in Apollonius' *Argonautica* depicting the Acherousian Headland, the entry to Hades on the coast of the Black Sea which the Argonauts sail past (2.727–49). The pictorial details add up to a precise mental image: the promontory rises high to overlook the Black Sea; at its base smooth, sea-washed rocks stand firm amid the roar and surge of the surf; its summit is lined with spreading plane trees; a hollow glen slopes down from the promontory inland; a cave leading to Hades is covered by trees and rocks, and from it a freezing draught deposits rime which does not melt even at mid-day. Here is the mouth of the River Acheron. From the scholium we can probably assume that Apollonius is borrowing from a description of the headland by the historian Nymphis, in which case the poet is not dependent on autopsy for his pictorial precision and scientific accuracy of observation regarding rime and cave temperatures.[42] This degree of interest in spatial layout and geographical detail is not equaled in painting and sculpture, as far as we know, until the first-century Nilotic mosaics,[43] and it seems here again that in fact poetry preceded visual art. And the atmosphere created is dwelt upon to an extent which makes us think of the Odyssey landscapes of two centuries later.

The use of landscape and reaction shots to provide three-dimensionality and spatial depth is something that the visual art of the period does not explore to the same extent. In the case of painting, we have the actual examples (discovered in 1978) of Hades' rape of Persephone in "Vergina Tomb I" and the hunting scene of Tomb II. It is perhaps significant that these scenes, both datable to the second half of the fourth century, reveal little interest in the space in which the incidents occur, giving only a context in space in which the characters can act. This confirmed what was known from the Alexander mosaic, generally assumed to go back to a late fourth-century painting. Here the scenery is limited to a leafless tree and some objects in the foreground.[44] Even if painting influenced the landscape scenery of the Telephus frieze,[45] we shall see that the results of such inspiration were in fact quite limited. Scholars have sometimes argued from the alleged "painterly" eye of Apollonius (in his descriptions of, for example, the scene of the launching of the Argo) that early Hellenistic painting was more advanced than we had thought. This is alleged to be demonstrated by Apollonius' use of color contrasts and his making the sky, land, and sea meet, to continue with the example of the launching scene.[46] But such arguments are close to circular (Apollonius' eye was educated by third-century painting, so his descriptive passages are a guide to it); they neglect the indicators which make us suspect that in some ways the poets went further than the artists themselves with their creation of visual effects in the depiction of landscape, especially in their pursuit of the poetic aim of *enargeia*. An overwhelming interest in landscape as a fully realized backdrop is not found in painting till the Odyssey landscapes.

Apart from isolated antecedents in sculptured friezes and painting,[47] the first significant and datable work of visual art that we have which exhibits a developed interest in such matters is the choragic monument of Lysicrates, of 334 B.C. The scene of Dionysus' punishment of the Tyrrhenian pirates contains landscape elements like trees, rocks, wine-mixing craters, and waves whose purpose is simply to locate the event and the figures in it. Suggestions that these features are more than stage props and are meant to show Dionysus' power over nature[48] are impossible to sustain. Of greater interest for us is the fact that Dionysus is depicted looking on, reclining with his panther on rocky ground and watching his satyrs as they overwhelm the pirates, for here we have a moment where the use of landscape detail and the motif of viewing coincide. As has often been remarked, moreover, this is in striking contrast with the "canonical" version of the myth, the *Homeric Hymn to Dionysus,* where the god (in the form of a lion) is directly involved in the action on the pirate ship while its men are transformed into animals as they jump overboard.[49] Thus, the presentation of the god as observer appears all the more remarkable, and his reaction shot gives a sense of depth of field in a way that the landscape elements really do not.

The Tyche of Antioch, reported to have been the work of Lysippus' son and pupil Eutychides,[50] featured the Hellenistic deity seated on a rock while Orontes swam below. If the statue was, as Ridgway suggests,[51] set up in connection with a pool, perhaps the nymphaeum mentioned by an ancient source, its base rock may have been fashioned to fit in with its setting, but the effect would no doubt have been in part to enhance the unprecedentedly daring casual conception of a goddess and the sense of her accessibility, rather than to draw major attention to the scenery itself.[52] The background details on the Telephus frieze of c. 165–159 B.C., the next monument showing a marked interest in setting, include altars and trees, the latter much more individualized than those on Lysicrates' monument. Again, however, though such details are elaborately executed, their principal aim is subsidiary to the narrative, locating the action outdoors in the country or inside a building, as the altar locates the scene inside a sanctuary. They are not there to be dwelt upon for themselves, as with Theocritus' evocation of the harvest festival, though, as we have seen, they do play a part comparable to the contrast between the beauty of the country setting and the ugliness of Amycus in *Idyll* 22.

The same may in general be said of the "Farnese Bull" group (Ill. 12), commonly regarded as a Roman adaptation of an original from the mid-second century, though scholars have recently lowered the date to 42 B.C.[53] This group depicts Zethus and Amphion punishing Dirce by tying her to a bull. Rocky scenery supports Dirce's drapery, and here the scenery is in the round, not just in relief, as on the Telephus frieze (a natural limitation of the medium). There may have been some attempt in the original to locate the harsh punishment in an appropriately desolate setting, but the scenery details are still not foregrounded in the way that they are in the *Thalysia*. Such effects are achieved only in the Nilotic mosaics of around 110 B.C., though the distinct possibility must be borne in mind that these had archetypes from Alexandria itself dating from the latter half of the third century B.C., and that these models had extensive backgrounds for their depictions of animals. It has been conjectured that their rendition of scenery was in the style of the Vergina hunt scenes.[54] The *Thalysia*'s interest in natural settings is also detectable in descendants of the Telephus

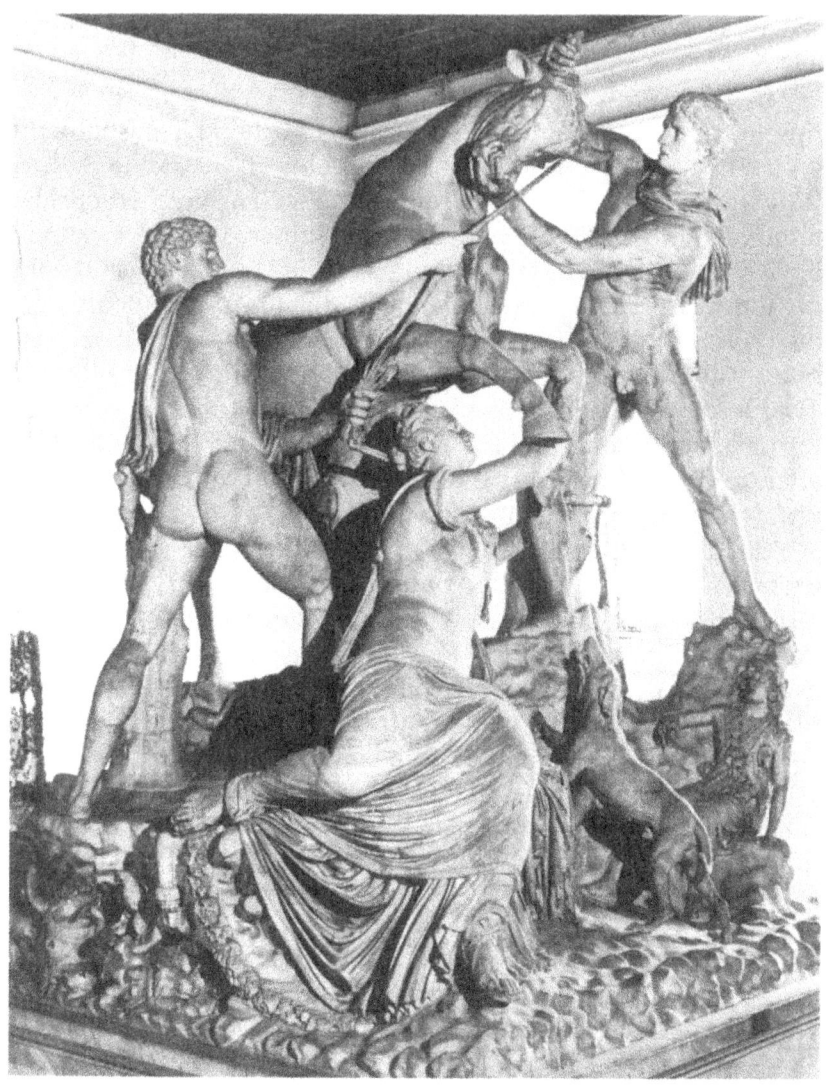

12. Farnese Bull. Museo Nazionale, Naples. Schwanke, DAI negative number 85.644

frieze:[55] the first-century B.C. friezes depicting a peasant watering his cow at a fountain, and the Munich peasant driving his cow to market, with its inward-stretching perspective, scenery, and rustic shrine.[56] Von Hesberg, for example, has mounted an impressive case, mentioned in chapter 1,[57] for believing that the Munich relief's gate with a tree growing through it, the temple, and the dilapidated wall were intended to suggest that *pax* and *pietas* were ideals which the Augustan age valued positively—not utopian but within the grasp of all ranks in society.[58]

We are obviously at the mercy of archaeological survival here, but from the extant evidence it looks as if early Hellenistic poetry's mode of vision was more developed than that of contemporary visual art in this respect.[59] This interesting possibility might perhaps be explained by a combination of factors. First there is the matter of narrative. This is essential to epic in any period, but not so elaborately integral to representational art until we have the continuous narrative of the Telephus frieze.[60] Second, the epic of the third century evinces a desire for the most precise pictorial presentation and spatial disposition of subject matter which is unprecedented in earlier epic, as we found in Theocritus' setting for the boxing match and Apollonius' description of the Acherousian Headland;[61] as we shall see, the poets on occasion actually demand that the reader visually supplement the setting.[62] This delight in visual detail is a sign that the poets regarded it as helping their readers feel as if they were in the presence of the subject, a quality which seems to have been formalized in the literary concept of *enargeia* to address precisely this effect. With late Classical statuary like the Cnidia (see Ill. 9) or early Hellenistic pieces like the Barberini Faun (see Ill. 10), we feel ourselves to be in the presence of the subject in a physical sense, sufficiently "located" without detailed backgrounding. Poetry strove for the same sense of orientation, but it had to use different means to achieve it.

Another particularly fascinating source of visual detail, and sometimes also of thematic perspective, is the exploration of optical effects, especially those involving mirror images and the reflection of light. We saw a hint of this interest in Theocritus' description of the pebbles gleaming under the clear water of Amycus' spring in *Idyll* 22. A straightforward but striking example of the fascination with actual mirroring is the passage in Callimachus' *Acontius and Cydippe*. The bulls to be sacrificed before the marriage of Cydippe to a suitor other than Acontius (the ceremony fails because Cydippe has inadvertently promised herself to Acontius) are said to be terrified when they catch a glimpse of the sacrificial knife reflected in the water in the lustral bowl (*Fr.* 75.10–11 Pfeiffer). Significantly, the motif appealed to that connoisseur of Hellenistic poetry's visual quality, Ovid, who uses Callimachus' image twice: in the *Fasti* he wonders whether the Agon of the Roman calendar is derived from the "agonized" fear of the sacrificial victim who sees the knife's reflection in the water (1.327–28); in the *Metamorphoses*, Pythagoras puts Callimachus to use to create pathos and revulsion at the suffering of the sacrificial bull as part of a sweeping attack on meat-eating ("the victim stains with his blood the sacrificial knives which he has perhaps seen before in the clear water," 15.134–35). Whether Callimachus was knowledgeable about animal psychology or not (Ovid deftly absolves himself from the charge of credulity by his "perhaps"), his ingenious detail rests on his imaginative "catoptrics." The reflected face of the dying Persian in the Alexander mosaic (Ill. 13) creates pathos in a parallel manner.

But perhaps the most prominent examples concern Aphrodite. The most notable is the description of the vignette, as it appears on Jason's cloak in Apollonius' *Argonautica*, of the goddess holding Ares' shield, in which her image is reflected (*Argonautica* 1.742–46). I once tried to bring out the sophistication of the levels of artistic representation implied, calling it "a poetic description of a reflected image in a woven picture,"[63] but Denis Feeney, subscribing to the view that the description is meant to evoke famous statuary, has now gone one better: he defines the description as "a representation in words of a representation in cloth of a representation in marble of a goddess — and her reflection."[64] We are told that the fastener of the goddess's tunic is unclasped and has fallen onto her left forearm and below her breast. Then we are told that "opposite her an accurate image of her, just as she was, could be seen on the bronze shield." We are left to assume that the picture of Aphrodite's décolletage is what appeared on the depiction of the shield. Interestingly, we are not told that Aphrodite is actually looking at the reflection of herself, a fact which ought to be addressed by the scholars (like Simon) who postulate direct influence from the Capua Aphrodite (Ill. 14), where the goddess is narcissistically perusing her reflected beauty.[65] One way ahead might be the word "opposite" (ἀντίον), which would probably (but not necessarily) permit us to infer that the image was "opposite" her upper body, and that she is holding the shield up to inspect the image on it. In any case, we can certainly talk of the eroticism involved in the indirect portrayal of the goddess's beauty, a masterstroke in this description of a work of art.

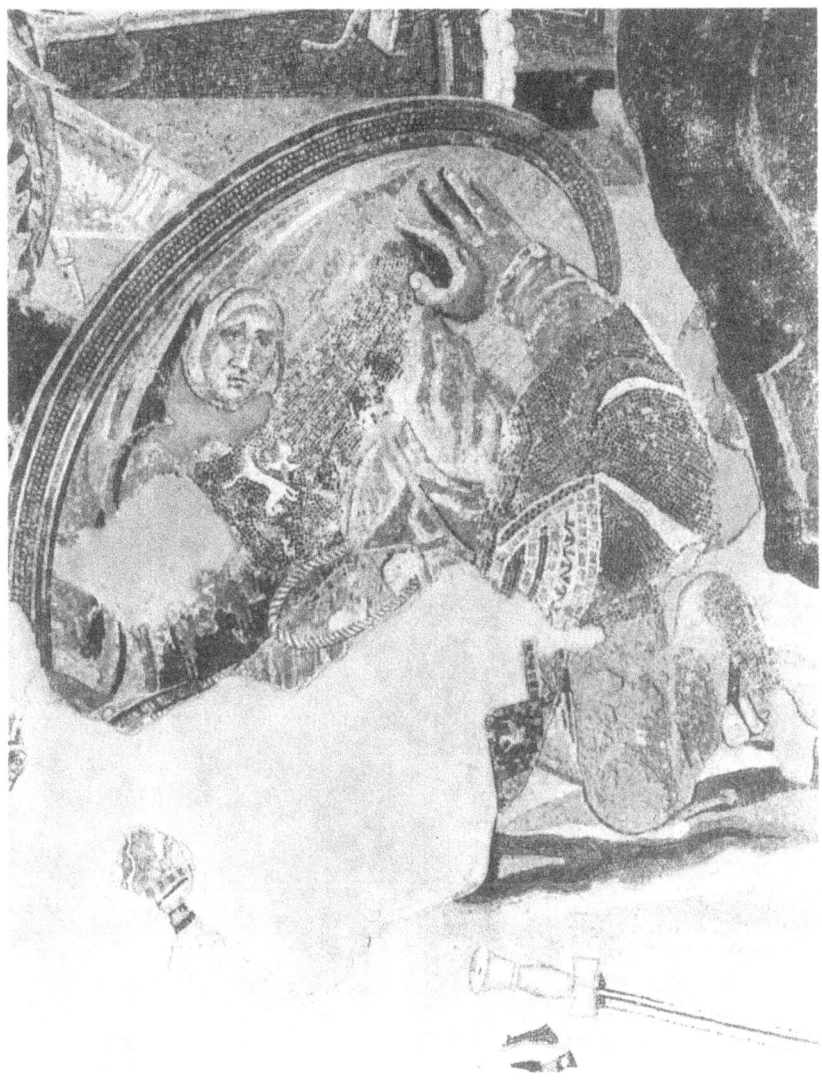

13. Alexander Mosaic: reflected face of Persian. Museo Nazionale, Naples.
Bartl, DAI negative number 58.1855

The theme of the mirror image as the special preserve of love is also to be found in Callimachus. In the *Bath of Pallas* the celebrant instructs the attendants not to bring Athene a mirror since she is always beautiful,[66] as was witnessed by her preparation for the Judgment of Paris. On that occasion neither she nor Hera had any use for a mirror or a reflection in a river's water, while Aphrodite

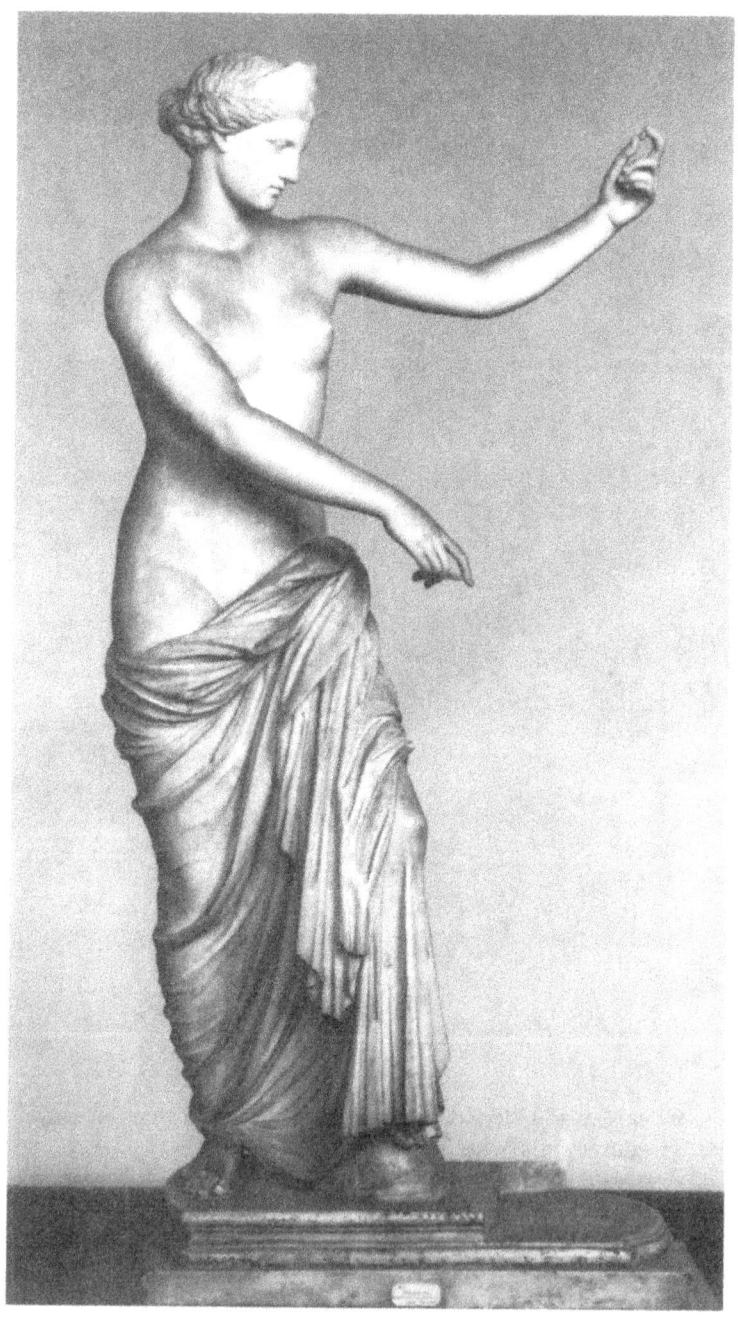

14. Capua Aphrodite. Museo Nazionale, Naples. Schwanke, DAI negative number 83.2259

"took a shining bronze mirror and often re-arranged the same lock twice" (*Hymn* 5.13-28), the implication being that artifice rather than natural beauty was what really won the day.

In visual art we have already noticed the Capua Aphrodite, which on Christine Havelock's recent down-dating comes from the first century B.C.;[67] here the goddess stands engrossed in her reflection on Ares' shield, and the motif of narcissism is quite explicit. It would be of the greatest interest if we knew for a fact whether Aphrodite's reflection was painted on the original of the shield, or whether, even more naturalistically, the bronze shield was polished so that it had an actual mirror effect. But the bottom line is that Aphrodite was presented as viewing the reflection of her own image. To follow Ridgway's conclusion: "On her projecting left thigh she must have balanced a large shield in which she admired her nude torso."[68]

An early Hellenistic work of art exhibiting an interest in reflections, and one also proposed as an actual model for the Aphrodite on Jason's cloak, is the lost painting of Thetis by Theon of Samos. Havelock reconstructs it from the Pompeian painting in Naples as depicting Thetis in Hephaestus' workshop, looking into the completed shield of Achilles, on which her image is reflected.[69] In the Pompeian painting Thetis' garment is slipping off her right shoulder on to her right breast: this is similar to Apollonius' evocation of Aphrodite, but a completely bare breast would have been inappropriate for a Thetis. Alan Shapiro has argued that Theon's painting was "probably" a source for Apollonius, though he regards it as possible that the debt was not only to this painting but to the numerous versions of the subject in the various media, in part attracted to it by the motif of the reflected image.[70] This is part of Shapiro's overall intention to show that the description of Jason's cloak is as much concerned with contemporary principles of art as with the deeper thematic preoccupations of the *Argonautica* as a poem. With this general conception of art's influence on Hellenistic poetry I am in the greatest sympathy, as should by now be quite apparent.

For further examples of Hellenistic art's fascination with reflected images we have reports of paintings of Narcissus from the Hellenistic period and later originals which feature the reflection of Narcissus' face in the water (Ill. 15).[71] The later originals, at least, show that the painters sometimes obeyed rules of perspective and catoptrics in rendering the reflected face.[72] These again reveal the age's fascination with the kind of eroticism associated with the indirect gaze at physical beauty to which Narcissus gave his name. More distant in effect, though not in technique, is the reflected image of the face of the dying Persian in the foreground of the Alexander mosaic (see Ill. 13). Here the indirect portrayal, which does not comply with the laws of the angles of reflection in perspective,[73] underlines the pathos of the warrior's plight.

Of analogous execution but with inverse effect is the moment described by Damoetas' Polyphemus in Theocritus' sixth *Idyll* when the Cyclops claims that he is not as ugly as people say. His evidence is that the other day he looked into the water when the sea was calm. His chin and one eye looked handsome, "in my opinion," and the water reflected the whiteness of his teeth, which gleamed brighter than Parian marble (35–38). Here the mirror image is willfully distorted into conveying the precise reverse of the visual truth—that the Cyclops is ugly. Moreover, while Daphnis in the companion song had addressed Polyphemus with the words "Un-beauty often appears beauty to love" (19), raising the enticing possibility that Galatea might be a victim of love's delusion, we now find that the commonplace has a more immediate application to Polyphemus, whose own judgment has been clouded by his desire to be attractive to his beloved Galatea. To a Hellenistic audience there may have been an element of surprise in seeing such a wrong reading of "true" information supplied by something objectively as faithful as a mirror image.

The sixth *Idyll* features another mirror image. Daphnis tells Polyphemus that the bitch that watches over his sheep is barking as she looks out to sea at Galatea, and the waves of the sea as it quietly laps onto the shore reflect the dog's image as she watches (10–13). This atmospheric detail also involves self-deception, for whereas Polyphemus replies in Damoetas' song that he made the dog bark at Galatea to soften her by reminding her of the time when the dog whimpered and nuzzled up to her hip (29–30), we are free to infer that the dog, as the guardian of Polyphemus' flock, is indeed more likely to attack Galatea when she comes on to the beach, as Daphnis suggests (13–14), in order to protect Polyphemus from emotional suffering. The interplay between the faithfulness of a mirror's image and the false interpretation to which it is subject is, therefore, a highly engaging element in the *Idyll*.

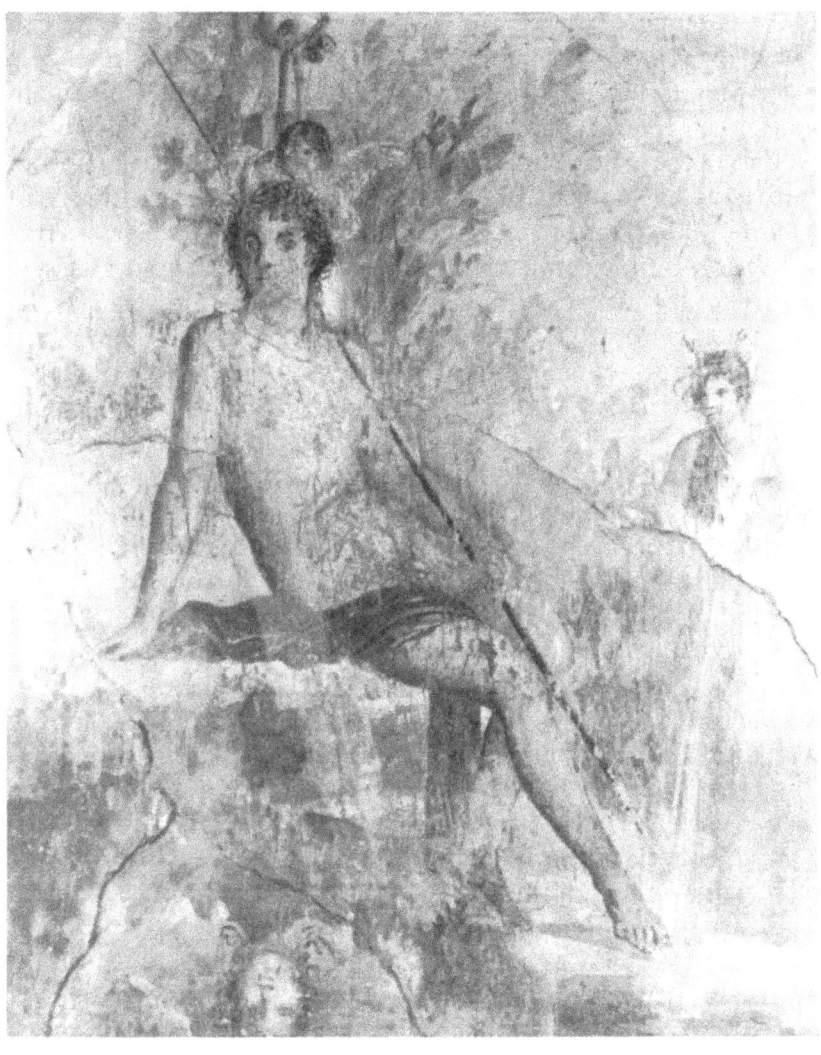

15. Narcissus' reflected face. Museo Nazionale, Naples. Anger, DAI negative number 89.84

A related preoccupation, again common to Hellenistic poetry and art, is with the visual effects of reflected light. In poetry, Apollonius is our major source of instances. The most striking example is to be found in the passage describing the rape of Hylas by the nymph of the spring called Pegae. As Hylas prepares to gather water in the dark of evening, "his beauty and sweet grace" are made to blush red by the light of the full moon, which catches him as it shines from the sky. His beauty, thus enhanced, motivates the nymph's desire (1.1230–33). The effect is again erotic. Hardly less so is the moment when Jason picks up the golden fleece for the first time. In the night, the gleam of its wool throws a red glow like flame on his fair cheeks and forehead (4.170–73). The erotic aspect of the image is brought out even further by the simile comparing Jason's delight to that of a girl who rejoices in the radiance imparted to her dress by the gleam of the full moon (4.167–70), another telling instance of Apollonius' interest in the aesthetic potential of reflected light.[74] Yet another example is the passage describing the local nymphs who, carrying many-hued flowers on their white breasts, decorate the cave in which Jason and Medea make love on the golden fleece. They are "all surrounded with the fleece's radiance like a fire's, such was the glow that sparkled from its golden tufts, and it lit sweet desire in their eyes" (4.1143–48). Scholars[75] have rightly observed that Apollonius shares this interest in reflected light and chiaroscuro with Hellenistic painters like Antiphilus, who actually served under Soter, and whose Boy Blowing on a Fire is described by Pliny.[76] The work is said to have been admired for the way the artist made the house and the boy's face reflect the glow. Pliny mentions the painter Philiscus as working with the same theme, a painter's atelier where a boy is blowing on the fire.[77]

Visual effects of this kind are not found in earlier Greek poetry, including Homer. They attest to the new viewing preoccupations of the early Hellenistic period. The age's fascination with light effects and the play of colors in general is illustrated beautifully by the epigrams dealing with gemstones which are preserved on the new Posidippus papyrus. In one poem (I 30–35 Bastianini-Gallazzi) Posidippus admires a honey-colored stone carved by Cronius which lights up (?) a woman's pendant "so that on her bosom a honey-colored light shines together with her white skin." In another (II 29–32 Bastianini-Gallazzi) the poet comments in positive terms on the visual trick a certain gem plays: if it is wetted, a light encircles its body; when it is dry, the image of a Persian lion blazes out as bright as the sun. And a cornelian gem "lets its light shine forth from within" ([φ]έγγος ἔνερθεν ἄγων), and would hold its own against Indian rubies if it were tested with illumination from an identical light source (I 36–II 2

Bastianini-Gallazzi). Clearly the Hellenistic eye was unprecedentedly alert to these color and light effects in both life and art.

The simile comparing Jason to the girl enchanted with the play of moonlight on her dress is an instance of Jason's frequent association with light and star imagery. This imagery begins in another love context, the moment when Jason, as he approaches the city of the Lemnian women, is compared to the bright star Hesperus, whose red brilliance, together with its associations with marriage, charms young unmarried women and the virgin whose betrothed husband is abroad, filling them with feelings of romance and yearning (1.774–81).[78] And when Jason at last appears to Medea for their assignation, he is compared to the brilliant star Sirius, whose rising heralded the hottest days of summer (3.956–60); its destructive aspect, despite its beauty and clarity, is reinforced by the reminiscence of Priam's sighting of Achilles as he bears down on Hector for their last encounter (*Iliad* 22.25–32).

Medea is associated with a similar set of images, as when the effect of her first love for Jason is compared to the way a flame leaps from a small brand on which a poor woman wool-worker has heaped up dry twigs, and the flame consumes them all, so that the woman has bright light in her dwelling during the night (3.291–95).[79] A comparison of this simile with its original, the simile at *Iliad* 12.433–35 featuring the poor widow's efforts to have her wool weighed accurately so that she can earn enough to feed her children, shows Apollonius' far greater emphasis on the lighting effects of the scene, though in the other simile inspired by the Iliadic passage (*Argonautica* 4.1061–65) Apollonius suppresses the motif of the flame's light, concentrating this time on the widow's lamentations for her children and her misery at the loss of her husband. Jason and Medea share the image at 3.1017–19, where she is said to have been willing to help Jason and to have rejoiced in his need of her, "such was the love that flashed forth its sweet flame from the son of Aeson's fair head and snatched the bright glances of her eyes."

But not even these images are so precisely observed as the simile describing the fluttering of Medea's heart as Jason undergoes the trial of yoking Aeëtes' bulls. The palpitations are compared to the way a sunbeam is reflected off the surface of water just poured into a bucket and dances on the walls and ceiling of a house (3.756–59).[80] The simile warrants quotation in full as a particularly

telling illustration of Apollonius' interest in the effect of light re-
flection.

ἠελίου ὥς τίς τε δόμοις ἔνι πάλλεται αἴγλη,
ὕδατος ἐξανιοῦσα τὸ δὴ νέον ἠὲ λέβητι
ἠέ που ἐν γαυλῷ κέχυται, ἡ δ' ἔνθα καὶ ἔνθα
ὠκείῃ στροφάλιγγι τινάσσεται ἀίσσουσα

Just as inside a house a ray of sunlight,
Reflected from water which has just been poured
Into either a bowl or a bucket,
Quivers and darts now here, now there, as it is shaken
     in the swift eddy . . .

True, Apollonius seems indebted to the formulaic couplet in the
Odyssey describing the palaces of Menelaus and Alcinous, ὥς τε
γὰρ ἠελίου αἴγλη πέλεν ἠὲ σελήνης / δῶμα καθ' ὑψερεφὲς, "just like
the sun's or the moon's was the radiance throughout the high-
roofed palace" (*Od.* 4.45–46, 7.84–85). But there is no concern for
the effects of reflected light in the *Odyssey*'s formula, and to that
extent we can fairly conclude that the optical motif in Apollonius
is unprecedented in earlier Greek poetry. It is equally unprece-
dented, as far as we know, in the way it vividly evokes Medea's
less "tangible" physiological and emotional state.

Significantly, Hellenistic poetry and visual art's interest in
these precisely observed optical effects coincides with scientific
inquiry associated with Alexandria. A *Catoptrics* is attributed to
Euclid,[81] and his authorship of an *Optics* is beyond doubt, as is his
activity in Alexandria (floruit under Soter).[82] Archimedes (floruit
c. 250), who resided at least for a time in Alexandria,[83] is also cred-
ited with a *Catoptrics*.[84] The fascination with mirror images and
reflected light that we have discovered in early Hellenistic poetry
and art was therefore part and parcel of the Hellenistic intellec-
tual and aesthetic culture in general.

May we go the next step and ask what the source of the Hel-
lenistic interest in such images might have been?

Plato in *Republic* 10 (596d–e) assumes mirrors to offer the "tru-
est" images, so that *a fortiori* any artistic mimesis is the more vul-
nerable to his strictures against objects and their appearances as a
guide to truth and reality. The only trouble for him is that not even
the original mirrored objects are "true": rather, as Glaucon puts it,

mirrors offer mere imitations of an appearance, not even imitations of things, but of how things appear. Moreover, Socrates' discussion of painting stresses its deceptive capacities, which are thus already implied in the sorts of images mirrors produce. But for Hellenistic poets and artists, the mirror's intrinsic "truth-to-nature" is a datum which is far less problematic in terms of ontologies. So, as we have seen, they exploit the capacity of a mirror to give multiple true images of the same subject, perhaps from multiple perspectives; this was probably part of the interest of the reflected face of the Persian in the original of the Alexander mosaic. But they also see potential in the paradox that the act of perception can distort a mirror's true image when emotions like love are at play. Love in particular can lead to sometimes drastic misinterpretations of the mirror's true report: the mirror image can be perverted to serve as an aid to the artificial improvement of the original as it exists in nature (like Aphrodite's face), or distorted into offering the precise opposite of its "truth" (as with Polyphemus' self-deception), or loaded with associations, especially emotional, that have nothing to do with the pure reflection of an image or light rays as subject to natural laws (as with the special eroticism of Narcissus or the heightened sexual attractiveness of Hylas or Antiphilus' young boy or Philiscus' studio-hand).

This range of possibilities was appreciated and exploited by the poets and artists of the Hellenistic period to an unprecedented degree. Classical Attic red-figure and South Italian and Sicilian vases, for example, do indeed depict mirrors, or objects which look like mirrors.[85] Many are unremarkable, but a few do contain scenes where Eros is present while a woman (sometimes Helen) gazes at herself. Mirrors often appear on pottery associated with weddings (e.g. the *lebês gamikos*). Certainly there are erotic connotations here, but no multiple views or such effects. The focus is instead on the woman herself: we typically see the back of the mirror only, and there is no instance of the rendering of a reflected face.

I conclude that it is in this discovery of the huge potential of the mirror image for multiple perspectives, for paradox, and for the light it can shed on emotional states that the origin of the new, specifically Hellenistic interest in mirrors is most reasonably located, rather than in the framework of some larger (meta)comment on the function of mimesis, or of art in general, for which

Plato had used mirrors. People clearly now found the world in which they lived quite real and fascinating enough. If anything, therefore, the Hellenistic poets and artists seem to have felt not merely that they could better the achievements of the naked mirror, but that they could exploit them for their own aesthetic purposes.

To end this section, let us consider whether the poets of the period show any interest in the artists' groundbreaking achievement in moving beyond fully realized surfaces to an inner essence, making surface detail convey inner ethos. Pollitt has explored this phenomenon in visual art and has aptly called the result the "psychological portrait."[86] The main subjects are intellectuals and rulers. Most interesting for our purposes, perhaps, are the sculptures depicting the great poets of the past recently studied by Paul Zanker. Zanker refers to "the little rippling muscles that seem to be in continual irregular motion" on the head of a Roman copy of a statue of Homer from around 200 B.C. in the Boston Museum of Fine Arts. The portrait, with the inward gaze suggested by the blind eyes, evokes "a fervid imagination in high gear." The bust of Homer in the Museo Nazionale in Naples stresses the "frailty of old age," but here too "the visionary aspect is linked to a sense of agonizing struggle."[87] The busts thus use the arresting surface features to enable us to make equally powerful inferences about Homer's mental state and inner genius. Lysippus' portraits of Alexander provide a clear and famous example of the process in the presentation of Hellenistic rulers. Plutarch records that antiquity judged Lysippus' statues the most accurate likenesses of the king, capturing features like the neck's slight turn to the left, the head's upward tilt, and the melting glance of the eyes, and conveying the king's "real character (*êthos*)," "essential *aretê*," and "manly and leonine quality," even though, as Stewart has recently emphasized, Alexander was in fact only moderately tall and handsome, and Lysippus was demonstrating his mastery of subtle physical distortion in turning these distractions to his advantage.[88] Do we find anything analogous in the period's poetry?

Two epigrams, both in fact on portraits of Alexander by Lysippus, make it clear that the Hellenistic poets at least admired the strategy in sculpture. One, reluctantly ascribed to Asclepiades by Gow and Page on the grounds of its being a "commonplace rhetorical quatrain,"[89] comments that Lysippus "has captured the daring and the appearance of Alexander in its entirety" (ὅλαν ... μορφάν), and the bronze, as it gazes heavenward, looks like someone who is about to say, "The earth I place under my command, Zeus, but you take Olympus." Important here are the insistence on the completeness of the likeness and the way the statue's appearance invites the viewer, as it does the epigrammatist, to read the statue's mind, and to give form to the reading by imputing to the mind the kind of utterance with which it would express itself verbally, an effect which simultaneously emphasizes the lifelike quality again. Significantly, the poem is quoted by Plutarch when he says that Lysippus apparently brought out Alexander's "real character" and "essential excellence," which confirms that people in antiquity read the poem as a comment on the art of capturing the subject's essence through the observation of external body language — an art which Paul Zanker has accurately labeled "spiritual physiognomy."[90] The other epigram, by Posidippus (18 *HE*), remarks that the bronze which Lysippus has cast in the form of Alexander "has a fiery look," which excuses the Persians' flight: "cattle may be forgiven for fleeing a lion." Again the essential leonine character is stressed, suggested by the fire in Alexander's gaze.

The process we see at work in the busts of Homer is admired and emulated by two epigrams on another "ancient" poet, Anacreon. Theocritus (in 15 *HE*) commends the visitor to tell people at home that on Teos he saw the statue of Anacreon, "an outstanding figure if ever there was one among the poets of old"; all the visitor has to add is that Anacreon's thing was young men and he will have accurately described the whole man (ὅλον τὸν ἄνδρα).

Θᾶσαι τὸν ἀνδριάντα τοῦτον, ὦ ξένε,
    σπουδᾷ, καὶ λέγ' ἐπὴν ἐς οἶκον ἔνθῃς·
' Ἀνακρέοντος εἰκόν' εἶδον ἐν Τέῳ
    τῶν πρόσθ' εἴ τι περισσὸν ᾠδοποιῶν '.
προσθεὶς δὲ χὤτι νέοισιν ἄδετο
    ἐρεῖς ἀτρεκέως ὅλον τὸν ἄνδρα.

Stranger, take a serious look at this statue,
    And when you return home say

"I saw a likeness of Anacreon on Teos,
    An outstanding figure if ever there was one among
    the poets of old."
Add also that he took pleasure in young men
    And you will accurately describe the whole man.

The emphasis on the rift between poets of the Classical period
and the present is indeed notable, as Peter Bing and Paul Zanker
have stressed (though Theocritus 14, on Archilochus, and 16 *HE*,
on Pisander, evince the same sense of rift).[91] But at least equally
important is the logic of the thought embedded in the piece: if you
just add the biographical detail of Anacreon's pederasty, the
statue is so complete in its depiction that you will carry away an
accurate picture of the whole man—that is, his external appear-
ance and his character.

"Character portraits" were clearly *en vogue* for the Hellenistic
poets; they liked the way the artists saw. Leonidas' poem on Ana-
creon (31 *HE*; epigram 90 is an iambic version) spends much more
space on the statue's actual appearance: Anacreon's love of ine-
briation comes out in the details of his wine-sodden state, the
loss of one shoe and his letting his robe trail right down to his
ankles, while his old age is referred to explicitly and implied in
the detail of his wrinkled foot. His pederasty comes out clearly in
the statue's lewd and languishing gaze, and in the remark, in its
way less realistic than the inscriptional supplement in Theocritus'
epigram, that Anacreon is depicted as actually singing of boy-
loves (the element of an address is reserved for the concluding
prayer to Dionysus to guard his own). More directly than the
Theocritean poem, therefore, Leonidas' epigram illustrates the
movement from the surface image to the underlying character of
the ancient poet. The contrast here with the athletic mid-fifth-
century figure of Anacreon in the Ny Carlsberg Glyptotek in
Copenhagen starkly illustrates how the paradigmatic public im-
age gives way in the Hellenistic period to display as a source of
private enjoyment; the more human, intimate context must in
turn have been a vital element in the development of the "psy-
chological portrait."[92]

Nor were the statues of the ancient poets the only types ad-
mired by the Hellenistic epigrammatists. The new Posidippus
papyrus graphically illustrates that "ethical portraits" of con-

temporary poets were also valued. There is the fascinating poem on Hecataeus' statue of Philitas of Cos, which Posidippus describes as "a bronze identical to Philitas in every respect," Φιλίτα χ[αλ]κὸν [ἴ]σον κατὰ πάν<θ>᾽ (X16–25 Bastianini-Gallazzi). Philitas is probably said to look as if he were about to speak, "so great is the character with which he is represented," ὅσῳ ποικίλλεται ἤθει. Given that the poem sees that character as marked by its perfectionism (ἀκρομέριμνον) and insistence on truth (ἀληθείης ὀρθὸν [ἔχων] κανόνα), and given that Hecataeus is credited with the same qualities (ἀ]κ[ρ]ιβὴς ἄκρους [ἔπλ]ασεν εἰς ὄνυχας,/ καὶ με]γέθει κα[ὶ σα]ρκι τὸν ἀνθρωπιστὶ διώξας / γνώμο]ν᾽), it seems likely that there is some truth in the conclusion that the sculptor is conceived as having artistic tastes which were congruent with Alexandrian poetic tastes,[93] and that would in turn suggest that in certain respects the Hellenistic poet felt that contemporary poetry was indeed proceeding analogously with contemporary art.

But however much the epigrammatists may have admired the new method of expressing the inner man, there is on this occasion comparatively little that could strictly be called analogous in other Hellenistic poetry. In poetry, especially narrative epic, character had, as Aristotle reminds us (*Poet.* 60a5–11), been best depicted in the exemplary manner of Homer, who allowed it to reveal itself by words and actions, in a "dramatic" fashion. Hellenistic poetic narratives in general employ this technique, even introducing dramatic stichomythia and antilabe into formerly nondramatic genres, as in the "epic" of Theocritus' mimes and the *Dioscuri*.

We have a fascinating exception to this rule, however, and significantly it involves a philosopher. In Hellenistic art, thinkers were prime subjects for the character portrait, and representation of them became so formalized that it is known nowadays as the "philosopher-type."[94] This is the depiction of Thales in Callimachus' first *Iambus*, where the resurrected Hipponax tells the story of how the Arcadian Bathycles donated a golden chalice to be given to the best of the seven wise men. Bathycles' son, Amphalces, first travels to Miletus to award it to Thales, who refuses it, whereupon it does the rounds of the other wise men. They likewise refuse to accept it, so it comes back to Thales, who dedicates it to the Apollo of Didyma (*Fr.* 191.31–77 Pfeiffer). Amphalces first encounters the old Thales in the temple of Apollo, drawing a diagram of a geometrical theorem in the ground with his stick (56–58);[95] his work interrupted, Thales strikes the ground with the stick and then with his free hand strokes his beard (69-71). The gestures detailed thus graphically are a clear index of the philosopher's mind and mental reactions: deeply immersed in thought when Amphalces comes across him, he is annoyed at having his train of thought interrupted, yet his beard-stroking shows the thoughtfulness with which he contemplates Amphalces' proposition. This last motif is in fact found in art, for the coins of Soli, usually dated around 200 B.C., depict Aratus stroking his beard with his left hand, though these portraits are too late to have influenced Callimachus.[96] All in all, we gain the clear impression of a thinker absorbed in his intellectual world, impatient at being jolted out of it, and confronting intrusions from the outside world with considered contemplativeness. Here we can legitimately talk of a shared interest in the figure of the intellectual, but more specifically of a close analogy between the poetic and the artistic modes of conveying mental and intellectual states.[97]

Apart from this striking instance, the focus of Hellenistic poetry's interest in psychological states is, of course, the emotion of love. Here visual details of external appearances can indeed be used to convey the underlying psychological state. A good example is again afforded by an epigram of Asclepiades' (18 *HE*), which proves the truth of the proverb "Wine is the test of love." At a symposium, Nicagoras gives away his unconfessed feelings by his repeated love toasts, by his tears, nodding, and downcast gaze, and by the way his garland keeps slipping from its place.

Οἶνος ἔρωτος ἔλεγχος· ἐρᾶν ἀρνεύμενον ἡμῖν
    ἤτασαν αἱ πολλαὶ Νικαγόρην προπόσεις·
καὶ γὰρ ἐδάκρυσεν καὶ ἐνύστασε καί τι κατηφές
    ἔβλεπε, χὠ σφιγχθεὶς οὐκ ἔμενε στέφανος.

Wine is the proof of love: though he denied to us that
    he was in love
    Nicagoras' frequent toasts found him out.
For he wept, kept nodding, and had a downcast look
    And his woven garland wouldn't stay in place.

Callimachus' thirteenth epigram, which is inspired by Asclepiades' poem, proceeds along the same lines, except that Callimachus makes the additional point that he is qualified to draw his inference because "it takes a thief to catch a thief," thus revealing his own susceptibilities.[98] The best-known example of the poetic portrayal of a woman in love is, of course, Apollonius' depiction of Medea's awakening love for Jason. This is conveyed to a certain extent by the rendering of the visual symptoms of Medea's passion—for instance, the longing glances she throws at Jason when Eros has pierced her with his arrow (*Argonautica* 3.287–88), the alternating pallor and blush on her cheeks (297–98), and her sidelong gaze at Jason as she holds her veil to one side (444–45).

Perhaps surprisingly, artistic depictions of people in love (as opposed to venting sexual lust) are rarely attested. There is a rough approximation to Apollonius' treatment of Medea in the Centaur and Eros group (see Ill. 3), where details like Eros riding on the old centaur's back and pulling his hair (and possibly whipping him with his right hand), the centaur's hands tied behind his back, and his tormented face, which turns backward to see his tormentor, visually but also allegorically point to the emotional and physical suffering that love brings to old age.[99] But the real method whereby Apollonius explores the movements of Medea's psyche is nonvisual, as in her wish-fulfillment dream and the speeches, gestures, and dialogue with her sister in which she expresses her struggle with her superego as she prepares to go against her parents and side with Jason (especially 616–824), though this is the occasion on which Apollonius introduces his remarkably visual simile of the sunbeam reflected from water on to the inside walls of a house (755–60). This nonvisual approach is in fact the main way in which the Hellenistic poets evoke psychological states.

Hellenistic poetry and art thus assuredly share a major preoccupation with "psychological portraiture." But the poets have different means at their disposal for achieving their effects in addition to visual signifiers alone, and to examine these nonvisual techniques, however vivid, would be beyond the scope of our inquiry.[100]

3

Reader or Viewer Supplementation

Art historians have recently drawn our attention to a remarkable and important departure in Hellenistic art from the traditional manner of presentation. As Peter von Blanckenhagen, Hugo Meyer, and Henner von Hesberg have shown, artists now frequently leave the context of single-figure images to be filled out by their viewers.[1] An excellent example of what these scholars mean is provided by a painting described in Aelian's *Historical Miscellany* (2.44), the famous painting of a hoplite by Theon of Samos. Aelian describes the terrifying look in the young warrior's eyes, the speed with which he dashes toward the enemy, and the readiness of his shield and sword. Aelian can state that the hoplite gives the clear impression (*enargôs*) that he is going into battle with tremendous commitment—"you would say he was inspired, like a soldier possessed by Ares"—and that he will spare no one. We see the commentator already importing his own interpretation of the hoplite's mental state. But then he makes the revealing observation that Theon adds nothing further to his painting of this solitary figure, thinking him sufficient to fulfill the demands of the picture. Aelian names the other things that Theon could have added, like the hoplite's fellow soldiers and commanding officers, cavalry, or archers. We may conclude that Aelian thought that Theon not only wanted to represent a warrior in an almost berserk state in his own right, but also wanted his viewers, like Aelian himself, to view the hoplite as one terrifying *pars pro toto* and put him in the context of the whole mêlée.

The idea of supplementation was certainly in Theon's mind if we can believe the story, which Aelian proceeds to tell, that the painter called in a trumpeter to play the call to attack at the unveiling, "the music making the impression (*phantasia*) of the charging man even more vivid (*enargesteron*)." As the modern art historians agree, moreover, Quintilian is very probably referring to this painting in particular when he claims for Theon supremacy among the fourth- and early third-century Greek painters in "conceiving visual impressions" (*phantasiai, uisiones: Inst. Or.* 12.10.6).[2] It is true that single hoplites in action go back to the statuettes of the archaic period, while warriors standing still, their spears at their side, appear on Classical Attic and Boeotian gravestones and are represented in the magnificent Riace bronzes. And in the late Classical period, in Ridgway's words, "warrior stelai, which traditionally showed the deceased triumphing over an enemy, may omit the opponent and show the dead charging from his naiskos against an imaginary adversary supplied by the passerby's imagination." This achievement is a precursor of the Hellenistic period's more widespread experimentation with both supplementation and statues which reach out from their own physical boundaries. But statuary could not easily have depicted a whole phalanx; only painting, especially on vases, appears to have depicted the formation regularly. And here is a principal source of innovation in Theon's painting: though he could easily have exploited his medium to include the rest of the hoplite's line, he has opted for the single figure, which invited the viewers to fill in the whole scene for themselves, perhaps, even, precisely because they were used to fuller battle contexts from the paintings on vases.[3]

This kind of "Einfigurgruppe," where one figure suggests the presence of other, unrepresented figures which we are invited to supplement, has been thought to include the Girl from Antium (Ill. 16), where the viewer is invited to put the young, isolated priestess-figure in the context of a whole sacrifice.[4] Timotheus' Leda makes a gesture of defense against the unrepresented swan;[5] in the case of the Sleeping Ariadne, we must imagine a deserting Theseus or an arriving Dionysus;[6] the Sleeping Endymion stirs as if in premonition of Selene's approach. For the Barberini Faun (see Ill. 10), von Blanckenhagen attractively argues that we must mentally supply "the countryside, the noon-tide silence of

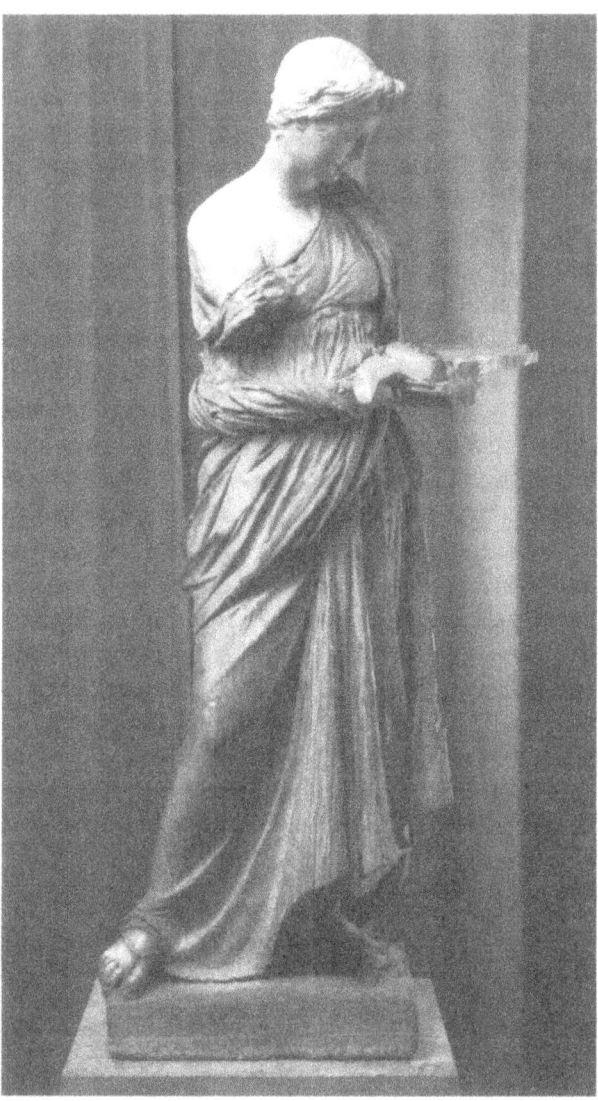

16. Girl from Antium. Museo Nazionale Romano
(Terme), Rome. Koppermann, DAI negative 65.1120

Arcadian desertedness, in which Pan once frightened the shep-
herds," though Ridgway for one canvasses the distinct possibility
that the faun was an actual garden decoration in Hellenistic times,
so that the setting may have suggested his natural habitat more
directly.[7] A more contentious example for sculpture is, as we have

already noticed, Hugo Meyer's reconstruction of the "red" Marsyas statues (see Ill. 7b), where Meyer argues that the Scythian was not represented but is all too easily supplemented from Marsyas' downward gaze of horror at his executioner. The observer is to some extent forced to take on the latter role, while Apollo's supervision would be implied rather more remotely.[8]

Praxiteles' version of the Marsyas theme on the base of the sanctuary in Mantinea had a strikingly different approach. Praxiteles had depicted the contest itself as well as the preparation for the punishment, Marsyas' agonized desperation being contrasted visually with the indifference of the Scythian and the serenity of Apollo.[9] Finally and quite persuasively, Stewart has now argued that the Nike of Samothrace (Ill. 17) depicts a moment in a continuous narrative which she is designed to help the viewer to supply. In this case there seem to have been props for the viewers' imaginative reconstruction, like rocks which were possibly meant to suggest a maritime setting. Stewart paraphrases the implied narrative as follows: "A great sea battle has taken place, and we, the citizens, wait anxiously on the shore for news. A ship pulls into view: Is it one of ours or an enemy? Suddenly, Nike alights on the ship, rushes forward, and throws out her arm to greet us with the news: The battle is won!"[10] Thus the full-scale narrative "includes the spectator—for we are the focus of the entire composition." Here we gain an idea of the naturalness with which viewer-supplementation merges into viewer-integration, a subject that we shall examine separately below.

From Pergamene sculpture we have the Large Gauls, dedicated on the acropolis of Pergamon in the 220s,[11] and the Small Gauls (including the Trumpeter, Ill. 18), probably erected by Attalus I close to the south wall of the Acropolis at Athens.[12] The Large Gaul figures included the Suicidal Gaul and his wife (Ills. 19a–b).[13] His upward gaze precludes von Blanckenhagen's thesis that it is directed at approaching victors whom the viewer is to supply in his or her imagination, though von Blanckenhagen helpfully reminds us that in the high Classical motif of the collapsing warrior supported by a comrade, which is the model for the inventive Hellenistic group, the supporting warrior's gaze is indeed focused on the battle raging about him, at friends who might come to his rescue, and at the threatening foe.[14] A perennial reconstruction, represented by R. R. R. Smith but going back

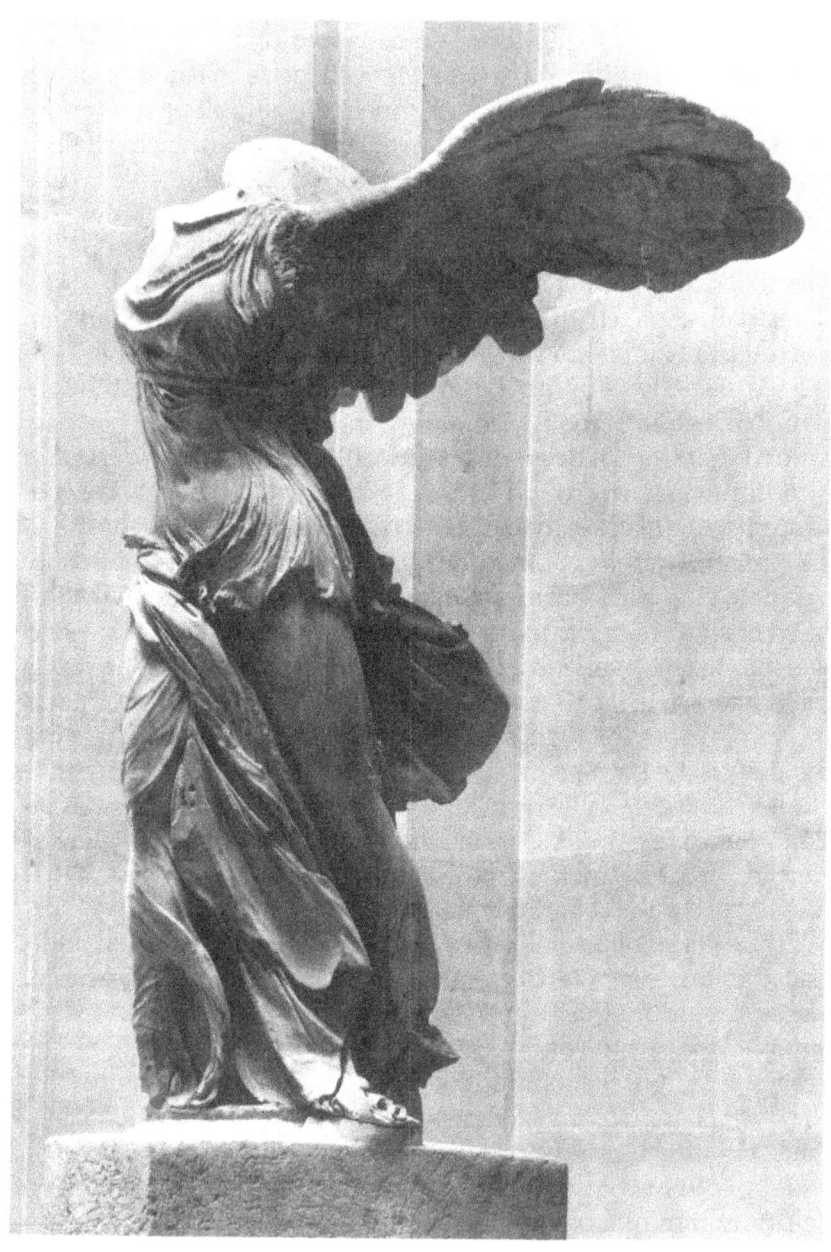

17. Nike of Samothrace. Musée du Louvre, Paris. Hirmer 561.1029

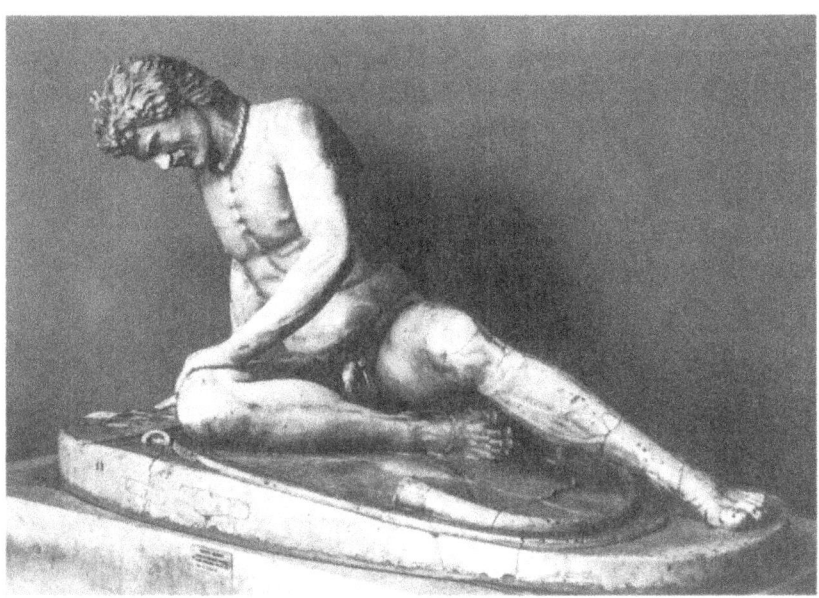

18. Dying Celtic Trumpeter from the Small Gauls dedication.
Museo Capitolino, Rome. Singer, DAI negative 70.2122

to nineteenth-century scholarship, would have it that the whole picture, including the victors, was to be completed by the viewer's imagination: "In this group, the viewer was thereby tacitly invited to assume the rôle of victor."[15] This suggestion, if true, would bring us to the Hellenistic technique of actually integrating the viewer, as in the case of the Samothracian Nike.[16] The trouble is that, however admirably this reconstruction illustrates what is meant by viewer-supplementation, it is unlikely to be correct. For, as scholars like Andrew Stewart and Manolis Korres have now established,[17] the monuments at Pergamon, the one at Athens, and the Gallic monument in the agora of the Italians at Delos all included the victorious cavalry, so that the argument *e silentio* that (wherever they stood) the Large Gauls alone omitted the victors collapses: einmal ist keinmal! Yet, since the copies of *both* the big *and* the small Gauls were found without victors (the former apparently in the niches of a nymphaeum, where no victors could have been included), the obvious inference is that it was the Romans who omitted them. Romans of Trajanic or early Hadrianic times had no interest in Attalid victors, but every

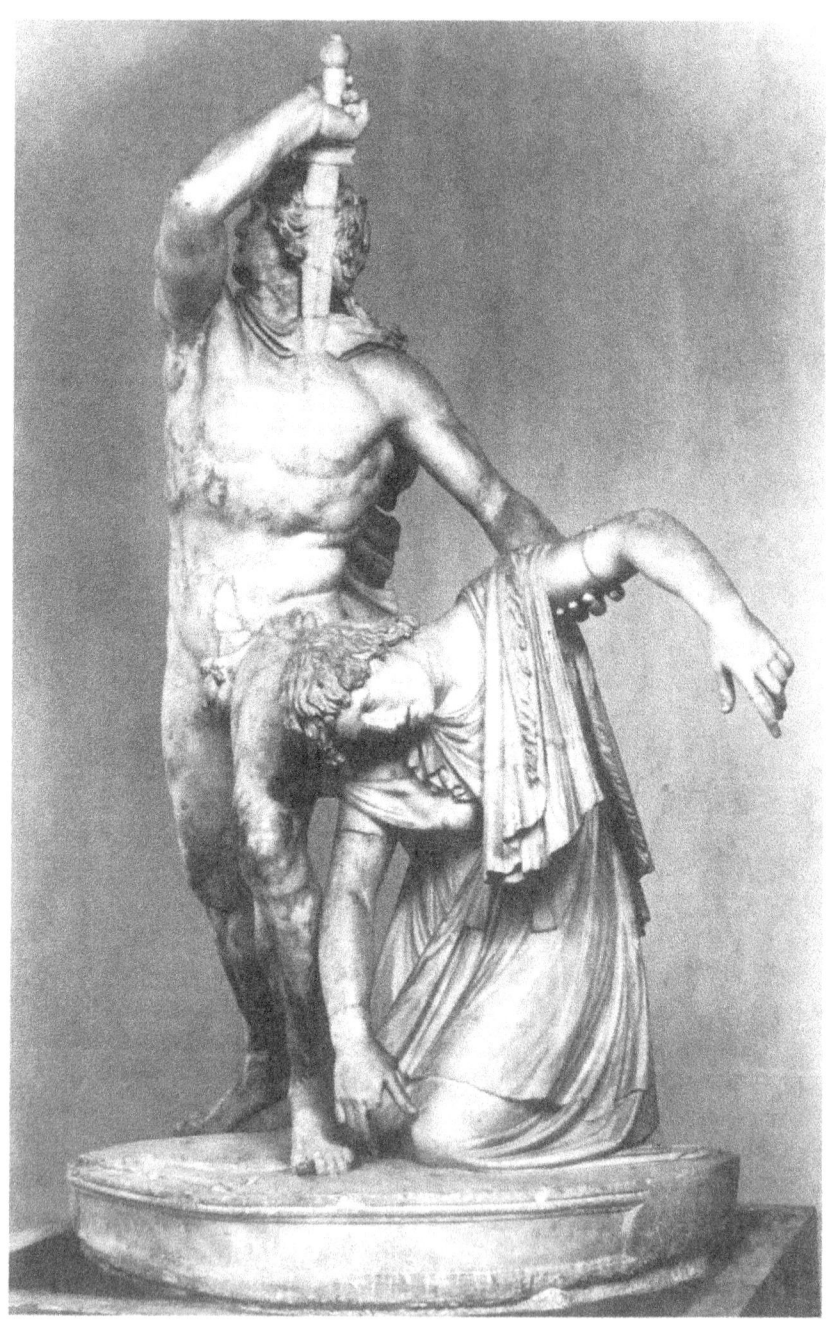

19a. Suicidal Gaul. Museo Nazionale Romano (Terme), Rome.
Sansaini, DAI negative 56.349

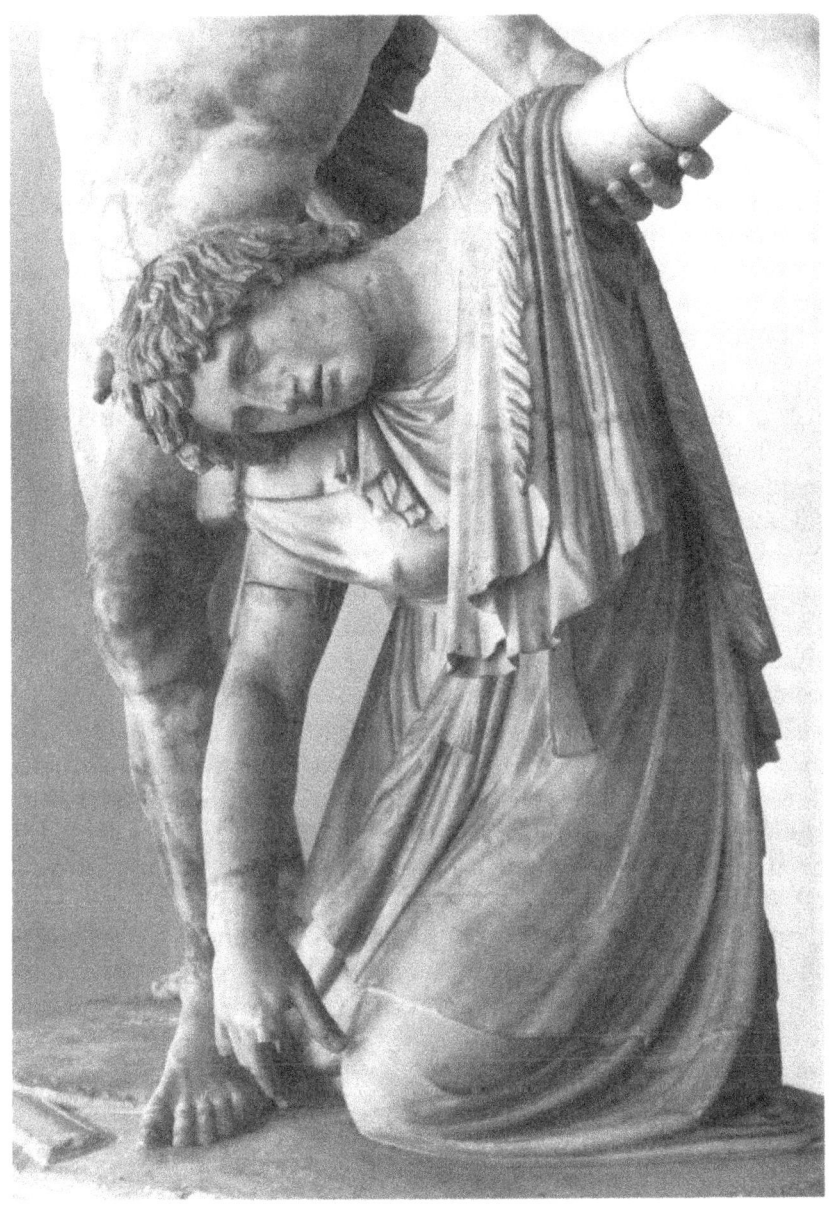

19b. Detail of dying wife. Museo Nazionale Romano (Terme), Rome. Hirmer 561.1096

interest in integrating themselves into a battle with northern bar-
barians. Viewer-integration in this case is therefore almost cer-
tainly a Roman innovation, not a Hellenistic one.

We are on safer ground with another Pergamene work of art,
the moment on the Telephus frieze where Auge looks on in de-
spair as the boat in which she and Telephus are to be exposed is
being built (Ill. 20). This is interesting because Auge's expression
seems to have obviated the need for the artist to create an *in ex-
tenso* depiction of the perils of her voyage, though she was almost
certainly shown being washed up on the Mysian coast, motivat-
ing the "to the beach!" scene on the next surviving panel (panel
10). In other words, Auge's downcast look has prefigured the
tribulations of the next stage of her story, which we can supple-
ment without its being depicted in detail. By contrast the Classi-
cal poet Simonides had earlier expatiated on the pathos of a hero-
ine in a similar plight, Danae, as she bewails her fate in the *larnax*
to her infant son, Perseus.[18] This method of abbreviating the nar-
rative, while doing full justice to the climactic story-unit, has close
analogies in the narrative poetry of Callimachus and the Theo-
critean corpus, as we shall see.

These examples are sufficient to demonstrate what historians
of Hellenistic art mean when they speak of viewer-supplemen-
tation and to illustrate the technique in practice. The discovery in
Hellenistic literature of the technique whereby readers are
prompted to supplement material has been more recent and
came about without reference to what had been recognized as a
characteristic feature of Hellenistic visual art, and without refer-
ence to the supplementation of specifically visual detail. One of
the first studies offering an analysis of one aspect of the subject
was published by Doris Meyer in 1993. Meyer drew attention to
an aspect of Callimachus' funeral and dedicatory epigrams: the
binaries which exist between their real author and reader, their
fictive author and reader, and their implicit author and reader.
The implicit reader, she argues, can "supplement" the discourse
between the fictive author and the fictive reader. In *Epigram* 15
Pfeiffer, for example, the implicit reader observes the fictive
speaker first reading the mere name of the tomb's occupant, Tim-
onoe, and then engaged in the act of processing the remaining in-
formation on the stele while speaking to the silent Timonoe.

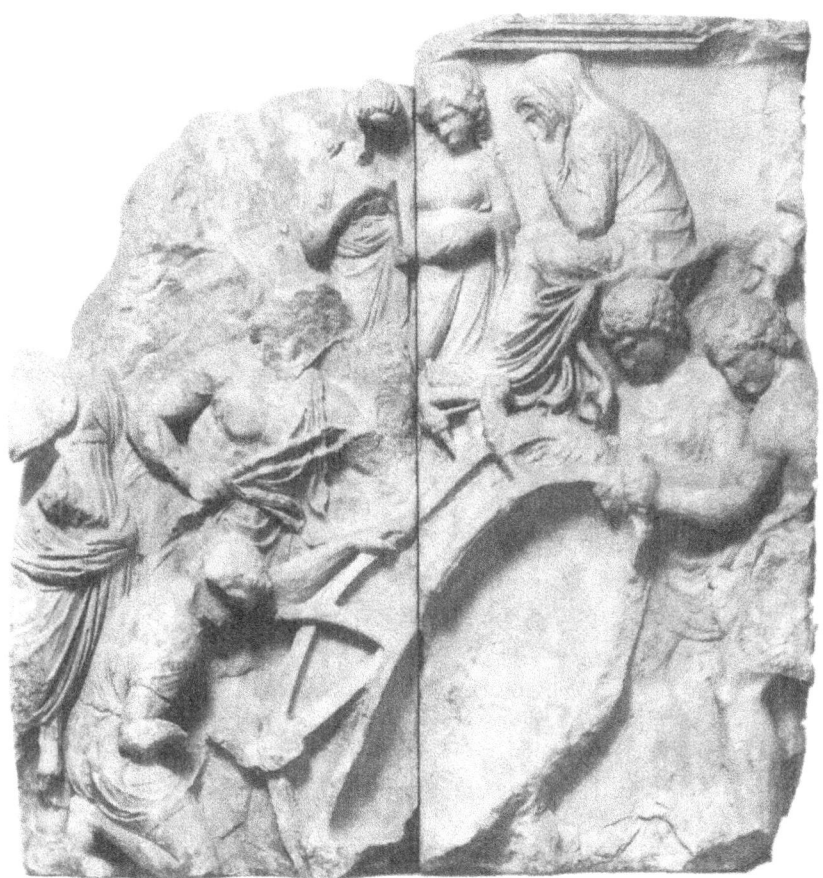

20. Auge and boat on Telephus frieze. Pergamon-Museum, Berlin.
Hirmer 214.1201

' Τιμονόη. ' τίς δ' ἐσσί; μὰ δαίμονας, οὔ σ' ἂν ἐπέγνων,
  εἰ μὴ Τιμοθέου πατρὸς ἐπῆν ὄνομα
στήλῃ καὶ Μήθυμνα, τεὴ πόλις. ἦ μέγα φημί
  χῆρον ἀνιᾶσθαι σὸν πόσιν Εὐθυμένῃ.

"Timonoe." Who are you? By the gods,
    I wouldn't have recognized you
    If the name of your father, Timotheus, weren't
Upon your headstone, and Methymna, your city.
    Deeply distressed indeed, I'm sure,
    Is your bereaved husband, Euthymenes.

The implicit reader has to supplement the content of the poem in-directly, through the subjective responses of the fictive reader. Thus the implicit reader can be identified with the well-known ideal of Hellenistic poetry, the "learned" reader, "dessen ästhetisches Vergnügen gerade in dem Einsatz seiner Verstehensfähigkeiten besteht."[19]

The activity of reconstructing the context of Callimachus' dedicatory and funerary book-epigrams was subsequently discussed in 1995 by Peter Bing, who illustrates the technique of "Ergänzungsspiel." (Bing had to invent a German term to cover what he had in mind, testimony to the novelty of his approach.) For example, in *Epigram* 58 Pfeiffer the reader is invited to supply more detail on the shipwrecked man for whom Leontichus has erected an anonymous tomb, and more on Leontichus himself, whose compassionate gesture was motivated by his own experience of the hazards of seafaring; indeed, within the poem itself, Leontichus has "supplemented" by seeing in the nameless corpse a reflection of his own doomed life as a mariner.

Τίς, ξένος ὦ ναυηγέ; Λεόντιχος ἐνθάδε νεκρόν
   εὗρεν ἐπ᾽ αἰγιαλοῦ, χῶσε δὲ τῷδε τάφῳ
δακρύσας ἐπίκηρον ἑὸν βίον· οὐδὲ γὰρ αὐτός
   ἥσυχον, αἰθυίῃ δ᾽ ἶσα θαλασσοπορεῖ.

Who are you, shipwrecked stranger? Leontichus found the
   corpse here
   On the seashore and gave it a burial by piling up this grave,
Bewailing his own hazardous way of life, for he can't live
   the quiet life either,
   But roams the sea like a seagull.

While little here is specifically visual, we can certainly allow that we are reviewing a procedure which is analogous to the supplementation we have seen in Hellenistic painting and sculpture.

Recent literary scholarship has also begun to explore a kind of reader-supplementation discernible in Hellenistic descriptions of works of art, especially epigrams, where it is left to the reader to supply his or her own interpretation of some work of art and a response to it even though interpretations and responses are represented within the description.[20] In particular, we have an essay in which Simon Goldhill, using the term "ecphrasis" throughout to denote "a description of a work of art," selects for preliminary consideration three funerary epigrams he feels to be "exemplary but little-known," or "all too often marginalized," claims which are a little inflated given Onians' treatment of exactly the same poems.[21] Goldhill's analysis of these epigrams, which serves partly as a build-up to a discussion of the "ecphrases" of the tapestries and the tableau of Adonis at the Adonia in the fifteenth *Idyll* of Theocritus, concludes that the "ecphrastic poetry" of the Hellenistic period demonstrates "a distinctive way of looking at things," which "becomes — with a characteristic self-reflexivity — itself the topic of poetry." This way of viewing contrasts with the polis-orientation of the fifth-century: now poets invite a personal "discourse" between reader, author, and the work of art described; poets engage in a "discourse" with one another, and in a "competition" with the poets of the past.[22] Most important for our purposes, poets like Theocritus in *Idyll* 15 distance themselves from commitment to interpretation by putting evaluative statements into the mouths of designedly naïve dramatis personae like Gorgo and Praxinoa, "which turns back on the reader the requirement of evaluative response (which so many epigrams celebrate)."[23] In this way we are, for example, left to our own devices to decide just how "erudite" the hymn-singer in *Idyll* 15 actually is: is the hymn an example of how badly people wrote public poetry[24] or "a serious evocation of 'the symbolic importance of the tableau'"?[25]

There is much in these conclusions with which one could scarcely quarrel, however questionable Goldhill's means of reaching them is at times.[26] Interpretative activity on the part of the reader is more generally involved when readers have to discover the relationship of a description of a work of art to its frame, like the cup description in Theocritus' first *Idyll*. Flora Manakidou, for example, contrasts the description of Europa's basket in Moschus' *Europa* with the description of the cup in Theocritus.[27] She points out how diaphanous the purpose of the former description is, compared with that of the cup, but she ignores the important fact that the cup description is offered by the Goatherd, not by Theocritus. This is another means whereby the poet withholds his own judgment, and apart from the poet's "silence," there is nothing exclusively Hellenistic about the need to relate a description of a work of art to its context: Simon makes a similar point about the descriptions of the shields in *Iliad* 18 and the *Seven against Thebes*.[28]

The significant point that emerges from these studies is the strikingly natural way in which the Hellenistic poets linked the act of viewing with more cerebral pursuits like being drawn into the discourse between fictive authors and readers in epigrams, interpreting visual symbols on a grave stele, or supplying an independent evaluation of a work of visual art. Poetic descriptions of art can also operate on a less rarified level, of course, and may help us channel our response to matters like the typology of the hero in epic and characterization. For example, the centrality of Aphrodite gazing on her own image in Ares' shield in Apollonius' description of Jason's cloak (1.742–46), the indisputable counterpart of Achilles' heroic shield, has an assured bearing on the way we construe Jason's heroism as he proceeds into the city of the Lemnian women. This episode ends up in the whole-scale lovemaking as the Argonauts "repopulate Lemnos," to use the appraisal of the canonical hero Heracles, who is impatient to get on with the heroic business of the quest (872–74).[29] Another *objet d'art* in Apollonius, the cloak given to Jason by Hypsipyle and used to lure Apsyrtus to his doom (4.423–34), plays a similar role, this time helping us fill out a feature of characterization. Interestingly, sight is not the only sense appealed to here, for the narrator says, "You could not satisfy your sweet longing by touching or looking on it, and it has an ambrosial scent" from the time when Dionysus and Ariadne made love on it. Jason woos Medea to his purpose by comparing her to Ariadne, who helped Theseus (3.997–1007); but he suppresses the story of Theseus' desertion of Ariadne on Naxos. Accordingly, we can, by back-projecting an act of supplementation from the cloak description, confirm our suspicion that Jason's use of the exemplum is calculatingly edited.[30]

The kind of supplementation talked about by scholars like Goldhill, Meyer, and Bing, whom I have cited *exempli gratia*, is unquestionably a strategy of Hellenistic poetry. Discussion of it is welcome indeed, and it illustrates the remarkable way in which scholars in the two fields of poetry and art can independently arrive at strikingly analogous conclusions. But however much it may operate from visual clues, it does not concern the attempt to help readers fill out a specifically visual image in their minds.

There are, in fact, moments in Hellenistic poetry when *objets d'art* are a major concern and readers are invited to supplement a visual mental image of them. A case in point is Herodas' fourth *Mimiamb*. Two women, Cynno and (probably) Phile, accompanied by their slaves, visit a temple of Asclepius in order to make a thank-offering. The two comment on the various sculptures and paintings that they see displayed there, including a painting, by Apelles, of a sacrifice. Certainly, Cynno's pronouncement on Apelles' "true hands" (72) brings us into the arena of Hellenistic art criticism, ἀληθινός *(alêthinos)* being a technical term,[31] but we seem to be invited to reconstruct the function and subject matter of the different works of art the girls see in the Asclepieion as well as to form a mental image of them from the girls' naïve responses; we are thus invited to supplement not only an evaluation but also an actual picture of them, from a nondescriptive exchange in the form of mime-drama.

From Cynno's opening prayer (1–18) we can easily call up an image of the girls before the altar-group of Asclepius and associated gods, with Asclepius "touching Hygieia with [his] right hand" (4–5), while Phile's exclamation of admiration for some other statues directs our mental gaze to a separate group with an inscription, which supplies the information that the sculptors were the sons of Praxiteles (Cephisodotus and Timarchus) and the dedicator one Euthies.[32] The subjects include a girl who looks as if she will faint if she cannot reach the apple she is longingly gazing up at (27–29), an old man (30), a boy squashing a goose, whom Cynno thinks would speak if he weren't a statue at their feet (30–34), and a female figure instantly identifiable as local girl named Batale; if anyone had never seen Batale, Phile remarks, he wouldn't need the original once he'd seen the statue (35–38). After Cynno's squabble with her slave, Phile apparently greets a statue of Athene, which she suggests the goddess herself has sculpted (55–58), and then comments on the lifelike quality of a painting (62), which Cynno is made to ascribe to Apelles (72–78). Phile singles out first a boy whose naked, pulsating flesh is represented so convincingly that it looks as if it would suffer a cut if Phile scratched the panel, and whose silver tongs[33] would fool thieves (59–65). She then turns to a sacrificial bull, whose gaze out of the picture almost causes her to scream in terror (66–71). Although this scene is conveyed by means of Phile's reactions, a surprisingly clear picture of a sacrifice emerges. Scholarly concentra-

tion on the girls' spontaneous reactions and aesthetic criteria has
diverted attention from the equally interesting process whereby
the reader walks among the art objects with the women and is en-
abled to reconstruct the visual image; it should, certainly, have
played a larger part than it has so far in the inquiry about the
mode by which the *Mimiambs* were performed,[34] for it may have
rendered stage-scenery unnecessary, or at least have helped re-
duce its scale.

Something like Herodas' strategy is at play in the mime-drama
section of Theocritus' fifteenth *Idyll*, for there too we are pre-
sented with Gorgo and Praxinoa's admiring inspection of the tap-
estries that they meet as they enter the palace: through their en-
thusiastic comments, we are led to postulate Adonis on a silver
couch as the main subject (78–86).[35] But we are also given the
scene of the Adonis tableau in direct description by the hymn-
singer (112–31). Theocritus' genre-mixing of mime-drama and
hymn thus permits both activities: reader-supplementation and
the poet's full image-drawing.

The technique of supplementation is, however, of more obvi-
ous use as a device in narrative. For art, broadly speaking, this
will entail the presentation of one moment that is made to suggest
a process by visual means. We have already briefly noted ex-
amples like Hugo Meyer's reconstruction (albeit disputed) of the
"white" and "red" Marsyas group (see Ills. 7a–b), as well as the
Nike of Samothrace (see Ill. 17). Poetry, which by its very nature
can handle processes more easily, may present a narrative and re-
quire its readers to supplement sections of it. In fact, the Hellenis-
tic poets often demand that their readers supplement narrative
units which are predominantly pictorial, sometimes also using
pictorial cues in the narrative to help readers reconstruct a sup-
pressed section.

We have already seen an example of the pictorial brilliance
with which the Hellenistic poets could describe movement and
continuous narrative: Theocritus' account of the boxing match of
Amycus and Polydeuces.[36] A more extensive, "filmic" continuous
narrative is provided by Apollonius in his remarkable narration
of the Hylas episode at *Argonautica* 1.1153–279, where the steps in
the story are motivated by visual means.[37]

The first step is the moment when Heracles breaks his oar as he
pulls the Argo along single-handed, having worn out the rest of

the crew in an endurance contest. The event motivates the narrative, for now the Argonauts must land so that Heracles can make a new oar. The felling of the pine which Heracles selects for the purpose is graphically detailed. He first puts down his quiver and lion-skin. He loosens the tree's grip on the ground by knocking it with his club, and then grasps it near the bottom, pressing his shoulder against it with his legs wide apart, the perfect stance for a man of Heracles' strength trying to drag a tree up by the roots. With tremendous effort he raises it, earth still clinging to its roots, then also picks up his bow and arrows, lion-skin and club, and heads home (1172–206).

Apollonius' narrative of Hylas' search for water and his subsequent rape is likewise in part motivated by pictorial details, as well as illustrating the poet's interest in the sensuousness of the light effects at the spring. The emphasis on the pictorial eroticism of the scene is immediately apparent: we can picture vividly the color of Hylas' face, gracefully blushing, and the enhancement of his beauty in the light of the full moon. Moreover, the pictorial element explains why the nymph falls in love so precipitately, thus bringing out the psychological motivation of the scene. A further telling detail is the way Hylas dips the pitcher into the stream, leaning to one side. In this position, which renders his footing unsure, he is seized by the nymph: she places her left hand behind his neck to kiss his mouth, grasps his elbow with her right hand, and pulls him down to the spring (1234–39). The whole episode is pictorially realistic, and the sequence of events is explained in pictures.

The final "shot" in the sequence comes when Heracles' companion Polyphemus tells the hero that he has heard Hylas' cry of distress. Heracles' reaction is expressed in the most visual terms: as he listens, sweat pours from his temples and the blood seethes deep within his heart (1261–62); he throws down his pine and runs in desperate search of Hylas. Meanwhile, at the sight of the morning star and the coming of dawn, the Argonauts set sail, so abandoning Heracles, Hylas, and Polyphemus.

This is a fine example of what the Greek rhetors were to call ecphrastic narration. The passage takes the time to draw a series of graphic pictures; sequence and causation are explained with particular reference to the visual. One effect of this is to define the myth's relation to perceived reality, right from the moment when

Heracles breaks his oar, which makes his separation from Hylas perfectly plausible by forcing him to go in search of a tree for a new one, till the appearance of the morning star, which motivates the Argonauts' departure. The emphasis on the visual for motivating narrative is not evidenced to such a degree in earlier Greek epic as we know it: the narration of Odysseus' encounter with the Cyclops is, as we have seen, brilliantly detailed, and offers an admirably clear exposition of the circumstantial details necessary to the development of the narrative, but close inspection of it reveals that the actual pictorial content is small in comparison with what we find in Apollonius' narrative of the Hylas episode.

These examples, which fulfill Hermogenes' later requirement that an *ekphrasis* describe what went before and what happened after,[38] will suffice to throw into deeper relief the narratives which require supplementation. The procedure is neatly demonstrated by a passage from Callimachus' *Aetia* in which the poet obliges us by directly explaining his strategy. This is the moment in the *Victoria Berenices* (*Fr.* 264.1–2 *SH*) where it has been argued persuasively that Callimachus avoids telling the story of how Heracles defeated the Nemean lion by stating that "[the reader] can imagine [all that] for himself, and cut down the length of the song."[39] The technique goes back at least to Pindar, specific allusion perhaps being made to *Pythian* 4.247–48, where the poet says he knows "a short cut," thus obviating the necessity of describing Jason's combat with the hydra and leaving it to the audience's knowledge of myth to supply the story. This allows Callimachus to concentrate on an evocation of Molorchus' more controversially heroic achievement in inventing the common household appliance, the mousetrap. Similar fastidiousness over rehashing the obvious can probably be seen in the *Hecale,* which appears not to have spent much time on Theseus' struggle with the bull of Marathon,[40] though we do have the fragments which tell us how Theseus forced the animal's horn to the ground (*Fr.* 67 Hollis) and perhaps how he broke one of them off with his club (*Fr.* 69.1 Hollis). Instead, the poet concentrates on celebrating Hecale's novel moral nobility in her déclassé, peasant circumstances.[41] In both the *Victoria Berenices* and the *Hecale,* therefore, the opportunity to describe the heroic beast-encounters is by and large foregone, and the episodes are left for readers to supply in their own imagination.[42]

An analogous technique is found in Hellenistic art, though from a period perhaps a hundred years after Callimachus. I refer once again to the Telephus frieze, which similarly selected only the key moments of the story of Telephus for depiction. For instance, long journeys are elided, merely suggested by the presence of a ship, as in panels 13, 32, 33, and 14, where Telephus journeys from the Peloponnese to Mysia, or, as we have seen, panels 5 and 6, where Auge's boat is under construction (see Ill. 20). And locations change abruptly — in the case of the northern wall from Tegea to the Parthenion mountains to the Peloponnesian coast to the shore of Mysia and back to the Parthenion mountains. It is interesting to see this kind of elision technique developed and entrenched in poetry before it takes such a dramatic form in the Telephus frieze.[43]

The most developed and sophisticated illustration of the Hellenistic poets' exploitation of the technique of telling an untold narrative, however, is provided by a remarkable miniature epic, the *Heracles Leontophonus,* which comes down to us as the twenty-fifth poem of the Theocritean corpus.[44] This poem gives an extensive, eighty-nine-line account of Heracles' slaying of the Nemean lion by means of a direct report from Heracles' own mouth (193–281). Heracles' report constitutes just over a third of the poem's entire length, but the setting of the narration is provided by the circumstantial events leading up to and away from the labor of the Augean stables: Heracles' meeting with the old Farmhand who gives the hero directions (1–84), his inspection of the dauntingly huge herds and encounter with the bull, Phaethon, the pick of Augeas' cattle (85–152), and his departure from the kingdom with Augeas' son, Phyleus, who has gone into exile with Heracles in protest against his father's reneging on the payment due to the hero (153–281).[45] It is striking that the poem thereby deals directly and in a highly detailed and pre-eminently visual manner with precisely the story that Callimachus passes over in the *Victoria Berenices,* while, as I hope to show, formally passing over the story of the stable-cleaning at the center of the framing narrative and at the same time providing the reader with all the clues — again of a predominantly visual nature — for the mental reconstruction of the untold episode.

Framed by the Farmhand's descriptions of the far-flung territories over which Augeas' sheep pasture and have their folds

(7–12) and of Augeas' extensive cornlands and orchards (27–33) is
the picture the Farmhand gives Heracles of the stables of Augeas'
cattle (13–26). They are standing in close view of the stables, and
the scene-change from the sheep pastures is made graphic by the
word ὧδε (*hôde*, "this way") (14); it marks the place of particular
importance to Heracles in his present business, and shows that he
has reached the setting of his Labor. The Farmhand describes the
scene with remarkable precision, as is appropriate for someone
giving directions to a stranger. He says that the stables are "here,
to your right" (18), "across the river" (19), "over there, where"
plane trees and wild olives are growing, and there is a shrine of
Apollo Nomius (20–22); in immediate proximity to the stables
(23) are the quarters of the farm laborers. The Farmhand specifies
the river earlier, when he talks about the rich grass on the
meadow watered by the River Menius (13–17). The Menius was
the river on which the town of Elis was situated; more particu-
larly it was, as Pausanias 5.1.10 tells us, diverted by Heracles to
clean Augeas' stables.

The place adverbs and prepositions certainly give a graphic
idea of the topographical layout of the scene. But the Farmer is
made to employ diction and phraseology evoking predominantly
visual images, which raises his description of Augeas' property
from the level of a map to a mental picture of a huge and fertile
farm. The pastures for the cattle, "despite their massive numbers"
(13), are "ever flourishing" (14); the mere by the Menius is "big"
(15); the grass that the dewy meadows "grow in abundance" (16–
17) is "honey-sweet" (15) and is of the rich type which "increases
the strength of horned cattle" (17); the river is "flowing" (19); the
plane-trees are "abundant" (20) and the wild-olive is "green" (21);
and the cattle stables on Heracles' right are "clear to see" (19).
With all this topographical precision and detail conjuring up the
richness of the farmland and its cattle, the reader is enabled to
view the scene as a "verbal landscape-painting," with the Farm-
hand on the viewer's left, Heracles facing him with his right
hand directed inward into the "painting," and the Menius and the
stables stretching into the background.[46] A coherent composition
can be made out in the mind's eye, reminiscent of Hellenistic por-
trayals of landscape. Such landscapes, as we have already no-
ticed,[47] are first significantly exemplified in moments on the
Telephus frieze and culminate in the Odyssey landscapes and the

Nilotic mosaics of the first century B.C. Here is one instance of the Hellenistic poet proceeding analogously with later Hellenistic art. Indeed, the analogy is so close that it might, anachronistically, look as if art had trained the author's eye in picturing his "landscape."

The Farmhand's description thus sets the scene before Heracles in impressive detail. But in fact it can be seen to have an even broader function: it also all but narrates the story of the stables (which is, of course, not told in the main narrative) by means of visual clues, again in a painterly fashion paralleled in later Hellenistic works like panel 6 of the Odyssey frescoes. There Odysseus meets Circe and threatens her with his sword, although the reason for this threatening behavior, the transformation of his men into pigs, has been omitted, and the narrative gap has to be bridged by means of the clues in the painting. The Farmhand's clues, together with his specification of the River Menius, which is not a pictorial detail but is introduced quite naturally into the Farmhand's speech, allow us to supplement an account of the labor of the stables, and to imagine the magnitude of the task before Heracles and the means by which it is performed.

Outside the Farmhand's speech, the poem offers further images which help the reader to form an even clearer impression of the unnarrated labor, and these too depend primarily on their pictorial impact. At lines 88–115 the poem offers the reader a detailed picture of the evening homecoming of Augeas' herds, which the king, his son Phyleus, and Heracles inspect. The picture begins with the impressive simile comparing Augeas' herds of cows to heavy rainclouds rolling across the sky (88–95). The plain that the Farmhand had described to Heracles earlier, when it was empty of the herds, is now completely filled (96–99). The impression of the size of the herd is further emphasized in the ensuing Breughelesque picture of the farmhands engaged in the evening milking and tending the herd (100–107).[48] The whole scene is vividly pictorial, and the main human characters within it are pointedly presented as watching: Augeas "watched" (108), and Heracles "marveled" (114), though he is not daunted. What is the function of all this emphasis on the visual? Is it really to be relegated to the status of a treat for the mind's eye? That will be at least part of it, but in addition it serves to build up an idea of the immensity of the task that lies before Heracles. That is also the role of the lines

describing Augeas' "inheritance" from his father Helius, the un-
surpassed herd which never succumbed to disease and had such
a high fertility rate (118–28).

  But the poem implies even more about the denouement of the
labor of the stables, and again the principal method is the evoca-
tion of a mental picture. First, Phaethon, the head of the herd of
twelve bulls who protect the cows against other animals, mis-
takes Heracles in his lion-skin for a marauding beast and makes
a charge at him (134–44). Stress is placed on the role of sight in the
encounter: Phaethon charges when he "sees" Heracles (142), and
Heracles responds in time because he is "watchful" (143); sight
thus also motivates the action. In the ensuing struggle, there is
much emphasis on the visual aspect of Heracles' moves and on
the visual effects of physical strain. Heracles uses Phaethon's left
horn to twist his neck down to the ground, and then puts his
shoulder into forcing the bull backward. We can visualize Hera-
cles on the bull's left, using his right shoulder for maximum
force. The use of the horn as a fulcrum, followed up by the brute
strength of Heracles' shoulder pushing against Phaethon's body
to make the bull go backward once his charge has been arrested,
is a convincing explanation of how the feat was achieved (145–
48). The muscles on Heracles' upper right arm, which must in-
clude the biceps, deltoids, and pectorals, stand out in tension be-
tween the tendons (148–49), a detail reflecting the Hellenistic
sculptors' interest in effects of physical exertion.[49] When Augeas
and Phyleus are confronted with the sight, their reactions are de-
fined pointedly with reference to their visual responses: they
"gazed in amazement, . . . having seen . . ." (150, 152), which
again foregrounds the importance of vision in the episode. More-
over, Heracles' strength, thus visually demonstrated, will *a for-
tiori* (since Phaethon is by definition the strongest of Augeas'
cattle: 136–41) be more than a match for the stable-cleaning. In
this pre-eminently ocular way, then, the successful outcome of
Heracles' errand is prefigured beyond reasonable doubt.

  Thus the role of the reader of the Farmhand's pictorial descrip-
tion in *Idyll* 25 does indeed present another form of the supple-
mentary participation on the part of viewers of certain pieces of
Hellenistic art and audiences of some at least of the period's po-
etry. *Idyll* 25, in a way analogous to, for example, the Sleeping Ari-
adne type, requires the audience to supplement an unrepresented

critical moment in the narrative of a myth; it is also analogous to the panel on the Telephus frieze showing Auge's sad gaze on the boat being made for her exposure at sea (Ill. 20): the scene obviates the need for the depiction of the rigors of the voyage. But an even closer analogy, and one which also involves the stables episode, is Lysippus' massive Tarentine Heracles, which, measuring 40 cubits in height, must have required some planned landscaping for a setting.[50] In the depiction of Heracles' deed on an east metope of the temple of Zeus at Olympia, Heracles appears actually on the job, working away purposefully with a pole or shovel, with his divine support, Athene, standing behind him. Lysippus avoids this directness, presenting Heracles in an off-moment as he rests despondently on his lion-skin, which is spread over a woven basket used for shifting the ordure. The accent has moved from the hero's steadfastness to the pathos of his weariness. And yet the viewer has enough of a clue in the visual detail of the basket to supplement the identity and magnitude of the labor from which the hero is seeking momentary respite.

One thinks also of the Farnese Heracles (Ills. 21a–b), where the hero stands alone and exhausted, having seized the apples that will give him eternal youth after his apotheosis. He holds the actual apples behind him, almost indifferently; one ancient spectator, Pseudo-Libanius (*Ecphrases* 15), didn't even notice them! We are thus invited to pity Heracles for having only barely succeeded in this, his final trial, despite all his enormous strength and intelligence, and also to remember, through the presence of the apples, his ascent to Olympus. Among the multiple ironies of this image: "The weakness of Heracles' own mortal flesh, magnified with his body to more than mortal scale, chains him to earth and distracts both him and us from what really matters: the Apples and their promise of heaven."[51]

Certainly, the depiction of heroes before or after the climactic moment had been a commonplace of earlier Greek art. We think, for example, of Exekias' Ajax amphora in Boulogne, with Ajax planting in the ground the sword with which he will commit suicide; or of the eastern pediment at Olympia, with Pelops' and Oenomaus' chariots before the race; or of Polygnotus' painting at Delphi of the Lesser Ajax at an altar protesting his innocence of the rape of Cassandra, who lies on the ground clutching the image of Athene; or of the same artist's depiction of Odysseus after

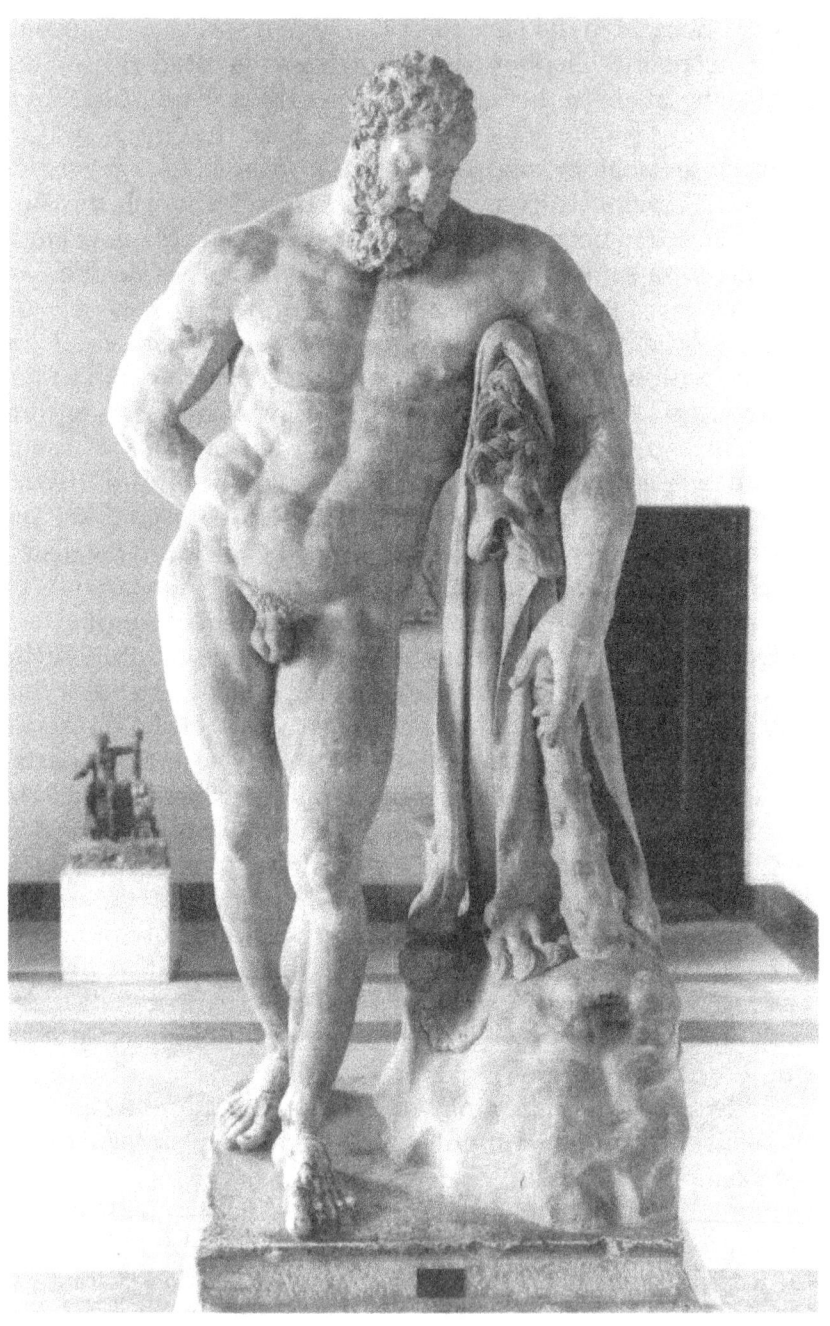

21a. Farnese Heracles. Museo Nazionale, Naples. Schwanke, DAI negative 80.2908

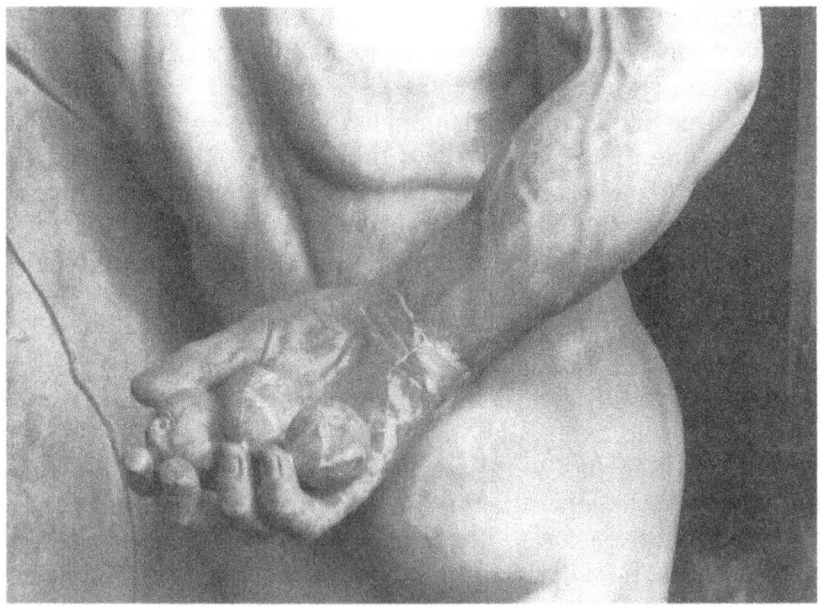

21b. Detail of right hand and apples. Schwanke, DAI negative number 80.2913

slaughtering the suitors; or of Timanthes' painting of Iphigeneia just before she is to be sacrificed.[52] What makes the Hellenistic examples new and distinctive is the degree to which the later artists emphasize the uniqueness of the moment by means of free-standing composition, and concentrate on the off-stage nature of the moments they have chosen to represent. They dwell on the psychological and physical states of the moment itself, making it every bit the equal of the climactic moment that has preceded or is to follow, but referring to the latter with the apparently casual but in fact deftly pointed use of an attribute.

The parallelism of the poet's and the artist's strategies could not be more striking, as the poet appeals to his reader's visual sense in particular to set the act of supplementation in motion. The Farmhand's speech, the simile of the clouds, and the pictorialism deployed in the description of the herds of Augeas all demonstrate how parallel the roles of viewers and readers were conceived to be, and how "plastic" the methods of the poet had become, even in the approach to narrative.

The novel Hellenistic literary form of the miniature epic was remarkably conducive to the narrative strategy under discussion.

This can be demonstrated further by a brief description of the technique used by Theocritus in his twenty-fourth *Idyll*.[53] The story of the ten-month-old Heracles' defeat of Hera's snakes is told in three highly pictorial "panels": the scene where Alcmena sings her lullaby to Heracles and Iphicles (1–9), the appearance and dispatch of Hera's snakes (10–33), and Alcmena and Amphitryon's discovery of Heracles' triumph and their putting the boys back to bed (34–63). In a way which is not nearly so prominent in Theocritus' models, Pindar's first *Nemean* and twentieth *Paean*, the feat is presented as a prelude of greater things to come — if this is what Heracles could achieve as a baby, what will he be able to achieve as an adult? The poem can then content itself with a brief reference to the twelve labors which is inserted — almost as an aside — into Teiresias' words of prophecy and advice on the purificatory rites Alcmena must perform to overcome the enemies of her household (64–102). "It is fated that, having accomplished twelve labors, he will dwell in the house of Zeus," says Teiresias (82–83), and no more. The next section of the poem deals with Heracles' education before his labors (103–40), and the fragmentary finale appears to have celebrated his apotheosis and marriage to Hebe after his earthly career (141–72). The intervening labors themselves were nowhere directly described, the need for a catalogue obviated by the proto-labor of the snakes. The undeniable Ptolemaic element in the poem, especially the prefiguration of Philadelphus and Arsinoe's incestuous marriage in Heracles' marriage to his half-sister, Hebe,[54] may indeed have predisposed Theocritus against cataloguing the labors, concentrating instead on the elements of Heracles' career which were of more immediate applicability to the regents, but this does not affect the analysis of Theocritus' technique of supplementation offered here.

It is interesting that the miniature epics are so often concerned with the off-stage moments of myth while suggestively alluding to the more central ones, and featuring the suppression and supplementation of the more spectacular moments in the heroes' lives. This is especially the case with the episodes involving encounters with animals: Heracles' defeat of the Nemean lion in the *Victoria Berenices,* his cleaning of Augeas' stables in the *Heracles Leontophonus,* Theseus' conquest of the bull of Marathon in the *Hecale,* and the entire labors of Heracles in the *Heracliscus.* The age's visual art reveals remarkably close correspondences in its approach to comparable material. Together, the sister arts in this respect illustrate a movement of interest from the heroic to the domestic that went alongside the many Gigantomachies, Amazonomachies, and Centauromachies on contemporary buildings. Poets and artists explore, as never before, what happened off-stage before or after the climactic moment.[55]

In the examples so far examined in this section, readers or viewers are meant to supplement "missing" climactic and grand elements from their fund of mythological knowledge in general. But in visual art there are cases where the knowledge required to contextualize a narrative or to supply its full meaning comes specifically from poetry. For instance, the original of the Pasquino group (Ill. 22), dated to the close of the third century,[56] depends for its very identification and context on the viewer's knowledge of Menelaus' rescue of Patroclus' corpse in *Iliad* 17.580–81.[57] Margarete Bieber observes that the group features "action in a fertile instant, full of movement and indications of earlier and following actions," an analysis which draws attention to the way the viewer's knowledge of the Homeric text aids in creating a narrative context of Patroclus' death at the hands of Euphorbus, Hector, and Apollo, Menelaus' slaying of Euphorbus, and his defense of Patroclus' corpse, which he will carry back to the Achaean encampment and Achilles. Again, it seems that in one way or another the Pergamene Gigantomachy was also shaped by a poetic text. The actual identity of the text is notoriously contentious; Simon's proposal of Hesiod's *Theogony*, mediated by Stoic interpretations by Crates of Mallos, has given way more recently to the quite old suggestion that a now-lost contemporary Pergamene court-epic, possibly the *On Giants* of Cleanthes, underlay the frieze's conception.[58] Whatever the actual poetic key to the Gigantomachy, viewers were guided in their reading by the unprecedented identification of the gods and giants by means of inscriptions. Yet another example of a sculpture dependent for its full effect on the viewer's knowledge of literature is the Nike of Samothrace (see Ill. 17), which carries connotations of the motif of the ship of state as spectators would have known it from their Alcaeus, Aeschylus, and Plato.[59]

A different method of basing artistic representations on specific poetic texts is exemplified by the "Homeric bowls," datable to

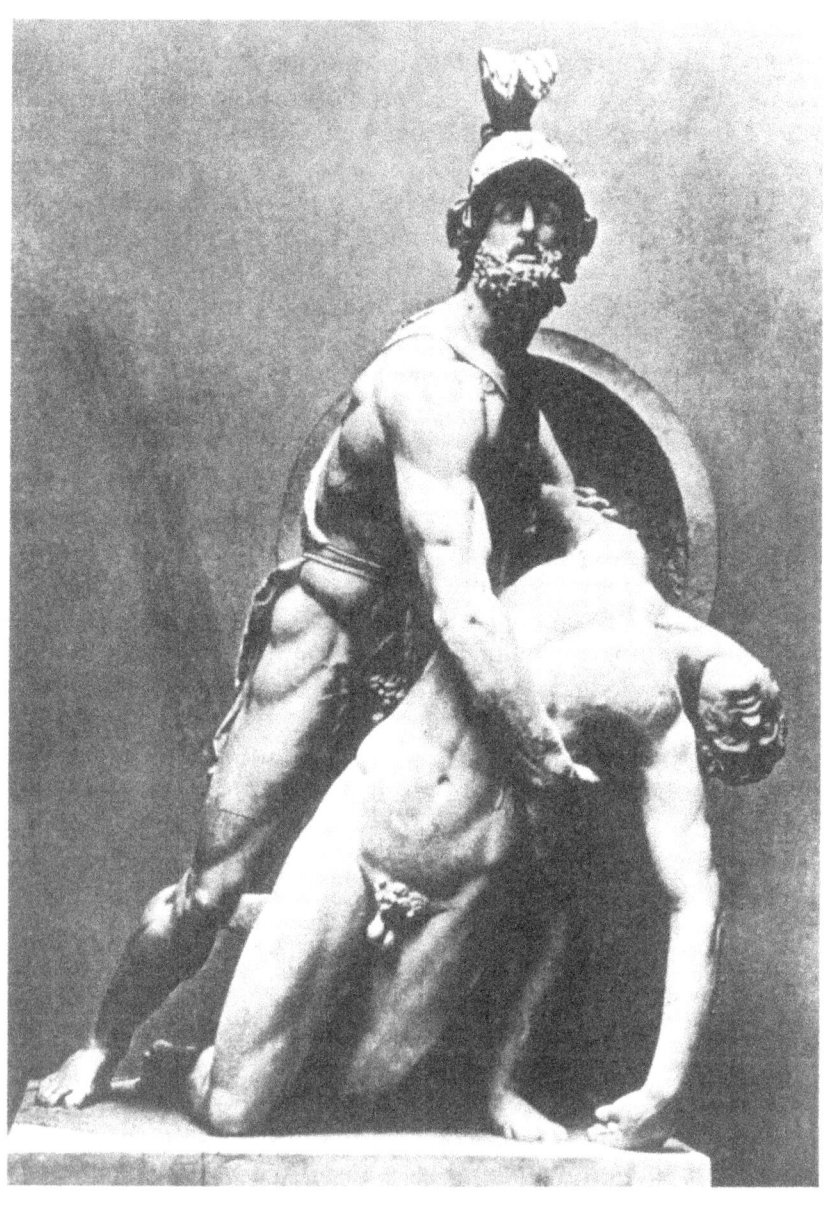

22. Pasquino group. Plaster-cast reconstruction by Bernhart Schweitzer, Antikenmuseum, Leipzig. DAI negative number 38.133

between 175 and 125 B.C., where, typically, the continuous narrative of an episode from Homer's epics is actually accompanied by the relevant verses. As cheap clay copies of Hellenistic silverware, these bowls were presumably intended for downscale symposia and middle-class consumers. In such a context, and given the small format of the friezes (one is only 7.3 cm high), scholars have recently concluded, "It is possible that the Megarian bowls functioned as symbolic reminders of the 'classics' rather than as depictions of them."[60] Similarly, the "Iliac Tablets," probably from the first century A.D., also illustrate scenes from epic with extensive inscriptional quotation of epitomized poetic texts from Homer and the Trojan Cycle.[61] Here, especially in view of the inconsistencies detected between the images and the texts, Richard Brilliant has found that their artisan worked "for a vulgar clientele that cared little for learning but appreciated the visual trappings of some familiarity with the 'classics'"—though the Tabula Iliaca Capitolina, with its emphasis on the flight of Aeneas, points toward the history of the formation of Rome, and is thus an expression of the treasured link between the hallowed Homeric past and the Roman present as celebrated in the *Aeneid*.[62] The two types of "illustrated classics," especially the Homeric cups, demonstrate that the continuous narrative technique in frieze, where one figure occurs in a series of scenes, was in widespread currency by the time of the Telephus frieze, but their rudimentary nature merely underlines the true achievement at Pergamon.[63] The Telephus frieze itself, directed as it is by scholarly mythological research, both offers full description and, in its elisions, demands viewer-supplementation, though the former strategy predominates.

We may, finally, note a related but separate strategy used by Hellenistic poet and artist. I refer to the supplementation of sense and meaning by the more generally intellectual interpretation of visual signs which constitutes allegory. On the whole, the poetry merely illustrates the process as experienced in visual art rather than actually adopting the procedure itself, for it does not normally dwell on visual description. Perhaps the most famous example of this in sculpture is Lysippus' Kairos. Here the abstract concept was personalized in a highly visual way: his hair, for instance, falls over his face, while the back of his head is bald. As he runs on his winged feet, he can be caught by the hair by those who confront him quickly enough, whereas those whom he has run past cannot catch him.[64] Poets admired the allegorical effect, judging by the emulation of it evidenced by Posidippus' epigram celebrating the Kairos (19 *HE*).

Τίς πόθεν ὁ πλάστης; Σικυώνιος. Οὔνομα δὴ τίς;
   Λύσιππος. Σὺ δὲ τίς; Καιρὸς ὁ πανδαμάτωρ.
Τίπτε δ᾽ ἐπ᾽ ἄκρα βέβηκας; Ἀεὶ τροχάω. Τί δὲ ταρσούς
   ποσσὶν ἔχεις διφυεῖς; Ἵπταμ᾽ ὑπηνέμιος.
Χειρὶ δὲ δεξιτερῇ τί φέρεις ξυρόν; Ἀνδράσι δεῖγμα
   ὡς ἀκμῆς πάσης ὀξύτερος τελέθω.
Ἡ δὲ κόμη τί κατ᾽ ὄψιν; Ὑπαντιάσαντι λαβέσθαι
   νὴ Δία. Τἀξόπιθεν δ᾽ εἰς τί φαλακρὰ πέλει;
Τὸν γὰρ ἅπαξ πτηνοῖσι παραθρέξαντά με ποσσίν
   οὔτις ἔθ᾽ ἱμείρων δράξεται ἐξόπιθεν.
Τοὔνεχ᾽ ὁ τεχνίτης σε διέπλασεν; Εἵνεκεν ὑμέων,
   ξεῖνε, καὶ ἐν προθύροις θῆκε διδασκαλίην.

Where did your bronze-sculptor hail from? Sicyon.
   What was his name?
   Lysippus. Who are you? Chance, the all-tamer.
Why do you walk on tip-toes? I'm always running.
   Why do you have a pair of wings
   On each foot? I fly with the winds.
Why do you have a razor in your right hand? As proof to men
   That I'm sharper than any blade's edge.
Why is your hair over your face? It's for men who
   confront me to grab,
   By Zeus. Why are you bald at the back of your head?
When once I've run past him on my winged feet
   No one will catch me from behind,
   for all that he might still long to.
Why did the artisan create you? Because of you people,
   Stranger, he placed me as his lesson right here
   at the entrance to the building.

Archelaus of Priene's Apotheosis of Homer,[65] where inscriptions identify some of the personificatory figures allegorizing Homer's supremacy in Greek life and culture, indeed constitutes allegory, but of a different species. The figures are not identified iconographically by attributes and by the group context as in the famous painting of Calumny by Apelles,[66] and indeed might be anybody, were it not for the inscriptions.

Within poetry, we have the description of Ate by Rhianus.[67] Rhianus' model is *Iliad* 19.91–94, where the picture is mainly intended to illustrate Ate's effect on men's minds; this it does by the graphic image of Ate's walking not on the ground but on men's heads. Rhianus increases the allegorical element through details, typically Hellenistic, which predominantly involve sight, like the goddess's invisibility and unnoticed approach, her appearance sometimes as a young sin among older ones, sometimes as an old sin among younger ones, and her bringing gifts to her masters, Zeus and Dike. In line with representations like the Kairos, the description entails an intellectual processing of visual details, and the greater intellectuality is demonstrated by the contrast with the Iliadic forerunner.[68]

Rhianus' Ate is, however, isolated in the extant remains of Hellenistic poetry as a personification allegorizing by visual means. In his fifth *Iambus* Callimachus employs allegory to dissuade a teacher from sexually harassing his (or Callimachus'?) pupils: "Put out the fire while it hasn't yet blazed up" is the general drift. But the imagery is not especially visual, and the poem does not use extensive visualization, nor does it describe personified allegorical figures, as Rhianus does with Ate.[69] On the other hand, Callimachus will perform the act of interpreting allegory when he sees it in visual art. At one moment in the *Aetia* he asks the statue of Apollo on Delos why the god is holding a bow in his left hand and the Graces in his right; the god explains that he is slower to punish than to dispense pleasantness.[70] Here we have a kind of personified interpretation of an allegorical motif, but the actual descriptive element is minimal. The process is paralleled by the interpretational work required for the full comprehension of Hellenistic funerary epigrams, whether real or imaginary, as we saw when discussing the studies of Meyer, Bing, and Goldhill.[71] For example, in the funerary piece by Leonidas on Peisistratus' stele with its proverbially low-scoring "Chian" throw of a dice, the fictive viewer makes a number of wrong guesses (Peisistratus was a Chian by birth or a hard-luck gambler) before satisfying himself that the real meaning is that Peisistratus died from drinking too much Chian wine.[72] Here again, the visual signs are merely catalogued rather than fully imagined, and simply provide a springboard for the more cerebral activity of interpretation.

These poems, therefore, all illustrate the way Hellenistic spec-

tators enjoyed decoding visual signs in art. In the cases of Posi-
dippus and Callimachus, readers arrived at abstract concepts. But
it must be concluded that pictorially allegorical effects, though
admired by the Hellenistic poets like Posidippus when praising
Lysippus' Kairos, are confined to the Rhianus passage as far as
we know. Generally, the poets were content to leave the actual
effects to art.[73]

4

Reader or Viewer Integration

Hellenistic artists and poets, as we have seen, drew viewers and readers into an image through invitations to supplement contexts and fill in narratives. Sometimes they went farther. Thanks in particular to von Hesberg, we are comparatively familiar with the artists' technique of physically integrating viewers into their compositions.[1] But again the lesson of painting and sculpture can be applied to facets of the period's poetry, where we shall find readers analogously turned into active participants in dialogues, descriptions, scenes, and narratives.

A glance at examples in visual art will illustrate and help us define the phenomenon, and will thus put us in a better position to appreciate its workings in poetry. A superb case in point is the Boy with a Goose (Ill. 23), of disputed date but generally accepted as being from the third or second century.[2] Some certainty can be attained in reconstructing its viewing context, an issue of great importance in this connection, for we must know as precisely as possible how the original viewers stood as they viewed the *objet d'art* in question in order to establish their spatial relationship to it. This we can infer from Herodas' fourth *Mimiamb*. We have already seen how Cynno comments excitedly on a dedicatory statue in the temple, "By the Fates, how the little boy is squashing the goose! If it weren't stone in front of our feet, you'd say the statue will speak" (*Mim.* 4.30–33). Given "in front of our feet," πρὸ τῶν ποδῶν, in line 32, we can agree with I. C. Cunningham that "the statue is therefore on the ground in front of them,"[3] though we should more correctly locate it on a low base, since there is no precedent for groups being exhibited "on the ground" itself.

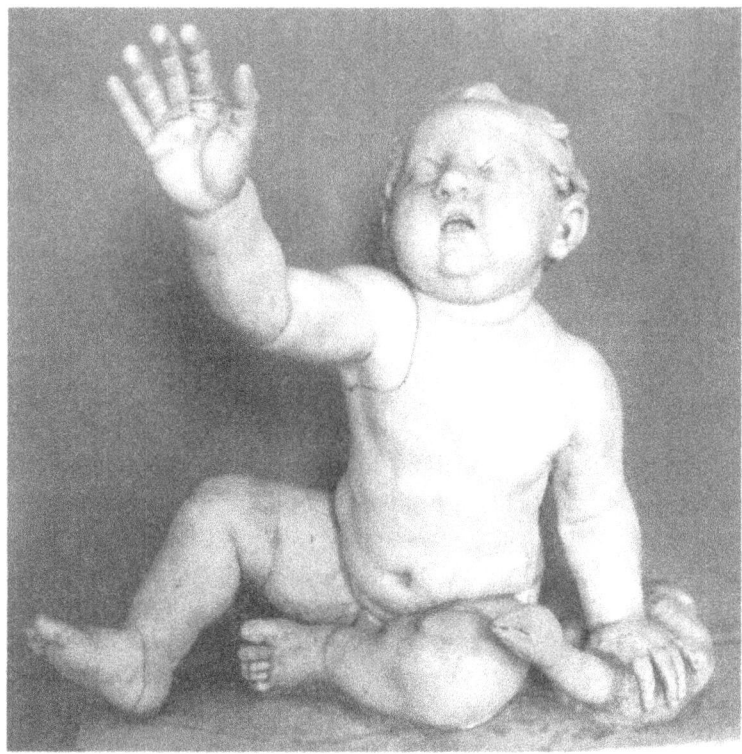

23. Boy with a Goose. Vatican, Rome. Author

Cunningham, moreover, identifies the statue which Cynno is looking at with precisely the group we are examining,[4] which would secure a firm third-century dating for it and help us invaluably in ascertaining what contemporary viewers saw in it. The identification is highly convincing. In any case, the passage demonstrates Hellenistic viewers' responses to such statuary in general.

Given that the dedicatory statue of the baby boy was originally exhibited on a low base, we can establish the viewer's relationship to him with real accuracy. The baby is reaching up with his right arm and hand, a gesture drawing attention to his imploring gaze, which is directed straight up to the viewer's and clearly signifies, "Pick me up!" The baby's mouth is open, and this is in fact the demand he will be addressing to the viewer. As we have noticed in passing before,[5] he compensates for the weight of his head, which is transferred to his left side because of the upward extension of his right arm, by leaning to his left and squashing his pet goose.[6] Through meeting the baby's gaze, the viewer is physically if not personally incorporated into the composition, and in a very real sense completes it. Once drawn into the baby's universe, the viewer can also respond to the group in terms of its lifelike quality and the tactile sensation created by the crushing of the bird. These are the main things to catch Cynno's eye.[7] Significantly, Phile is excited by a similar effect when she expresses her terror of the bull in Apelles' painting of a sacrificial scene: the bull is glaring sideways, and Phile interprets this glare as a threat to her personally (69–71). Here it is a flat, painted surface which encroaches on the viewer's personal space, so the effect was by no means confined to three-dimensional art.

Viewer-incorporation was intended by another statue, the bronze Boxer of the Terme Museum in Rome (see Ill. 8). A third-century dating of the statue has been proposed, though more recently it has been challenged by Nikolaus Himmelmann, who favors a first-century original.[8] Whatever the Boxer's original location was,[9] his seated position, with his marvelous shoulders slumping forward as he recovers after an evidently hard-won victory, makes full sense only if the statue was originally displayed on a low base at ground level, for the simple reason that its detail can be appreciated only if the viewer is standing and looking down upon it. From his location at floor level, the Boxer's gaze functions much like the little boy's in the Boy and Goose group. He looks upward, to his right, and catches our gaze as we move from his frontal aspect to our left. We are at first arrested by his gaze as he seems to address us, and, after we are over the initial surprise, we start to examine his cut and swollen facial features, beginning with his eyes. The left eye looks quite normal, apart from some cuts directly beneath it, but the right eye has been hit so hard that its lower lid has run together with the cheek in one huge, ugly swelling. Together with the evidence of the severe old and recent bruising on his body, his face is a narrative of the seasoned campaigner's career: he is still on top, but he is aging, and victory does not come without a tremendous effort and act of his utterly unbroken and defiant will. His gaze at us provides the point of focus and climax of our inspection. We are, perhaps, one of the awed spectators of the match he has just won; our presence is built into the composition and completes it.

We have already considered the Attalid victory dedications commemorating the Pergamene victories over the Celts: the larger-than-life group mounted on the acropolis at Pergamon in around 220 B.C. and the "Small Gauls" (see Ill. 18 for the Dying Trumpeter) dedicated on the Acropolis in Athens by Attalus I in 200 B.C. We have found that the likely original presence of the Attalid cavalry precluded their being examples of viewer-supplementation.[10] But even with the victors represented, the spectator could still have felt integrated into the tragic deaths of the Suicidal Gaul and the Trumpeter. Most commentators seem agreed that the Trumpeter was exhibited on a low base, because otherwise his trumpet, which lies on his shield, would not be visible to the viewer, as it was clearly meant to be.[11] In this case, the viewer would have been able to stand in front of the figure and look on the noble warrior's death. Yet the fragments of the base identified by Korres as the one on which the statues of the Pergamene victory dedications on the Athenian Acropolis were ranged show that the base was surprisingly high. Apparently the figures were elevated, and it would have been difficult to look down even on the supine forms. On the other hand, one might have been meant to look down on the Dying Trumpeter from a higher vantage point like the steps of a colonnade, for which there are precedents and parallels. It is likewise undeniable that the Suicidal Gaul (Ills. 19a–b) is optimally viewed in the round even if he was originally accompanied by a victorious cavalryman. Starting with the expression on the face of the chieftain's dying wife, we move left and follow his body-line upward to see the defiant expression on his face, which is obscured by his sword and right arm if one tries to see it from the best position for viewing his wife. Our gaze is directed forcibly, and we are led into the presence of the chieftain, for all his almost contemptuous lack of concern for ours.

The feeling that one was surveying a battlefield and the conquered foe was, however, an undeniable effect of what we know about the mode of display of the Small Gauls on the Athenian Acropolis. Estimates of the numbers of all four groups—Giants, Amazons, Persians, and Celts—vary considerably. Against the "maximalist" counts of the Celts attributed to the lesser dedication, Stewart now argues that only ten copies *in toto* can be accepted: one Giant, one Amazon, three Persians, and five Celts. On the other hand, he takes seriously the indications that each of the four groups must have totaled at least twenty-five or even thirty figures, and considers the footprints on the bases decisive proof that the victors were included.[12] On his reconstruction, the bases were set out in a line on the long, narrow, and high base along the inside of the south wall of the Acropolis, beginning about halfway along the Parthenon and stretching eastward toward the present museum. So to have walked along the dense and dramatic group must have created an overwhelming sensation that one was actually witnessing the massive defeat and surveying the battlefield at the battle's closing stages, with wounded, bleeding, and dead warriors — and their conquerors — everywhere.[13]

This "eyewitnessing" of an imaginary or past scene through arresting ocular impressions is precisely analogous to the later rhetors' conception of *enargeia,* as we remember from Dionysius of Halicarnassus' admiring comment on the visual brilliance with which Lysias reconstructed scenes from his cases: we think we are in the actual presence of what happened as it happened. Of course, this effect is subordinate to the dedication's overall aim, the glorification of the Attalids and the celebration of their Celtic victories, among other ways through the allusions to the themes of the Parthenon metopes: directly in the case of the Amazonomachy, by inference in the case of the Marathonomachy, and more generally in the case of the Gigantomachy. Hellenistic viewers would, moreover, have enjoyed the three-dimensionalization of the older reliefs, and their pleasure would have been increased by the added visual vividness that we have singled out for special consideration.[14]

Another victory monument which, according to a recent interpretation, involves direct address to the viewer and his incorporation within the composition is the Nike of Samothrace (see Ill. 17). As we have seen, Stewart argues that she greets the spectator with news of victory as she alights on one of the homecoming warships, throwing out her right arm toward us in a triumphant gesture.[15] Details like the dramatic movement of Nike's dress emphasize the immediacy and "realness" of her epiphany in the presence of the onlooker.[16]

But other statuary, on less bellicose themes, attempts to incorporate the viewer on a more intimate level. I refer to the different types of statues depicting Aphrodite surprised in various stages of nakedness, starting with the Cnidia (see Ill. 9) of the mid- to later fourth century, revolutionary in functioning as a cult statue while depicting the goddess nude. Although the Cnidia is a late Classical work, she adumbrates and inspires (like many other groups by Praxiteles) much statuary from the Hellenistic period. The specific features that the Hellenistic artists emphasize in their reworkings of the statue serve as an especially valuable index of actual Hellenistic concerns and preoccupations, among them the inclusion of the viewer into a statue's personal space.

With what we know from the literary texts was a smile and "dewy" eyes,[17] the Cnidian Aphrodite looks away to the spectator's right as she moves her right hand to cover her pubes, a gesture which the smile probably demoted to a pretense. In her study of the Cnidia and her influence, Havelock has recently reinterpreted the goddess as neither bathing, surprised, nor even trying to hide her sexuality by her right hand's gesture. Instead, the goddess is revealed in the full, confident potency of her divine authority, not coyly reacting to an unauthorized viewer.[18]

In the absence of other contemporary literary evidence for what it meant for humans to view a naked female deity, Havelock cites as her major authority Athene's blinding of Teiresias in Callimachus' *Bath of Pallas*. Havelock sees the goddess's motivation as encapsulated in lines 101–2: "Whoever sees any of the immortals when the god himself does not choose, sees him at a great price."[19] Havelock thus regards Athene as acting under orders, and not as reacting to an intrusion on her sexuality. But this is a loaded reading of the hymn, for Callimachus prepares us earlier for the kind of feminine beauty that Teiresias catches sight of when he describes in detail her athletic, roseate charm as she gets ready for the Judgment of Paris (17–28). Moreover, in her lamentation Chariclo specifically singles out Athene's breast and flanks as what Teiresias had seen. Despite Callimachus' characteristic avoidance of direct description, he in fact demonstrates the reverse of what Havelock sees in his poem, and he makes it quite clear that Athene is indeed responding to a sexual affront.[20] Crucially, however, Havelock's denial of a sense of intrusion ignores certain telling features of the pose of the Cnidia in all her copied representations—namely, the way she holds her knees together and crouches slightly, which can only denote a defensive attempt to conceal her genitalia.

The motif of covering, which serves also to draw attention precisely to the parts of the body meant to be hidden, is extended in the Capitoline Aphrodite (Ill. 24), whose original Havelock now convincingly dates to at least two centuries later than the Cnidia, 100 B.C. at the earliest.[21] We may agree with Ridgway's impression that "the goddess is protecting herself from impertinent glances,"[22] for her right hand covers her breasts while her left reaches over her pubic area, but in both cases the act of hiding is quite ineffectual: that is all part of the titillation. Her arms frame her stomach, which attracts our gaze all the more, and, as her torso leans forward, the focus of our gaze is brought even further inside her most intimate personal space. Her gaze is turned to her left and slightly downward; if she is turning away from the spectator, she presents an interesting case, since then she will be avoiding our gaze, possibly out of self-absorbed coyness.[23]

The Crouching Aphrodite (Ill. 25), of the second century,[24] must have produced a similar effect in directing the viewer's gaze into the interior of the composition. This is at least the case with the beautiful statuette in Rhodes of the goddess wringing out her wet hair, which the Crouching Aphrodite evidently influenced. Though our major copy of the statue, that in the Terme Museum, is too fragmentary to tell us about the actual object of her downward gaze to the right,[25] the viewer is still placed in the position of an accompanying figure, even if the goddess is as yet unaware of our appreciative presence and her pose is less sexually confrontational; Stewart has recently talked of her "cupped posture," which invites the voyeur's probing.[26] Whether because of the goddess's gaze or because of her pose in these groups, then, the spectator is strikingly incorporated into Aphrodite's very presence, and in the case of the Cnidian and the Capitoline types completes the composition.[27]

We have seen enough of the effect of spectator-integration achieved by Hellenistic art in our period to enable us to examine Hellenistic poetry for analogous procedures. One area has already been canvassed: Doris Meyer's and Peter Bing's demonstration of Callimachus' technique of integrating the historical reader into the dialogue between the fictive speaker and the fictive reader of funerary and dedicational epigrams.[28] The effect is

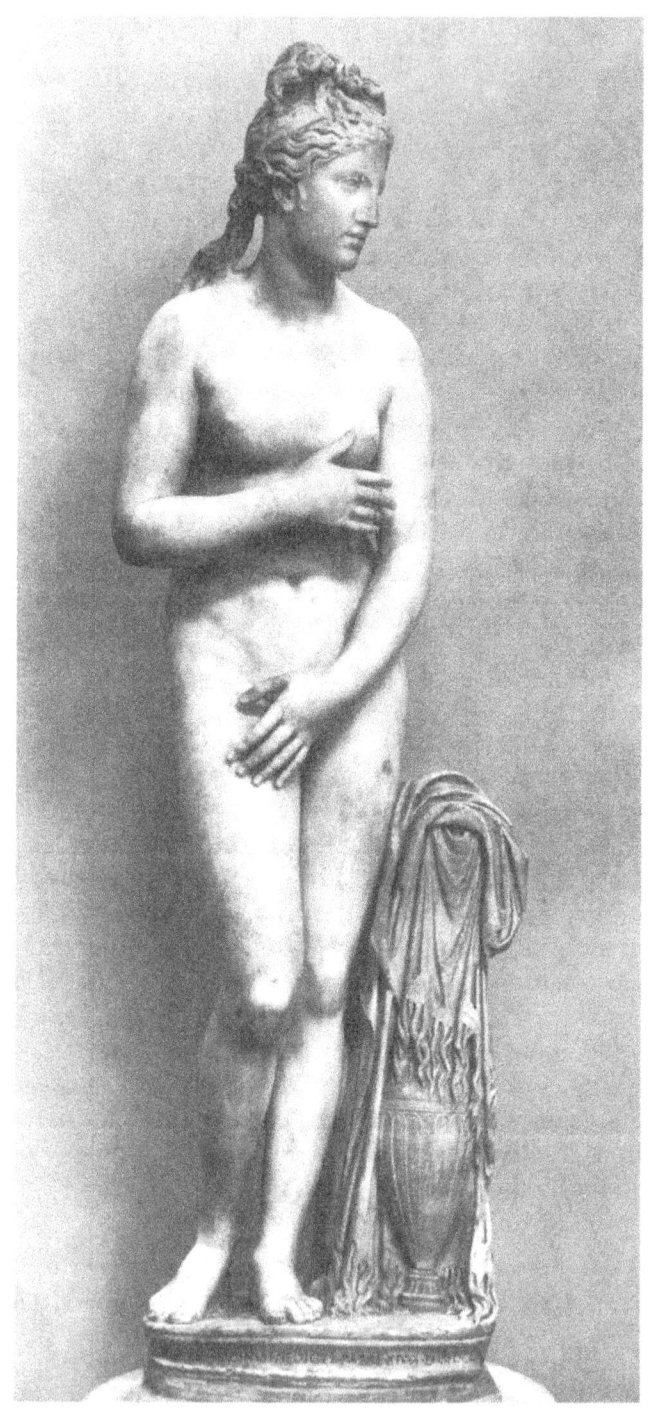

24. Capitoline Aphrodite. Museo Capitolino, Rome.
Sansaini, DAI negative number 57.720

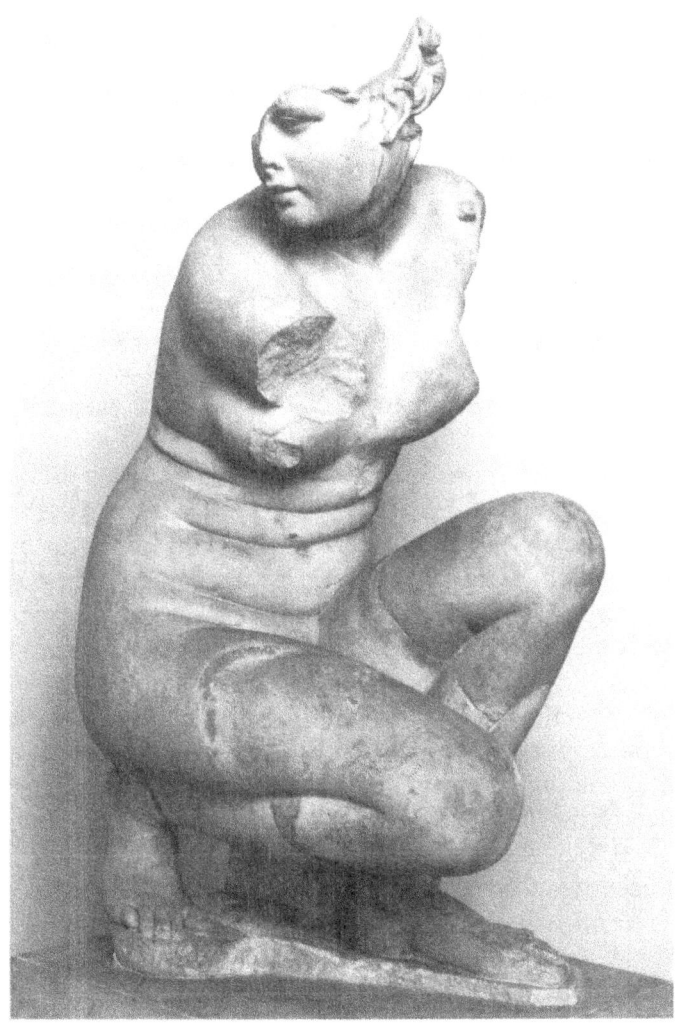

25. Crouching Aphrodite. Museo Nazionale Romano (Terme), Rome. Koppermann, DAI negative number 66.1682

akin to the experience of a spectator of a drama, passively hearing and engagedly and actively listening beyond a dialogue between two characters and thus playing a role and creating a new level over and above the interchange. And in fact it is interesting that instances of this kind of reader-integration are frequently to be seen where the Hellenistic poets experiment with dramatic forms.

To stay with epigram, we have Callimachus' poem (13 *HE*) which goes beyond its sympotic framework to become a symposiast's observation of a fellow drinker's behavior, his sighs and the roses falling from his garland inviting the conjecture that he is in love. It takes a thief to catch a thief, the symposiast remarks, thus commenting on himself as well. But the speaker's observations are not a monologue, for they are addressed to someone: "What deep, painful sighs he's drawing," he says, adding, "Did you see?"— εἶδες. With this single interjected word, Callimachus has included an onlooking interlocutor. Within the dramatic framework of the poem, this will be a fellow symposiast, but the question catches us by surprise. We feel at least momentarily that we are the addressee, and are thus subtly but strikingly involved in the scene, witnessing the lover's symptoms ourselves.[29]

More overtly dramatic is Meleager's epigram on a painting of the dying Niobids (128 *HE*). It unprecedentedly takes the form of a messenger-speech, as if from a tragedy. The messenger first announces to Niobe Apollo's slaughter of her male offspring, but then witnesses in horror, before his very eyes, the slaughter of the female Niobids around their mother, who is struck dumb and motionless like a stone through shock. The messenger vividly describes the daughters in their dying poses, one dead at Niobe's knees, one on her lap, one on the ground, one at Niobe's breast, another looking in horror at the arrow aimed at her, another sinking beneath the shafts, another still alive and conscious. His description of the events happening before his eyes integrates us in precise accord with the rhetorical conception of *enargeia*. Moreover, his account is strikingly similar in its effect to the experience original viewers would have had when walking among the dead and dying Niobids of Classical and Hellenistic sculpture (Ill. 26), which Ridgway once suggested were placed as a "scattered ensemble" in a late Hellenistic grove or garden,[30] or when walking past the stricken figures of the Attalid dedications on the Athenian Acropolis. A comparison with the inscriptional piece on the same subject by Theodoridas (18 *HE*), which is descriptive, static, and moralizing, brings out eloquently the extent to which the reader is visually integrated into Meleager's poem.

There are also the epigrams which describe works of art and explicitly call the reader's attention to certain features. A series of these by Nossis, from the early Hellenistic period, has not been

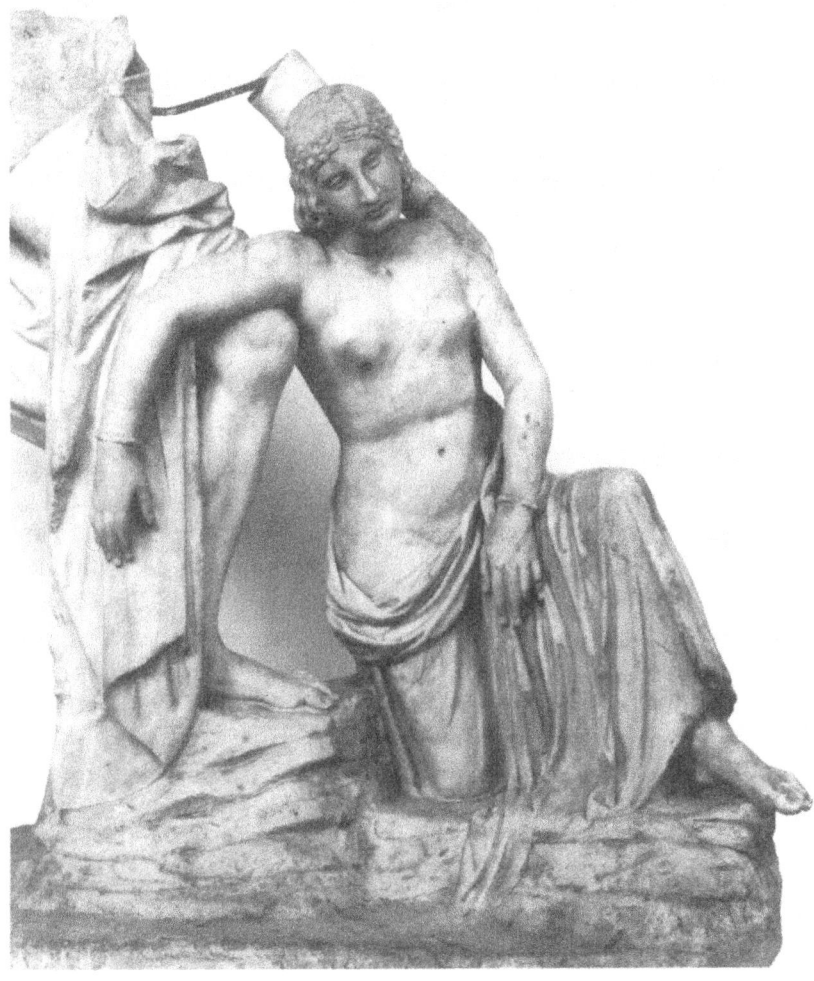

26. Dying Niobid. Vatican, Rome. Anger, DAI negative number 96 Vat 644

adequately discussed by scholars. In poem 4 *HE* the speaker, de-
fined in the first word as a woman, urges another woman, "Let's
go to the temple of Aphrodite and see how cleverly wrought in
gold is the goddess's statue" which the hetaera Polyarchis has
dedicated — Ἐλθοῖσαι ποτὶ ναὸν ἰδώμεθα τᾶς 'Αφροδίτας / τὸ βρέ-
τας ὡς χρυσῷ δαιδαλόεν τελέθει. Here the fictive speaker ad-
dresses the reader, whom she presumes to be female (reasonably,
in the circumstances), and directs her attention to the skill with
which the statue's metals have been rendered. Similarly, in poem

8 *HE* a viewer, whose sex is this time undetermined, asks a fellow spectator to see (ἴδ') how gentle Automelinna's face appears on her portrait: "she seems to be giving us[31] a sweet look": Αὐτο-μέλιννα τέτυκται· ἴδ' ὡς ἀγανὸν τὸ πρόσωπον. / ἁμὲ ποτοπτάζειν μειλιχίως δοκέει. Here the reader is surprised to be included in the speaker's address and very company, and even transported before the statue's direct, friendly gaze. In poem 9 *HE*, after remarking how true to life the portrait of Sabaethis is and how she can be recognized even from a distance, the speaker says, "Look (θάεο)! I think I'm seeing the wise woman and her sweetness here on the spot!"—thus inviting the reader to share his or, more likely, her viewing experience: θάεο· τὰν πινυτὰν τό τε μείλιχον αὐτόθι τήνας / ἔλπομ' ὁρῆν. More conventional is the address to the reader inviting him or her to notice (ἴδ') how Callo the hetaera's beauty is in bloom on her portrait (6 *HE*).

The new Posidippus papyrus yields a slightly more complex version of the motif in an epigram praising the statue of a colt who has won by a head at the Nemean Games (XI 25–28 Bastianini-Gallazzi). It begins with a command to the person reading the poem and viewing the statue: "Admire the determination of the colt, and how he draws his breath with the whole of the statue (παντὶ τύπῳ) and how his flanks are stretched to the limit (πᾶς ἐ<κ> λαγόνων τέταται)." Here the representation of the horse is identified with the actual horse as a guide to the animal's temperament in real life, and the reader is invited to view the statue and the horse as one and the same, thus feeling integrated into the real horse's presence.

Showing the process's further potential is the couplet dubiously ascribed to Asclepiades (39 *HE*): "This is the portrait of Cypris. —Come on: let's make sure it isn't Berenice's: I'm in two minds as to which of the two one should say it's more like."

Κύπριδος ἅδ' εἰκών· φερ' ἰδώμεθα μὴ Βερενίκας·
   διστάζω ποτέρᾳ φῇ τις ὁμοιοτέραν.

Here we can imagine a fellow viewer reading the first words aloud, as if it were the portrait's inscription—Κύπριδος ἅδ' εἰκών—but then turning to his neighbor or companion and asking him to share in his skepticism about inscriptional labels and the identification of the subject. These examples illustrate the variety and versatility of Hellenistic epigram's integration of the reader-viewer into a poem of even the smallest compass.

Another branch of Hellenistic poetry which approximates fascinatingly to the direct appeal of the Boy with a Goose (see Ill. 23) is the mimetic hymn invented by Callimachus. Again a Hellenistic poetic form draws on drama and invites the reader to be present and involved, this time with the process of cult rituals. Whether these poems were meant for reading in private, for performance outside the festival they celebrate, or for post-ritual recitation,[32] what concerns us here is that they are clearly meant, in a way that a traditional hymn was not, to create an illusion in the reader or audience of being present in the actual festival. The second and fifth hymns begin with the chief celebrant describing signs of the deity's nearness. Apollo's presence is indicated by the rustling of his laurel in the temple, the nodding of the palm tree, and the singing of the swan, and by the master of ceremony's command to the bars and bolts to slide from the temple door of their own accord (2.1–7); Athene's presence is "confirmed" by the neighing of the horses and the nervous creaking of the axles of the wagon drawing the cult statue (5.1–3, 14). In the *Hymn to Demeter* the chief celebrant, who is a woman, like her counterpart in the *Bath of Pallas*, tells her fasting retinue what to chant as the *kalathos* moves in the procession, warns all women to join in and watch the procession from the ground, not from rooftops, and draws attention to the evening star, Hesperus, who persuaded Demeter to drink during her search for Persephone, and who will end the fast by his appearance. In each case the audience is put into the scene as an observer of the festival — in fact, in a privileged position.

The chief celebrant then proceeds, in the hymns to Athene and Demeter, to tell her followers a relevant story about each goddess: the blinding of Teiresias by Athene the "Sharp-sighted," and Demeter's punishment of Erysichthon with insatiable hunger. The storytelling entertains the women until the next stage of the procession, the arrival of Athene's cult wagon or the commencement of the hymn to Demeter, which will conclude the fast. We are thus party to a "back-stage" moment in the proceedings. In the *Hymn to Apollo*, the master of ceremonies follows up the signs of the god's proximity by an aretology, but then concludes with the famous passage in which he makes the god of poets defend Callimachus' stance on poetry. Here there can be no doubt that the reader is addressed as a member of the festival of Carneian Apollo, but the lesson can easily be generalized to all three poems: we are integrated into attendance at the ritual evoked in each. Seen in this way, the mimetic hymns indeed provide analogues with the contemporary works of art which innovate so brilliantly by incorporating their viewers within them as part of their conception and composition.

The evidence of Hellenistic mechanical works of art, in particular temple gadgetry and automata used in royal spectacles, is capable of shedding valuable light on a problem which modern readers encounter in evaluating Callimachus' mimetic hymns. Are these poems designed to convey any serious religious or devotional feeling, or is their innovational nature to be seen as an aim in itself, shorn of any religious intention or effect? It might be felt that it is precisely the vividness and the sense of personal involvement that destroy the mystery of the religious experience that these hymns purport to recreate.

The real test case in this connection is the *Hymn to Apollo*, which begins with the celebrant commenting in terms of awe on the way Apollo's young laurel tree and the whole temple are shaking as, he supposes, the god strikes the door with his foot. The Delian palm tree has nodded, and the swan is singing in the air. The celebrant commands the bolts and keys of the doors to draw back by themselves, "since the god is no longer far away" (1–8). Whatever else one may say about this proem, it is undeniably an evocation of the religious and devotional atmosphere of a ritual. I have argued elsewhere that the passage exhibits features of *enargeia* in that it presents an image of an experience as if it were happening before the audience's eyes.[33] Callimachus has varied the format of the traditional hymn by making it a re-enactment of a festival rather than a song to be presented as a direct act of worship, though his celebrant's stories of Athene's and Demeter's interactions with mortals have forebears in the Homeric hymns. As such, Callimachus' variation on the hymn form gives his descriptive powers free play in putting the supernatural before our eyes, a by-product of *enargeia* recognized by Dio Chrysostom, as we have seen.

On what level should this form of poetry be read? I suggest that such an evocation of a religious moment in no way precludes a religious purpose or effect. Others disagree; Mary Depew summarizes her position by writing, "But the very realism of the conventions [Callimachus] adopts alerts us to the text's awareness of its own artificiality."[34] It is by now no news that Callimachus and the other Alexandrians in particular set great store by textual self-consciousness and artificiality. But Depew leaves the basic question unanswered: do artificiality and self-awareness necessarily preclude seriousness of poetic intent or effect, or religious or ethical truth and sincerity? The answer is clearly no, but we would welcome some other, preferably external, arbitration that might help to confirm that answer.

Of particular value in this connection are the mechanical gadgets actually used in the Hellenistic age to add to the impression of a divine presence in temples, shrines, and festival processions. These go even further in stressing the "realness" of divine epiphanies than an impressive piece of fine art like the Nike of Samothrace (see Ill. 17) in all its vibrant immediacy. Hero of Alexandria's *Pneumatics* is our main source on this topic.[35] Aristotle's pupil, Strato of Lampsacus, who was active in Alexandria under Ptolemy Soter,[36] discovered the vacuum, and engineers applied that discovery to, among other things, the manufacture of temple gadgetry designed to present worshipers with "awe-inspiring miracles." Hero's phrase "astonishing awe," ἐκπληκτικόν τινα θαυμασμόν (*ekplêktikon tina thaumasmon*), is itself significantly approving and points to the positive response of a Hellenistic mind—admittedly a late one, for Hero's floruit was 60 A.D.—to such machines in a devotional context.

In fact, several features of the opening of the *Hymn to Apollo* can be paralleled in the mechanical devices described in the *Pneumatics*. The sound of Apollo kicking the temple doors is comparable to the trumpet sounded when the temple doors were opened (*Pneum.* 1.17 Schmidt).[37] The singing swan finds its counterpart in the bird which was made to turn and whistle on the top of a shrine (*Pneum.* 2.32 Schmidt).[38] The self-opening doors recall the doors which opened automatically when a fire was lit on an altar (*Pneum.* 1.38, 39 Schmidt). Other aids to devotion included the use of a fire on an altar to make two figures pour a libation (*Pneum.* 1.11 Schmidt), and another altar fire which caused figures to pour a libation and a serpent to hiss (*Pneum.* 2.21 Schmidt).

These contraptions undeniably represented an attempt to actualize the divine presence: would any commissioner have both-

ered constructing them otherwise? The sacrificial vessel which
flowed when money was placed in the slot (*Pneum.* 1.21 Schmidt)
shows that worshipers were by no means put off by patently arti-
ficial effects.[39] If, then, such ways of inspiring devotion were tol-
erated or considered effective in the actual practice of religious
cults, why shouldn't their poetic counterparts, produced, equally
artificially, by *enargeia*, have similarly impressed their audiences?
And lest we think the temple gadgetry effective only for the
gullible, we should remember the famous statue of Aphrodite-
Arsinoe on Zephyrium, in the temple dedicated by the admiral
Callicrates to Queen Arsinoe, which held a drinking-horn in the
shape of the Egyptian deity Bes designed by Ctesibius so that it
played a musical note when water was poured from it.[40]

Also important in this connection are the Hellenistic mechani-
cal effigies of deities, like the Nysa who stood up, poured a liba-
tion of milk, and then sat down again on a float in the great pro-
cession of Ptolemy Philadelphus.[41] Von Hesberg says that Nysa
represented the omnipotence of Philadelphus,[42] as did other
gadgets for display in the intimate court ambience. This mode of
epiphany-simulation was clearly part of the Ptolemies' dynastic
and religious program, and hence to be taken seriously, even, in
all probability, among the intelligentsia of the Alexandrian court.
Its aims included the lifelike presentation of the divine, the ele-
ment of surprise, and the celebration of the royal house which
could produce such an object.[43] That such displays could be taken
as possessing a downright numinous significance is revealed by
the recorded reactions of onlookers when the contraption in ques-
tion failed. In 87 B.C. spectators recoiled in horror when the me-
chanical figure of Nike, which was to descend and crown Mithri-
dates VI Nikator, dropped the crown, smashing it to pieces on the
floor of the theater of Pergamon.[44] Nor was the "fixing" of the re-
ligious image necessarily thought preclusive of genuine religious
feeling in the period.[45]

The evidence of the religious gadgets should reduce some of
our modern disbelief in the ultimate religious seriousness of Hel-
lenistic poetic inventions like the mimetic hymns of Callimachus,
however they were actually performed. The *enargeia* of these
poems would have integrated Hellenistic audiences and private
readers even into the world of religious experience.

A moment in the mimetic hymns introduces us to one more aspect of viewer-integration: the motif of the image surprised by the viewer. I refer to the passage in the *Bath of Pallas* in which Teiresias unintentionally sees Athene bathing. We have already seen the most remarkable instances of the motif in visual art, the statues of Aphrodite artfully pretending (to judge by her smile as she looks away from the spectator) to be startled by our gaze into trying to cover her genitals (despite Havelock's attempts, discussed earlier, to disabuse us of this interpretation in the case of the Cnidia [see Ill. 9]). Describing the response of the Cnidia to the spectator's presence, Stewart writes: "Reducing [the spectator] to the igno-minious rôle of a Peeping Tom, . . . [her gestures] emphasize not only the uniqueness of the goddess's charms — the very fountain-head of her power — but also his own crude mortality by compar-ison."[46] As we have seen, Ridgway describes the Capitoline Aph-rodite (see Ill. 24) of two centuries later as "protecting herself from impertinent glances."[47] In these and other statues of the type, therefore, the viewer is physically made to encroach on the im-age's personal space and cause it to respond.[48] The goddess in each case inspires an erotic response in the viewer, and his gaze, which has thus been turned into the projection of his desire, causes her instinctive response. This can in turn have an effect that is the reverse of what she — but not the sculptor — desired, that of actually drawing our attention to the parts of her body which she is trying to conceal. The Hellenistic sculptors have, of course, other means of directing our gaze in such contexts. We catch the Aphrodite of the Beautiful Buttocks (Ill. 27) narcissisti-cally looking over her shoulder and admiring her bottom, which is tantamount to an invitation to admire it ourselves. In this case, however, the goddess does not know that we are observing her, and the motif of surprise is lacking, however much we feel our-selves to be in the goddess's intimate presence.[49]

As far as poetry can duplicate this effect, we gaze admiringly on the picture of Aphrodite drawn by Apollonius at *Argonautica* 3.43–47. Aphrodite sits alone at home in a chair opposite the door; she has a golden comb to order her hair, which she has let down over her white shoulders, and is on the point of plaiting her long tresses. Of course, we cannot interrupt the deity ourselves; that is left to other characters in the poem, in this case Hera and Athene, whom she notices in the doorway opposite. Up to a point, Hera and Athene stand in for the reader, who is clearly meant to have

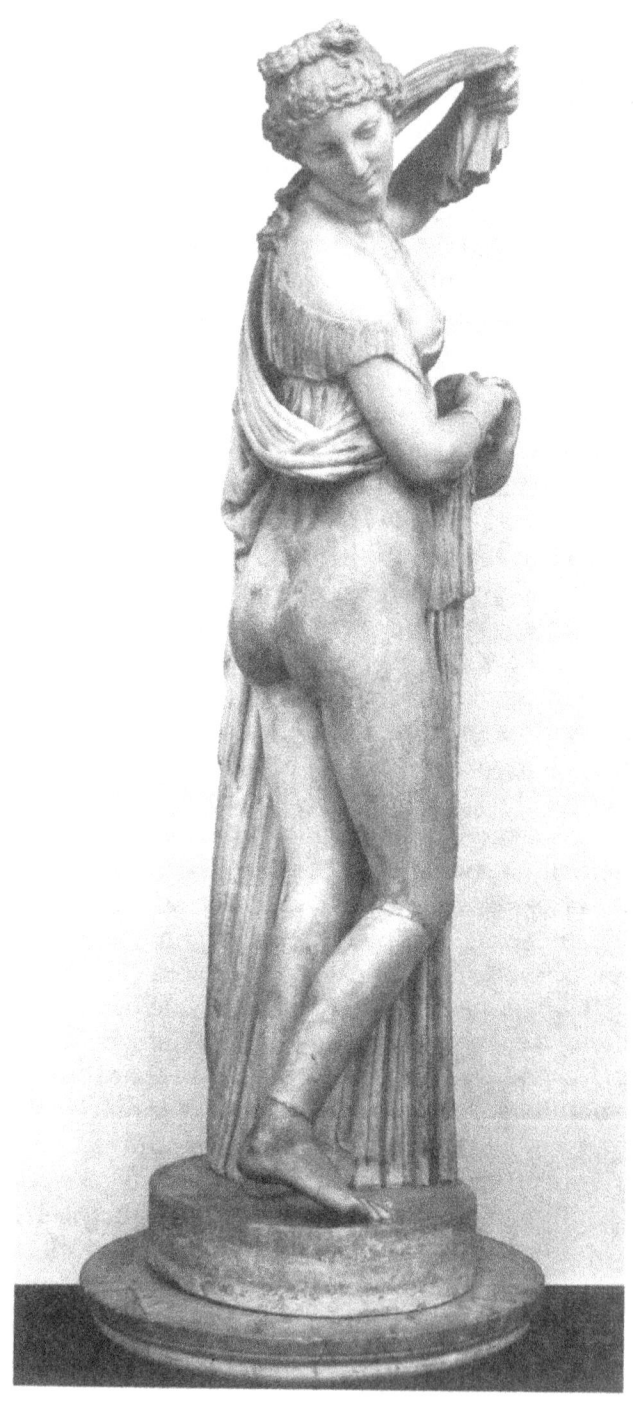

27. Kallipygos. Museo Nazionale, Naples. Hirmer
671.9234

dwelt on the soft, erotic charm of the scene and has, in a sense, intruded on the goddess's intimate moment. In the *Bath of Pallas,* the erotic element of the goddess's naked beauty is presented less directly, and the presentation of Teiresias' gaze is similarly indirect and implicit. Athene's beauty is extolled earlier in the poem, when the chief celebrant describes how the goddess still retains her fresh glow after a grueling training run (23–28), contrasting this with Aphrodite's less naturally emergent beauty. The reader projects the picture of Athene's lovely freshness onto what Teiresias sees as he stumbles across her bathing. The poet has no need to expatiate further on the goddess's beauty in that episode and can deftly leave that to the reader's imagination, through the clues in Chariclo's agonized cry: "My accursed child, you have beheld the breasts and flanks of Athene, but you will never see the sun again!" (88–89). The appraisal of Athene's beauty earlier in the hymn is something which the reader may respond to erotically here, whereas in Apollonius the reader has to respond to a mental image of the goddess, and the interruption is enacted more or less innocently by characters in the poem. To some extent, then, the reader is put emotionally in the position of Teiresias, who is, moreover, a male and a real if unwitting intruder, though he has a much more privileged knowledge of Athene's naked beauty (to his loss) than the reader. His response thus approximates even more closely to that of the spectators of the statues of Aphrodite.[50]

The surprise expressed by the image at our intrusive gaze is complemented in Hellenistic poetry and art by the motif, in erotic contexts, of the image surprising us. In art, this is perhaps most obviously the case with the Sleeping Hermaphrodite (Ill. 28). The viewer approaching the figure from behind is attracted by the sensuously undulant curves of (apparently) a female lying down, proceeds to view the figure from the front, and is surprised by the so-far hidden erect penis and testicles.[51] (It should be noted that one authority is not convinced that the type is a Hellenistic Greek original but thinks that it was perhaps actually created in Rome for the temple of Cybele.)[52] The Sleeping Hermaphrodite is one of those types that draw the viewer into a circumnavigation of the statue. In this it is like, for example, the Farnese Heracles figures (see Ill. 21), which hold the explanation of the hero's exhaustion in the hands hidden behind the hero's back: he has just retrieved

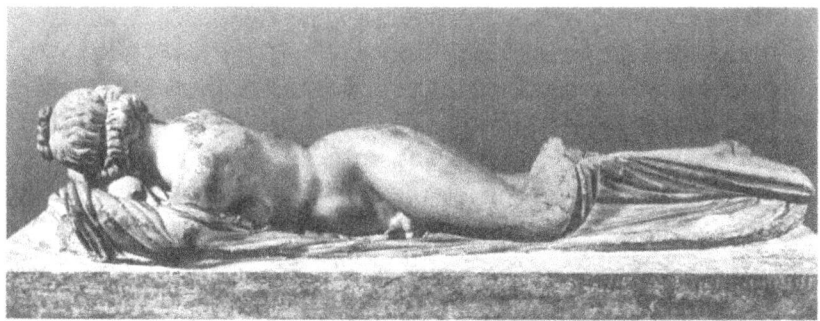

28. Sleeping Hermaphrodite. Museo Nazionale Romano (Terme), Rome.
Sansaini, DAI negative number 54.99

the apples of the Hesperides, so his apparent fatigue could be
seen as a liminal state representing his transition to an immortal
realm. In fact, there are probably some serious uses for the con-
structed experience involved in viewing the sleeping hermaphro-
dites. If we consider these statues in connection with Pompeian
wall-paintings of Pan being surprised by Hermaphrodite, whom
he has mistaken for a nymph, we may come closer to under-
standing one aspect of Hermaphroditus' function as an apotro-
paic entity.[53]

Of course, constructing the conditions for a visual surprise like
this is not a strategy that lends itself naturally to rendition in po-
etry even of the Hellenistic period. The closest analogue is pro-
vided by the fragmentary pastoral, insecurely ascribed to Bion,
called the *Epithalamium of Achilles and Deidameia*. The poem tells
how Achilles hid on Scyros in the female quarters of the house of
Lycomedes, wearing female attire in order to avoid call-up to the
Trojan war, and how he tries to seduce one of Lycomedes' daugh-
ters, Deidameia.[54] Our fragment makes it absolutely clear that
considerable titillation was featured in the later paradigmatic
warrior's masquerade as a woman who "learnt wool-working
instead of arms" and acted the woman, with a blush on his white
cheeks, adopting a girl's gait and fastening up his hair with a
veil—all the while having a man's mind and a man's sexual ap-
petites (15–21). The response to the inevitable revelation, not in-
cluded in our fragment, will presumably have been conveyed by
a character within the poem, who is likely to have mediated the

reader's response much as we saw happening in Apollonius' picture of Aphrodite.

In sum, we can better appreciate the context and function of the technique of viewer-integration in Hellenistic poetry through recent findings on the period's painting and sculpture. We have not, however, found any case in which we are necessarily led to postulate direct influence from specific works of art on specific moments in poetry. Rather, the conclusion emerges even more clearly that the artists trained the eyes of the poets in a more general way, and opened them to unprecedented possibilities and effects in viewing and imaging which could be emulated in ways amenable to poetry.

5

An Eye for the New
Poetic Genres, Iconographical Traditions

The innovations of Hellenistic artists and poets which we have already explored, remarkable as they are, are not the whole story. A good portion of the picture remains to be filled in, and that is the special task of this chapter and the next. This involves going beyond the Hellenistic optic nerve (physical or mental) and analyzing what the Hellenistic eye looked for and how it evaluated what it saw — particularly in terms of emotions. There undoubtedly were unprecedented, characteristically Hellenistic modes of viewing, and, as they evolved, so did a new and deeply engaging range of subject matters on which they were typically deployed. This in turn extended the age's vocabulary of viewing to a degree that would have been unthinkable for the preceding Classical period, however much the new effects depended on the most intimate knowledge of the earlier age's artistic and poetic icons.

Here again the conclusions of art historians will place often quite well known facets of the Hellenistic literary scene in valuable new perspectives, though the relationship between the two fields will prove to be of reciprocal benefit. We remember, for example, how poetic images of Eros, and expressed responses to the motif, helped us place the intention and tone of statues like the Sleeping Eros (see Ill. 1). Compare the tone of a pseudo-Theocritean poem which makes Aphrodite chide her little son — indignant because he has been stung by a bee: "Aren't you like the bees, you who are so tiny and yet deal cruel wounds?" (*Id.* 19.7–8).[1]

The new directions in Hellenistic art and the new subject matter on which it can draw are familiar from every handbook. The range of major statuary, for instance, is extended drastically and now includes new states of mind and body. Images of the gods are softened or conceived in casual moments, the cue here being works like Praxiteles' Cnidia or Sauroktonos (though the latter's traditional attribution to Praxiteles has recently come under reconsideration).[2] The most important developments, however, center on Aphrodite and Dionysus. These two deities are presented in contexts that emphasize their immediate relevance to personal human experience, and their iconography is now clearly intended to present them as enriching this in the most fundamental ways. Their entourages, especially the figures of Eros, Pan, satyrs, maenads, shepherds, nymphs, and hermaphrodites, are increasingly foregrounded.

Alongside these humanized deities are the all-too-human boy-jockeys, old boxers, poor fishermen, drunken old women, dwarves, cripples, and grotesques. The last three types touched their commissioners and owners in a particularly personal way. The terracotta cripples and so forth provided a kind of humor (which our own age deplores) and performed, in the case of dwarves, something of a phallic[3] and apotropaic function,[4] while the hunchbacks averted the evil eye[5] by simultaneously making it laugh and terrifying it by their shape and mordant repartee, much as Mr. Punch or the Italian *gobbo*, their descendants, amuse and terrify today's onlookers. They also served as negative exempla and counterfoils to their owners' enjoyment of life, and thereby underlined their prestige.[6]

The statues of fishermen (Ill. 29) had a similar effect, imparting by contrast high social status to their owners, probably being displayed in naturalistic settings like fishponds.[7] The drunken old women, especially the fascinating and moving example in the Munich Glyptothek (see Ill. 34), have also been convincingly interpreted as carrying the typically Hellenistic moral "Look after yourself."[8] And yet the age could also produce the heroic, "pathetic" monuments like the Gigantomachy of the Great Altar at Pergamon. What social context can be identified as explaining this explosion of *sujet* for visual appreciation and for mental and emotional response? What social context trained the eye of Hellenistic audiences and viewers to look for subjects so different from the

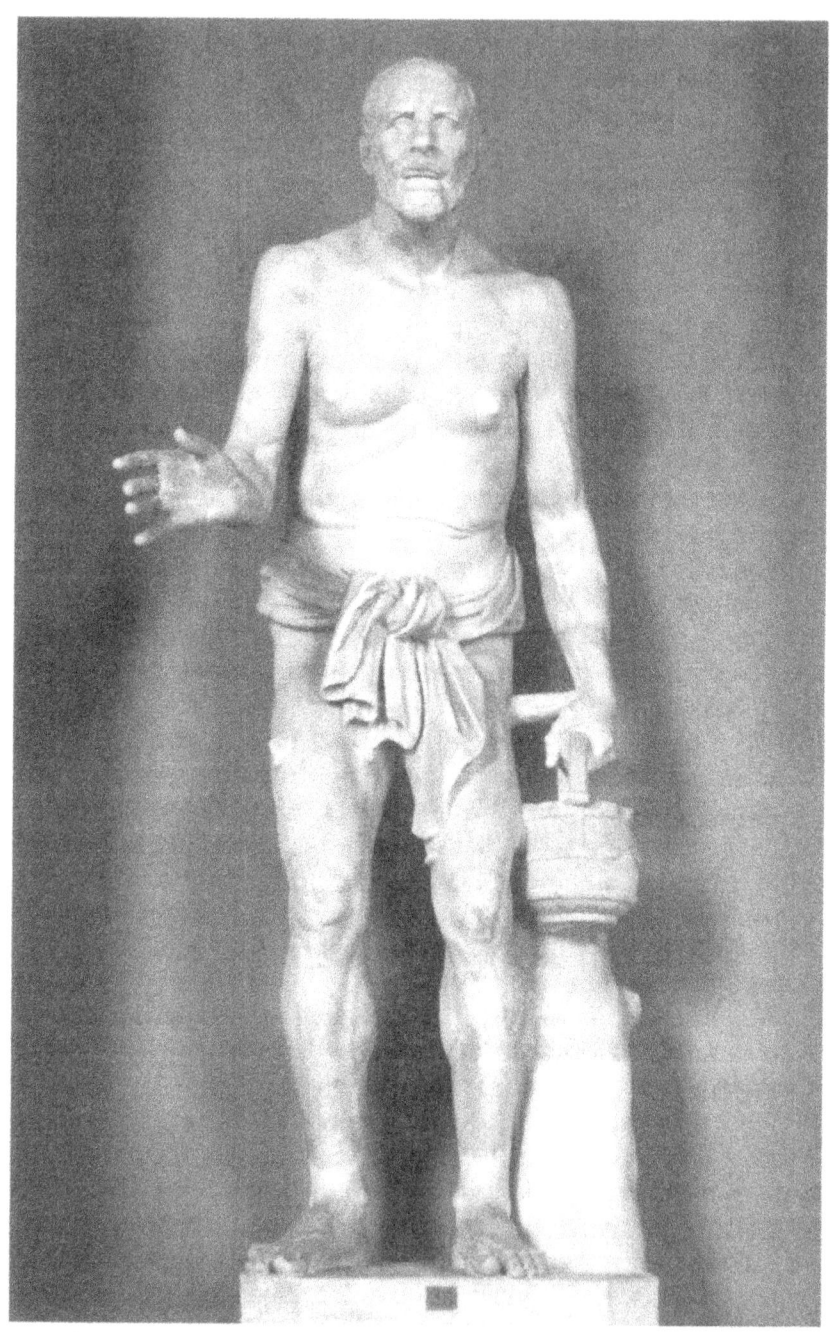

29. Fisherman. Vatican, Rome. Author

traditional repertoire, or to see traditional subjects or motifs in a new light, a new perspective, or a new setting which so vastly increased the tonal and emotional range of visual images in both poetry and art?

One explanation for the new interest in the *Kleinwelt* is that polis-life collapsed under Alexander and his successors.[9] The popularity of the comedy of manners and the growth of the new philosophies of individual self-fulfillment are commonly regarded as indicators of a retreat into private life. In the case of poetry, this movement might naturally be thought to coincide significantly with the growth of private reading, as opposed to hearing recitations at public venues like the Greek poetry competitions mentioned at the beginning of Plato's *Ion* (530a–b). Peter Bing has done the pioneering work in tracing the effect of this radical change on the way poets composed.[10]

This scenario is, however, something of an oversimplification, as might be expected of any such generalization. For one thing, a host of recent studies show that polis-life did not collapse—far from it.[11] For with the general acceptance of democracy as the proper way to govern a polis, internal politics were often more vital than ever before. Instead, the polis was supplemented by the court. Its external activities, like foreign policy, were often restricted, but they had often been so before, under the Persian, Spartan, Syracusan, and Athenian hegemonies. The numbers of poleis increased markedly owing to the settlement of the East, and megalopoleis like Alexandria appeared. "Supplementation" and "transformation" perhaps describe what happened better than "collapse." Moreover, Paul Zanker has done much to show that, going by the honorific portraiture of the period, the Hellenistic citizen-bodies still respected civic values and public services. In other words, there was by no means a total discontinuity from the Classical period in the matter of involvement in public life, no wholesale "cocooning" in Hellenistic society.[12]

As Zanker's study of grave stelae shows, however, alongside the pride in recognition conferred in the arena of public life was an equally positive value placed on private, individual fulfillment in the home and within the family.[13] Moreover, the influence of the portraits of the new personal philosophers is detectable in the portraits of private citizens.[14] Private life was in fact the main zone offering space for the remarkable expansion of the subject range of monumental art. In this context, however, it is above all the world of Aphrodite and Dionysus which figures most prominently in home decoration and acts as conclusive evidence for the positive value placed on the private enjoyment of what Zanker calls *tryphê,* the life of financial and personal fulfillment, success, and even luxury.[15] The same is true of the mosaic genre of the *asarôtos oikos* ("unswept room"), which evinces a clear and quite unashamed preoccupation with food and even conspicuous excess.[16]

At Alexandria, it is significant that the Ptolemies and their queens associated themselves with Dionysus and Aphrodite.[17] Philadelphus' *pompê* is a graphic instance of this, with boys mixing and dispensing Dionysus' wine among the onlooking citizenry in the stadium (Callixenus as reported by Athenaeus 5.200a–b) and, as part of the procession, wine and milk gushing from two springs on the float depicting the cave of the Nysaean nymphs, the nurses of Dionysus (Callixenus ap. Athenaeus 5.200b–c). The city's court-poetry, moreover, includes not only Callimachus' *Lock of Berenice,* which stressed Berenice's association with Aphrodite-Zephyritis, but pieces like the exquisite epigram on the dedication of the nautilus shell to Aphrodite-Arsinoe for showing favor to Selenaea (Call. 14 *HE*). And in Theocritus' poems we have not only the women visiting the Adonis festival in the palace of Arsinoe, but also the praise of the queen mother, Berenice, in *Idyll* 17, where the deified queen is presented as a protégée of Aphrodite, who is "gentle to all mortals and inspires soft loves, and makes light the cares of the yearning lover" (51–52). The Ptolemaic royals clearly sensed the spirit of the times and used the identification in public iconography and display to infiltrate the private and even intimate lives and loves of their subjects.[18]

The state art of Pergamon indeed provides a stark contrast. But in fact the drive behind the contrasting scales, styles, and subjects may not be so utterly different after all. Seen within the context of the Attalids' cultural program to authenticate the Greekness of their city or even outbid the achievements of mainstream Hellenic myth and history, the Great Altar can be viewed as an attempt to link Pergamene life with the world of traditional Hellenic mythology. Whatever the precise interpretation of the Gigantomachy may be,[19] the Telephus frieze definitely makes every conceivable effort to associate the modern city and the mythical past, in certain respects despite the most adventitious connections. Thus the Attalids also will have been responding to a personal cultural need.

One factor in the contrast of the pathetic state art of Pergamon and the cheerful private art in Hellenistic Greek homes may have been the difference in the accessibility of the Attalid and Ptolemaic royal palaces to the subject populace.[20] At Pergamon the Attalids' palace was a residence, and the regent presented himself to his common subjects as king only outside it, though of course he will have entertained his select *philoi,* held audiences, received petitions, and so forth on a regular basis. But he could not be presented as his common subjects' king "at home," and he had no chance of staging small-scale and intimate art for *en masse* display within his residence. And his monuments, like Eumenes' Gigantomachy or his magnificent two-story temple to Athena Nikephoros, had to be correspondingly and "appropriately" impressive. In Alexandria, however, as Theocritus' fifteenth *Idyll* shows, the queen could invite the ordinary populace into the palace (or at least sections of it) for an intimate viewing of a sensual rite and tableau with erotic appeal. The Ptolemies and their queens could therefore show their relevance to the common populace within their own dwelling, "intimately," if with lavish outlay. For their part, the poets at Alexandria were clearly conforming to Ptolemaic taste when they depicted "domestic" material in poems meant for private recitation to élite court audiences, though it is interesting that Theocritus' *Heracliscus* (*Id.* 24), which the Antinoe papyrus shows the poet concluded with a prayer to Heracles for victory in a public competition, quite possibly the Basileia,[21] also placed the regents firmly within the context of the *Kleinwelt,* for there are clear points of identification between Philadelphus and the ten-month-old baby hero.[22]

The Ptolemies' own state art can be viewed in much the same light as the Attalids'. The imposing Pharos lighthouse, for example, was clearly an impressive statement of Ptolemaic supremacy, good governance, and energy, whoever the actual dedicatees were,[23] but the chief beneficiaries were sailors, for whom the monument must have been as welcome a sight as the San Francisco Golden Gate Bridge is to their modern counterparts. The connection with the Proteus of *Odyssey* 4, who was the hero of the island on which the lighthouse was built, will have reinforced for the populace of Alexandria the sense of continuity with mainstream Hellenic culture much as the Telephus frieze was later to do for Pergamon.[24] And the grand procession, while being a demonstration of Ptolemaic wealth, could also reach into the life of the private citizen, given its emphasis on *tryphê* and the more tangible largesse dispensed in the form of wine. This aspect of Hellenistic state art is often understressed.[25]

The foregrounding of the individual was also cardinal in the imaging of the heroic mythical past. Not only are Dionysus and Aphrodite brought into the sphere of personal and sensual experience, but the paradigmatic strong-man hero, Heracles, is introduced into their world of *tryphê*, whether as a baby in a domestic setting, as in Theocritus' twenty-fourth *Idyll*, where as we have just seen Heracles is a likely candidate for identification with Philadelphus, or as relaxing after his toil, eating, drinking, manifesting the effect of the last activity on his bladder, or marrying Omphale in the most luxurious, indeed feminine, attire. This domestication of the Classical ideal in turn has ramifications for certain features of Hellenistic poetry and art. In poetry, it entails "genre-crossing," especially the housing of lowly material in meters and forms classically associated with the depiction of grand characters and themes; in visual art, the citation of iconographical traditions for the varied purposes of humor (Heracles urinating) or pathos (Heracles resting, exhausted).

So far in this study, it has more often than not been our understanding of developments in Hellenistic art which has helped us to gain a more comprehensive context for some of Hellenistic poetry's more innovative techniques of visual presentation. But in the case of genre-crossing we are far better informed for poetry. Our experience of the poets' experimentation should be used for the light it may shed on the artists' strategies.[26] Surprisingly, the comparison has never been made on any systematic basis.

One example will illustrate the process in poetry. Theocritus' fourth *Idyll*, a dramatic dialogue between two herdsmen, Battus and Corydon, is written in hexameters. The noble medium would therefore have been felt to be in tension with both the dramatic mode and the lowly personnel of the *Idyll*. We know from Aristotle that the hexameter was not considered suitable for the presentation of ordinary conversation. In the *Rhetoric* he contrasts it with iambics: "Of all the meters the heroic meter is grand and lacks the rhythmical structure of ordinary speech" (*Rhet.* 3.8.4). In the *Poetics* we read, "The heroic meter is the stateliest and most weighty of all the meters" (*Poet.* 59b34–35). Theocritus seems, moreover, to have gone out of his way to add to the impression of artificiality created by the meter in which he makes his rustics speak, using a Doric dialect which is highly literary, however generally appropriate it may be to the Doric-speaking regions in which this and other low-life *Idylls* are set.[27] And yet *Idyll* 4 presents the herdsmen passing the time of day, reminiscing, needling one another, and catching up on the latest rustic gossip, the culminating item of which involves Corydon's report of how he discovered the father of the owner of the flocks he is tending *in flagrante delicto* with a country girl near the byre (58–63). It is inconceivable that this detail, with which the poem closes, was not intended humorously as a means of outraging the last vestiges of the expectations traditionally entertained of the hexameter.

The clash between the grandeur of the meter and the comic nature of the dramatic mode is the first major element in the tension. The second is that between the kind of people traditionally thought appropriate for depiction in the hexameters of epic poetry, whom Aristotle defines most succinctly in the *Poetics* when he says, "Epic followed tragedy inasmuch as it was a metrical representation of superior people" (*Poet.* 49b9–10). The fact that Battus and Corydon are placed so emphatically on the low end of the social scale flies in the face of traditional expectations of epic and the meter associated with it. The hexameters of *Idyll* 4 act as a ground bass over which Theocritus can improvise deliberately incongruous themes. By themselves they cite the tradition of epic and thereby increase the sense of rift between the subject matter and tone we expect of such a noble form and those currently on offer. Here the dominant effect of disappointing our expectations is humor.

This is generally true of all of Theocritus' low-life mimes, whether rustic or urban. Sometimes the epic tradition is cited explicitly. The *locus classicus* is the closing moment in *Idyll* 5 when Comatas the goatherd, threatening one of his goats with castration if he doesn't stop trying to mount the nannygoats, expresses his readiness to be called Melanthius if he doesn't fulfill his threat. Odysseus' punishment of the disloyal goatherd Melanthius by cutting off his genitals and throwing them to the dogs (*Od.* 22.475–77) may be ironically appropriate to Comatas' expressed resolve, but given such prominence it merely serves to underline how far down we have come in the epic world. This is more specific than genre-crossing, the use of a grand form to represent low subject matter and tones: it is the citation of a tradition, which I have called "genre-marking."[28]

Hellenistic poetry's interest in everyday characters, moments, and themes seems to have stemmed from the same socio-political motivation as visual art's. There, as we have seen, Paul Zanker illustrates how the new preoccupations are associated with the value placed on *tryphê* in the home.[29] We can see the shift in interest in the poetry itself, where productions like Callimachus' mimetic hymns can accommodate not only recitation to an audience but also private reading with no context of public ritual required, a function that goes naturally with the growth of a reading public. The encomiastic poetry of Alexandria, with its celebration of, in particular, the queens as Aphrodite, is also a valuable index of how the Ptolemies now use poetry as one means of reaching into the homes and personal lives of their subjects. Hence, at least in part, poetry shares with visual art a fascination with the world of children, everyday and ordinary people, people in reduced circumstances, like Callimachus' Hecale or, very differently, the drunken old women of the fictional funerary epigrams, and the *demimonde* of Herodas' *Mimiambs*. The new interests carry over to the poetry on mythological themes, in which Arnd Kerkhecker has discerned the workings of *Fußnotendichtung*. By this he means the kind of poetry that explains the down-to-earth realities of the heroic world: where Theseus might have spent the night before his confrontation with the bull of Marathon, or what a heroic family might have done if there were snakes in the children's room.[30]

But to return to *Idyll* 4, a scene that is of special interest to us is the one in which Battus treads on a thorn while his attention is focused on a heifer (50–57). Out of the dialogue emerges a strikingly visual picture. In his pain, Battus asks whether Corydon can see the thorn; Corydon replies that he can and that he has it in his fingernails, and then proclaims, "There it is." Couched in the hexameter, this exchange, together with Corydon's portentously superfluous moral that Battus shouldn't walk barefoot on a hill where thorns grow, illustrates the process of genre-crossing clearly enough. But so does the mental scene which is evoked, the actors and their banal action being totally and intentionally out of kilter with anything Theocritus' audience would have expected of the traditional ways in which the hexameter was deployed.

Inevitably, connections have been made here with certain well-known products of Hellenistic visual art, and perhaps most convincingly with the Spinario (Ill. 30) and with the Pan and Satyr groups in which Pan inspects the sole of the satyr's foot for a thorn.[31] In fact, given the later dating of the Pan and Satyr group to sometime between the mid-second and first centuries,[32] and of the Spinario to around 100 B.C.,[33] any inspiration is more likely to have been from poetry to art. But direction of influence is of less importance here than the analogous execution. R. R. R. Smith briefly makes the right connection when he remarks, "As in literature, the statues aim to make a telling contrast of subject and medium. Theokritos wrote of shepherds and whores in recondite Doric hexameters, and fine, technically exquisite bronze statues represented derelict fishermen."[34] The analogy drawn by Smith warrants closer scrutiny.

The Pan and Satyr groups do indeed evidence exquisite composition and execution, and are of course presented in traditionally noble materials.[35] And yet they feature lowly country deities engaged in a trivial, quotidian activity. The materials and style would traditionally have awakened expectations of a far grander subject, and these expectations are dashed. The true analogy with poetry in this case is with poetry's genre-mixing. And, just as the clash of form and content created a new range of tones in Theocritus' fourth *Idyll*, so works of art like the Pan and Satyr groups played much more aggressively than is commonly thought on live expectations of the appropriateness of the subjects on which one might lavish such "serious" materials and workmanship. True, experimentation with presenting humbler moments in the grand style had been an area of long development, reaching back at least to Cephisodotus' Peace,[36] onward through Praxiteles' Sauroktonos, if the traditional attribution is accepted,[37] Lysippus' Silenus and Baby Dionysus, Praxiteles and Lysippus' developments in depicting satyrs and Eros,[38] and the Hellenistic "rococo";[39] but it remains the work of the Hellenistic artists to have developed these effects to their logical conclusion.

Be that as it may, the expectations entertained of the appropriate deployment of subject mater, style, and materials seem to have retained their actuality in Hellenistic art, just as much as they clearly did in Hellenistic poetry. We remember that at least part of the point of the cup description of Theocritus' first *Idyll* is the shock that the "goatherd's miracle" could have been executed so inappropriately in wood, the only material available on a rustic's budget. Significantly, too, art historians talk of how lowly subject matter "by its nature lends itself better to small than to monumental size."[40] Regarding the unusual two-thirds lifesize scale of such figures, R. R. R. Smith suggests that "smaller size might assuage any sense of impropriety at the representation of such lowly subjects in fine statues."[41] I would suggest, rather, that, to judge by the poetic analogy, "impropriety" was a goal.

This comes out with more clarity, though with incomparably more subtlety, in the Spinario (Ill. 30). Its noble materials, meticulous composition, and exquisite execution would all, on traditional thinking, have been "meant" for the depiction of a grander subject than the rustic boy absorbed in his insignificant activity. Yet the sculptor took a step which emphasized the clash of traditional expectations awakened by the medium and the reality of the untraditional content. He "cites" the iconographical tradition of the Classical ephebe statue. This is effected in the treatment of the head of the Spinario in the Palazzo dei Conservatori, which is in the severe style, though the other type copying the same original, the Castellani Thorn Puller in the British Museum, has a head which is naturalistic. As Paul Zanker says, the charm of the Spinario in Rome is its self-contradictory eclecticism: in the casual motif there is severe composition, "im Kopf des Hirtenknaben das früh-klassische Ephebenbild."[42] But with the example of genre-marking from poetry in mind, we can perhaps describe the statue's rationale with even more precision by saying that the Spinario consciously marks itself as being in the tradition of the classical ephebe by citing the tradition, and then willfully goes its own untraditional way, the explicit citation adding to the sense of shock caused by the disappointment of traditional expectations.

At least in the case of the Spinario, moreover, the severe and Classical styles evidently carried associations of grandeur for the artist who cited them, in a way analogous to the Hellenistic poets' view of Homeric epic and Classical tragedy as the grand poetic

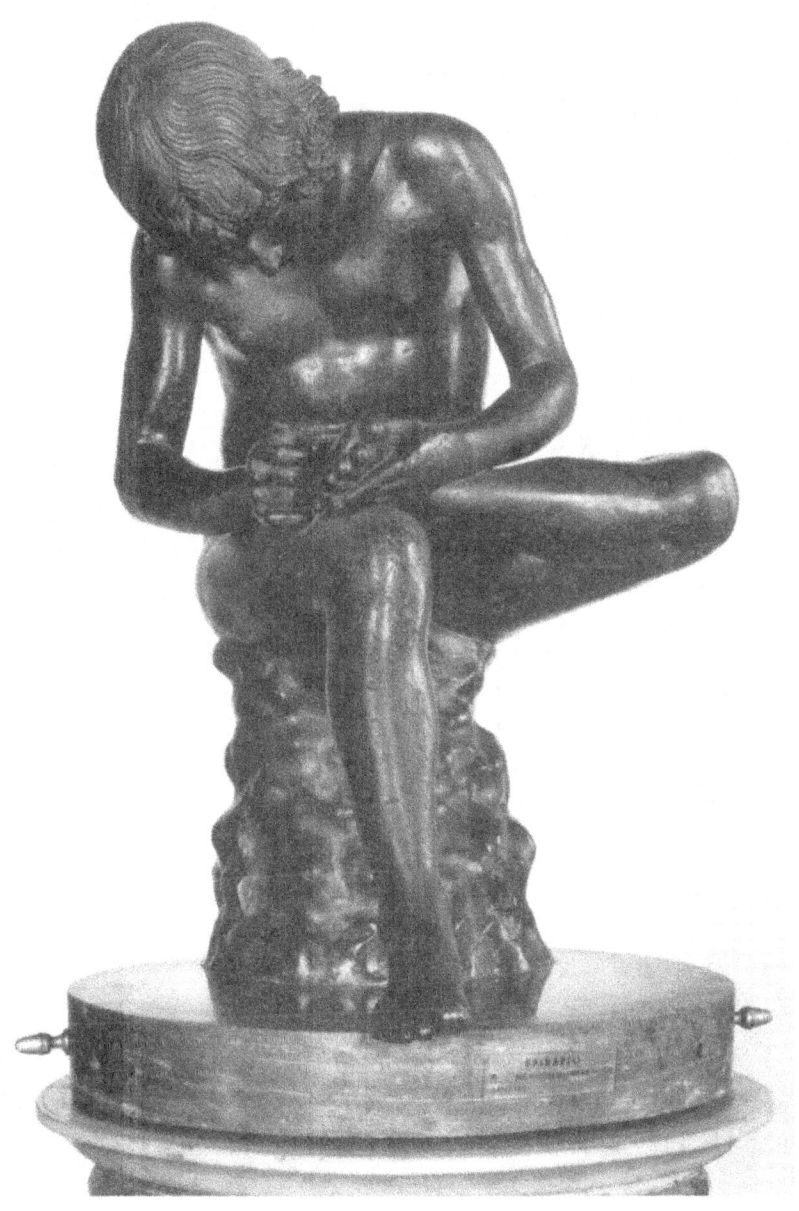

30. Spinario. Palazzo dei Conservatori, Rome. Hirmer 671.9358

genres. That is at least part of what these earlier styles meant to the artists who reworked them, and the grandeur of the tradition thus cited must have thrown the incongruity of the Spinario into even deeper perspective. True, reusing an earlier ephebic head type is typical of a lot of Hellenistic "archaizing" or "severizing" sculpture of the second and first centuries B.C., as in the youth depicted by Stephanus,[43] but no examples of eclecticism other than the Conservatori Spinario lavish such features on the body of such a socially low figure as a country boy pulling a thorn from his foot. Perhaps a parallel, admittedly minus the social aspect, is provided by the "neoclassical" Melian Aphrodite (Ill. 31).[44] The fusion of her realistic body and idealized head, adorned with hair in the simple Classical style,[45] might have given an added dimension and piquancy to the goddess's beauty.

The process can, however, be seen in works from the early Hellenistic period like the Boy with a Goose (see Ill. 23), which is definitely early third-century. Here we must take into consideration the function of the statue. It was a dedicatory offering, perhaps for a child who has recovered from illness, "probably . . . inside the temple," to judge from Herodas' fourth *Mimiamb*.[46] Traditionally, the boy would have been presented wearing a cloak, as a citizen-to-be. In terms of its function, therefore, the statue stands in a clear iconographical tradition. But now the child is presented in a sanctuary naked, with his pet, begging the onlooker to pick him up, as if the statue were alive, as Phile says in Herodas' poem. The original Hellenistic viewer would have seen none of the expected exemplary beauty ascribed to a future citizen here: instead, he would perhaps have remembered Aristotle's down-to-earth observation that the reason babies cannot walk upright is that their upper bodies are not well proportioned in relation to their lower parts and "because they are in every respect like dwarves."[47] In this early Hellenistic work, too, we can see a sculptor shocking his viewers' expectations by citing the iconographical tradition — this time the one associated with dedicatory statues set up in a sanctuary.

As in poetry, it should be noted, such flouting of expectations can lead to much more serious effects. Aristotle, as we have seen, did not feel that epic was the proper place to give serious representation to figures low on the social scale, but Callimachus introduces a figure like Hecale, who is made to share center stage

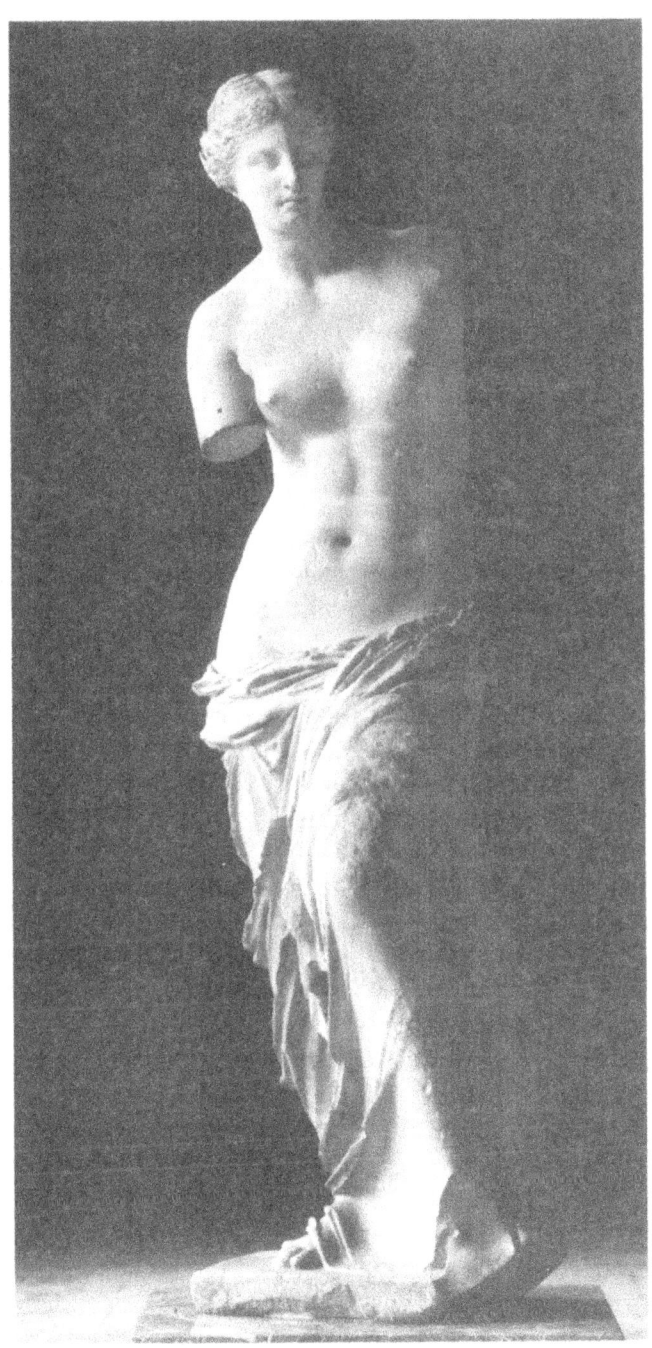

31. Melian Aphrodite. Musée du Louvre, Paris. Hirmer
561.1039

with "canonical" heroes like Theseus. The elevation is an impressive shock, and we admire the old woman's humble generosity and moral goodness, and feel the pathos of her situation, a matter which we shall examine at greater length in chapter 6. If we look at the visual art of the period, we find strikingly analogous procedures, with a broad range of emotional effects. The fact that realism in early Hellenistic poetry produced pathos and a serious tone should be considered for the light it might shed on the old problem of placing the tone of works like the old fishermen (see Ill. 29) from, perhaps, the first half of the second century B.C.[48] The fisherman on the Goatherd's cup in Theocritus' first *Idyll* has shown us that a poor old man's undaunted pursuit of a livelihood could be admired, but the *Hecale* illustrates a technique by which such a figure could be appraised positively, and we should consider whether it had a role to play in art.

Obvious starting points are provided by the fishermen and the Terme Boxer (see Ill. 8). These remarkable statues, whatever their setting and function, represent figures from the lower social orders and are nonetheless rendered with the highest degree of execution and in noble materials. Do the execution and medium at least in part ennoble their lowly subjects, engaged in their day-to-day but still, in their own way, heroic struggles? If we accept the *Hecale* as in any way analogous, the possibility becomes a serious likelihood. Genre-marking is arguably also at work. As we shall see, Hecale stands in a line of epic heroines reaching back to the *Odyssey*'s Eurycleia, but she also cites grander epic personages — specifically Hecuba and Thetis — deepening the pathos of her circumstances. So the fishermen cite the iconographical tradition of kouros and korê portraiture. Though of course they stand at the opposite extreme from the autonomy, beauty, and youth of these Archaic statues and their progeny from the Kritios Boy to the Peiraeus Youth and beyond, it is precisely the shock of the citation that throws the pathos of their situation into even deeper relief.

In the modern criticism of the poetry of the Hellenistic period, the concept is known, quite unproblematically, as *oppositio in imitando*: the "model" provides a benchmark for assessing the circumstances of the new subject, and the comparison forcibly brings out the difference by a kind of chiaroscuro effect. Similarly, the Boxer cites the tradition of athlete statuary, but the contrast between the idealism of the tradition and the realism of an athlete whose victories are increasingly hard-fought-for places the tradition in a striking new perspective. In much the same way, Lysippus made statues of Heracles in states of exhaustion, and the Attalids commissioned victory monuments celebrating their achievements by presenting not merely victorious Pergamene generals and warriors but also the reverse: conquered, suffering Celtic foes.[49]

Another instance is possibly to be found in Meyer's reconstruction of the "white" Marsyas group (see Ill. 7a), in which, Meyer argues, Apollo's Scythian slave is featured.[50] Critics have been quick to point out that in the Classical period major art avoided the foreground depiction of slaves,[51] though they are ubiquitous in background contexts, possibly even appearing on the Parthenon frieze.[52] Foregrounding a figure of such status as forcefully as in the case of the Scythian helps define the group's novelty and would certainly have added to the impression of the extreme cruelty of which a god is capable.

In all these works of art, viewing is enriched in ways unprecedented in Greek art, just as the analogous procedure of genre-crossing and marking in poetry, which has helped us to appreciate what precisely is afoot in viewing these Hellenistic statues, is unprecedented in Greek literature.[53]

The example of poetry can also help us gauge the original aesthetic effect of visual art depicting the Hellenistic rulers, from Alexander onward, as gods. What precisely was the effect of Lysippus' creation of the "ruler-hero" statue-type representing Alexander? What was the effect of a production like Apelles' painting of Alexander as Zeus Keraunophoros, aside from reminding its viewers in the temple of Artemis at Ephesus not only that Alexander was the son of Zeus, but that his power on earth was "like that of Zeus, universal, invincible, and omniscient"?[54]

The Hellenistic poet's handling of the genres of the hymn and the encomium provides a key. In Classical thinking, these two types of poetry were strictly distinct. For example, when Plato makes Socrates say that all poetry will have to be banned from the ideal state except for "hymns for the gods and encomia for good men" (*Rep.* 607a), he was really only reflecting, from his own moralistic point of view, generally held ancient Greek sensibilities about the two poetic genres, especially the idea that the two should be kept separate. In the *Laws* Plato is a witness to the sense of breached decorum when such things are mixed, for he complains about how moral and poetic decay set in when poets mixed, among other contrasting genres of poetry, laments with hymns, which had formerly been considered "opposites" (*Laws* 700a–e).[55] Here again is the quite traditional thought that there were specific types of poetry for immortals and specific types for mortals. What strategies, then, did the Hellenistic poets adopt when they were faced with humans who had pretensions to deity?

Obviously, one way ahead was simply to address the mortal as a god whom one could see, not merely in the form of a statue, as the Athenians did with Demetrius Poliorcetes in Hermocles' ithyphallic hymn to the "liberator," recorded by Athenaeus (7.253d).[56] It is significant that Demetrius is presented as *"theos epiphanês,"* "god manifest," thus paving the way for the appearance of this epiklesis on Hellenistic inscriptions and coins. But there are more subtle approaches, which, as Theocritus' *Encomium to Ptolemy* and Callimachus' *Hymn to Delos* demonstrate, involved playing with the traditional expectations of the hymn and the encomium, and actually mixing them together.

For an encomium, Theocritus' seventeenth *Idyll* contains quite remarkable hymnic elements. The very exordium illustrates this by the way it compares Zeus as the most prominent immortal and Philadelphus as the most prominent mortal, but then continues with the statement of the poet's intention to "hymn Ptolemy, for hymns are the reward of the immortals themselves as well" (1–8), as if it were somehow even more the poet's brief to sing hymns to mortals. The poem's closing lines bid the king farewell, as a hymn traditionally does to a deity, but the poet claims that he will mention Ptolemy no less than the other demigods, and finally asks him to pray to Zeus for excellence, as if the "demigod" were subordinate to Zeus after all (135–37). It is as though Philadelphus were not yet established as a god, but is on the way to deification. The Theoi Soteres are mentioned, Soter pictured in the company of Heracles and Alexander after a party on Olympus, and Berenice presented in her cult function as facilitator of mortals' love lives (34–52). The poem thus probably just pre-dates the establishment of the Theoi Adelphoi, which P. M. Fraser dates to 272/1.[57] In view of all the ambivalences, it may have been a kite-flyer for the idea of Philadelphus' deification.[58]

Callimachus' *Hymn to Delos*, on the other hand, shows how encomiastic elements can be incorporated into a hymn. Here the unborn Apollo warns Leto not to give birth to him on Cos, for the island is reserved by fate for the birth of "another god," Philadelphus, who will rule a vast kingdom and will aid and abet Apollo's repulse of the Gauls from Delphi by stranding and starving mutinous Gallic mercenaries on an island in the Nile (162–95).[59]

The two poems thus deliberately flout the Classical separation of hymn and encomium when confronting the new monarch, thereby actively raising him to the recognizably divine status appropriate to the hymn genre, and furthering his political aims. On a more purely aesthetic level, the audience must have experienced a sense of shock at hearing the hymnal mode used for the mortal regent in the more traditionally appropriate context of an encomium, to take the example of Theocritus' piece, or at hearing a god singing a hymn to Philadelphus in the hymnic context appropriate to Apollo, as in Callimachus' *Delos*. Given Classical sensibilities as reflected by Plato, the juxtaposition of the two genres must have added to the feeling of a creative collision. The striking nature of this procedure, however, must have depended on a live acceptance of the rules of the game: otherwise, intentionally flouting them would be pointless. And it is this element of unexpectedness and surprise that, I suggest, originally had an analogy in the visual arts.

Up till now, we have not been able to point to a comparable kind of genre-crossing in the visual arts. We have had to look at sculpture in terms of iconographical traditions, like the tradition of ephebic statuary cited by the Spinario. But with the rules for the depiction of gods and mortals we are for once on remarkably similar ground to the principle "hymns for gods and encomia for good men." The Greeks of the Classical period distinguished firmly between ἀγαλματοποιία (*agalmatopoiia*, "the making of beautiful objects for the gods") and ἀνδριαντοποιία (*andriantopoiia*, "the making of statues of men").[60] Poetry in fact both attests to and plays with the fixed expectations of *agalmata*. We have already considered an epigram in which this can be seen, the poem of doubtful ascription to Asclepiades (39 *HE*): "This is the portrait (εἰκών) of Cypris. —Come on, let's make sure it isn't Berenice's: I'm in two minds as to which of the two one should say it's more like." The word for portrait here, εἰκών, *eikôn*, had traditionally been neutral as to the divinity or humanity of its subjects, but a statue of Aphrodite was her *agalma*. And yet the subject of this *agalma* can be mistaken for a human, which is a clever way of complimenting the Ptolemaic queen's human beauty and elevating her to at least near-divine status. An epigram of Meleager (110 *HE*), of admittedly later date, plays with a similar conceit: though the great sculptor Praxiteles made an *eikôn* of the god Eros, Eros has now, having made a portrait of himself (αὐτὸν ἀπεικονίσας), created as a "living *agalma*" (ἔμψυχον ἄγαλμα) the poet's beloved, who is coincidentally named Praxiteles. The poem thus explicitly speaks of an *agalma* of a human, hinting at the proximity to the divine of the poet's boyfriend.

For sculpture, therefore, and presumably for painting, there were two "genres" for each type of subject, determined by subject matter and formal features like occasion, social function, and material, roughly as epinician poetry was considered to be a genre distinct from hymns by virtue of their differing subjects, performance settings, and meters. And the two "sculpture genres" were traditionally kept meticulously separate. As a consequence, works like Apelles' Alexander Keraunophoros must have provoked the shock with which we have seen Theocritus and Callimachus experimenting in poetry. The subject matter up till now considered appropriate for *andriantopoiia* is all of a sudden graced with the medium and attributes of *agalmatopoiia*, and the consequent collision of the genres and the expectations associated with them is likely to have deepened the sense of surprise—and awe. In fact, we have it on record that contemporaries of Apelles felt precisely this way: Lysippus famously criticized Apelles' painting on the ground that Time would rob it of its glory—kings die too![61] Clearly, Lysippus felt the attribute to be inappropriate.[62]

This shock must have been even more drastic when a private citizen was honored with, for example, a statue in a temple dedicated to him. Diodorus Pasparus, the Pergamene politician who steered Pergamon through the confused period after the death of Attalus III and during the conversion of the kingdom into a Roman province, saving the city from the devastation of the Mithridatic wars, was also given an *agalma* "enthroned with the gods" in a gymnasium.[63] The process is taken to an instructive extreme in the realm of coins, moreover. In particular, we have the gold octodrachms of Ptolemy III Euergetes and Ptolemy IV Philopator. Multiple divine attributes — the aegis, sunbeams, and tri-dent — show that the two regents are at once like Zeus, Helios, and Poseidon on earth.[64]

Only with an effort of the imagination can we recapture the full effect of this real genre-crossing in visual art. But the analogue of Hellenistic poetry alerts us to the likelihood that it was remark-ably dramatic, as striking as Hellenistic art's humanization of the gods will have been in its own, different way.

6

Viewing Pleasure and Pain

Of all the gods and heroes endowed with human traits in Hellenistic art and poetry, Aphrodite is pre-eminently and the most sensually so.[1] Her novel nakedness in the late Classical Cnidia (see Ill. 9), which was especially admired at least in later antiquity for its equally gratifying viewability from all angles, heralds a new attitude to the female figure, and a new genre in the art of the Hellenistic period which enthusiastically followed the Cnidia's example.[2] The metamorphosis of her son from a slim young man into the Hellenistic putto with whom we most readily identify the god nowadays fits naturally enough into the new taste for "child art." Behind his apparent accessibility and vulnerability, however, there often lies an unstated but implied power and potential cruelty. In this last he is truly his mother's son, for it is likely that even in the Cnidia the goddess's might was a potent subtext.

Just how are we to read the Hellenistic artists' innovations in the iconography of Eros and Aphrodite? Here again the written word and written narrative of the poets can help us appreciate the range of associations and responses that were current in the age and might underlie the artistic images. They can, moreover, give us a clearer idea of the means by which visual art achieved these effects.

The first thing to note is the remarkably parallel manner in which poets and artists avail themselves of genre-crossing and genre-marking (in the case of poetry) and citing and mixing iconographical traditions (in the case of art) to achieve their new effects. The art involving Eros and Aphrodite has never before been analyzed from this vantage point, which has been used exclusively for the criticism of poetry. The presentation of the goddess in the sculpture of the Hellenistic age in fact provides us with many examples of the strategy. Its ancestry reaches back at least to Phidian practice, as seen on the East Pediment of the Parthenon (Ill. 32). There we have the famous motifs of the goddess's voluptuous reclining pose and the drapery falling off her right shoulder. Elements of the presentation of the goddess's sexuality are indeed present. The cue is perhaps taken up in the Fréjus Aphrodite of around 410 B.C. (Ill. 33), whose left breast is bare and whose drapery might as well not exist.

But it is Praxiteles' Cnidian Aphrodite of between 350 and 340, with the goddess depicted nude before or after her bath, which takes the final step on the path to full nudity. The balance toward total nudity in a representation of a goddess is tilted tentatively in the Fréjus Aphrodite, but tipped firmly in the Cnidia. The drastic break with traditional representations of the goddess and the well-documented response of the Coans who took the draped option[3] can be appreciated fully only when we consider the traditional expectations entertained of a representation of a divine epiphany: traditionalism as much as prudishness is likely to have guided their decision. And this flouting of expectations is as likely as anything else to explain the statue's appeal to the Hellenistic taste. As we have seen, breaking with traditional expectations became a vital element in the age's special creativity in both representative art and poetry. To name only one example in Hellenistic art, we have, from admittedly perhaps as late as the first century, according to Havelock's impressive down-dating,[4] the Capua Aphrodite (see Ill. 14), whose upper torso is bare down to the right slope of the mons Veneris. R. R. R. Smith detects "revisionist 'modesty'" in the drapery,[5] but Ridgway is probably correct to conclude that "the conception of the bare female torso reflected in a shield does not convey a spirit of modesty, and the residual clothing acts as a foil rather than as a cover."[6]

In the more private arts, too, the shift of emphasis in the portrayal of Aphrodite is very evident. We have, for instance, the "domestic" Aphrodite scenes in fourth-century vase-painting. The Meidias Painter's hydria, with Adonis casually reclining on the goddess's body, and Aphrodite sitting on his knee amid

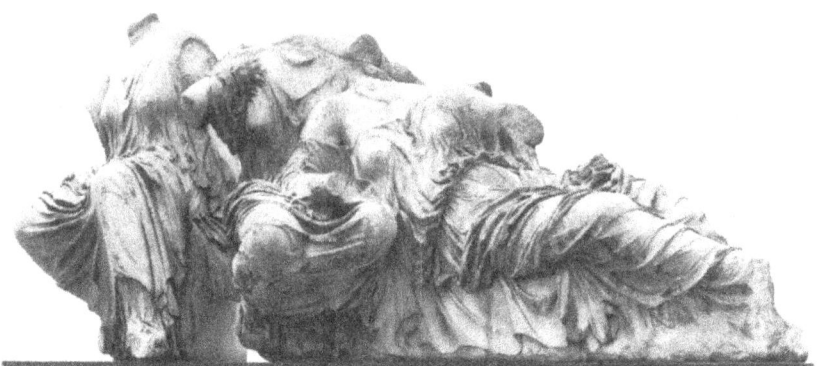

32. Aphrodite reclining, East Pediment of the Parthenon. British Museum, London. Hirmer 561.0108

attendant female figures who play with a mirror or a pet bird, is a good example for us. The scene strikingly anticipates and complements the tableau of Aphrodite and Adonis described by the Singer in Theocritus' fifteenth *Idyll:* "Cypris embraces Adonis and the rosy-armed Adonis embraces her; the groom is eighteen or nineteen years old; his kiss does not scratch, for the golden down still grows around his lips."[7] Similarly intimate moments in the goddess's love life are also displayed on mirror-cases.[8] Havelock surveys the popularity of Cnidia-style statuary in private houses, gardens, and fountains, and even tombs.[9]

Aphrodite décolletée, Aphrodite bathing, Aphrodite admiring her image in the shield of Ares, Aphrodite, that is, depicted in attitudes of emphatically human sexuality—what student of Hellenistic poetry is not reminded of his or her Apollonius or Callimachus? Leaving aside for the moment the question of which medium is inspired by the other, the undeniable fact remains that the rationales of presentation are analogous. Aphrodite playing with her locks in preparation for the Judgment of Paris at *Hymn* 5.21–22 is characterized as fussy and trivial, and part of the effect is achieved by the depiction of Aphrodite's behavior in a hymn, and by the contrasting numinousness of Athene when bathing. Apollonius employs the same approach in his depictions of the deity looking at her reflection in Ares' shield and preening herself when Hera and Athene visit her, though I for one have stressed

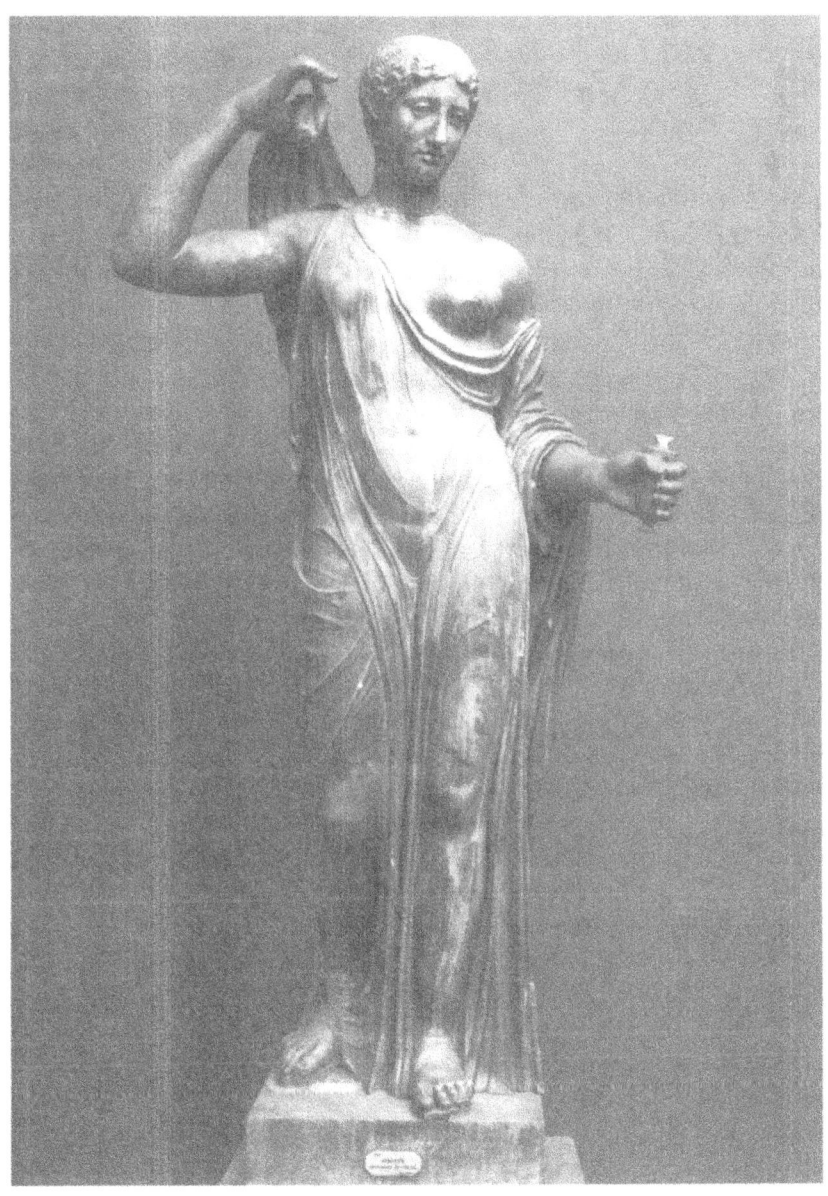

33. Fréjus Aphrodite. Museo Nazionale, Naples. Singer, DAI negative number 70.1512

that behind the appearance of triviality lies a dangerous force well beyond our control,[10] an effect which R. R. R. Smith discerns in the Cnidia and her followers.[11] The poets have proceeded analogously. While the sculptors teased out hints in the Phidian Aphrodite, making them into the main message, the poets took cues from texts like the song of Demodocus and the *Homeric Hymn to Aphrodite* 60–66, emphasizing these motifs and tones to a degree unprecedentedly "inappropriate" in the elevated context of traditional hymnic or epic poetry.

So much for the means by which a novel range of effects was opened up in the poetic and artistic presentation of Aphrodite. But what precisely were these new effects? Here we must address the direction of inspiration. The Fréjus and the Cnidia are dated to the late fifth century or the mid- or late fourth century; the poets' interest in a coquettish or narcissistic Aphrodite, unprecedented to this degree, is securely located in the first half of the third century. Thus, there can be no real doubt that the general inspiration for this conception of the goddess came from art. We should bear in mind, however, that Havelock's persuasive arguments for dating the Capua later than the Melian Aphrodite of 120–100 B.C. and for similarly lowering the dates of the Capitoline and Medici Aphrodites, the Croucher, the Sandal Binder, the half-draped and nude Anadyomenes, the Melian, and the Kallipygos[12] mean that these other statues post-date the poetic evocations of the goddess by a considerable timespan. Simon's postulation of the Capua as an actual model for the image of Aphrodite in the *Argonautica*[13] is a particularly notable casualty of this reading.

But we need have no hesitation in accepting the original direction of general inspiration as being from art to poetry where the depictions of Aphrodite and Eros are concerned. Here the artefacts for private use, like the vases and mirror-cases mentioned above, will have brought the new ways of depicting the two deities into more immediately accessible currency. Nonetheless, the real point at issue for our purpose is that the poetic texts give us more explicit evidence than the art objects for Hellenistic spectators' range of responses and associations. Once recovered, these will in turn help us locate the original meaning conveyed by icons of Aphrodite and Eros.

The opening of the third book of the *Argonautica* is particularly useful in this regard. It contains the famous scene in which Hera and Athene visit Aphrodite in order to get her to make Medea fall in love with Jason, and features the picture of Aphrodite combing her hair in preparation for plaiting it (7–110). It cites the moment in *Iliad* 18 when Thetis visits Charis and Hephaestus to obtain new armor for Achilles.[14] Apart from the general similarities of narrative, there are clear verbal echoes. Aphrodite's needling greeting, "My dear ladies, what purpose and need bring you here after such a long time? Why have you come here? You have not visited me much in the past, since you are pre-eminent among the goddesses" (52–54), builds colorfully on Charis' welcome to Thetis, "Why have you come, so respected and beloved? You have not visited us often in the past" (*Il.* 18.385–86, repeated by Hephaestus at 424–45). We therefore have explicit citation of the tradition, and, significantly, the moment cited has perhaps the most light and chatty tone in the whole of epic.

Moreover, the dynamics of the relationship between the three goddesses in Apollonius are charged with added significance in that they are made to foreshadow the rivalry caused by the Judgment of Paris.[15] The tone of frivolity — here with more than a hint of ironical self-effacement — is amplified when Aphrodite offers to help in whatever way her "feeble hands" can (81–82). But this is also the deity whose "cunning aid" the prophet Phineus has told the Argonauts that they must seek, "for the glorious success of your expedition depends on her" (2.423–24). Hera and Athene realize that they are at an impasse without her. For all her frivolity and self-professed weakness, Aphrodite is presented as the key to the successful outcome of the mission.

Aphrodite's portrayal in the *Argonautica* thus illustrates the Hellenistic fascination with her playful superficiality on the one hand and her irresistible potency on the other — and with the way her lighter aspect masks the ultimate power of her darker side. This effect is something we have already noticed in the portrayal of Eros in the poem. His laughter at his success in a game of knucklebones with Ganymedes on Olympus is the same laughter he indulges in when he has inflicted the agony of love on the mortal Medea.[16] Aphrodite is, of course, as much the instigator of the narrator's "Cruel Eros, great cause of misery" outburst as Eros himself, for it was she who originally got her problem child on the job, threatening to break his bow and arrows, and promising the toy ball with which Zeus played as a baby, with recourse to the child psychology that any human mother is from time to time obliged to use.

My second example illustrating the Hellenistic dual vision of Aphrodite is Thyrsis' song "The Sorrows of Daphnis" in Theocritus' first *Idyll*. When Aphrodite first appears to the dying Daphnis, she is described as "craftily smiling, but withholding heavy wrath" (96). This might serve as a key signature for Hellenistic portrayals, for it captures her surface gaiety and her simultaneous deeper purposes. Daphnis' response to her entails references to two humans who exemplify the misery reserved for mortals on whom Aphrodite bestows her love. Anchises, to whom she made love on Mount Ida, where "bees hum sweetly near the hives," was punished cruelly, possibly even being blinded by bees. Adonis, who "hunts all kinds of beasts," was killed by a boar sent by Artemis or Ares.[17]

But Daphnis' third example is of a very different kind: her encounter with Diomedes at *Iliad* 5.330–430, where for once a human gives the goddess a hard time, in this case wounding her and driving her from the fighting before Troy. Now that she has conquered Daphnis, the mere cattleherd, he says sarcastically, she is qualified to demand a re-match with the heroic Diomedes. But her wanton exercise of power over Daphnis backfires, for we read that at Daphnis' death Aphrodite "wanted to raise him up again" (138–39); she has thus been the real loser in their dealings. As we have noted, Apollonius uses genre-marking in citing the Charis episode in *Iliad* 18 for the conference between the three goddesses and its "at home" tone, soon to be dissolved into something incomparably more serious. Here we see Theocritus genre-marking in order to give a deeper significance to the present situation: Aphrodite has as much right to claim the title of victor over a mere cattleherd as she has to demand a second contest with Diomedes. In each case the duality of frivolity and potency is vitally emphasized by genre-marking.

This extreme contrast in tones is unprecedented in the earlier tradition. Aphrodite might demonstrate her cruel supremacy in *Iliad* 3 by forcing Helen, despite her defiant protest, to welcome Paris back into her bed after the duel with Menelaus (395–420). And a note of comedy is introduced in the *Odyssey*'s song of Demodocus, with its element of at least superficially comic voyeurism as Apollo and Hermes enjoy the spectacle of the goddess enchained to Ares.[18] But the *Iliad* strictly rules Aphrodite out of contention for the kind of heroic action for which she is responsible in the *Argonautica,* as can be seen from Zeus' words after her wounding by Diomedes: "The works of war have not been given to you, my child, but instead attend to the lovely works of marriage, and let Ares and Athene concern themselves with all these things."[19] And in no poetry before the Hellenistic period's is the element of eroticism presented with such frivolity, nor are her two aspects brought into collision so directly and confrontationally.

So it is, I suggest, with the age's artistic images of Aphrodite. The Cnidia (see Ill. 9) had most certainly been meant to celebrate the goddess's unmatched beauty, but behind her untroubled but concentrated gaze at her onlooker and her noticeably unhurried attempt to cover herself we are at liberty to sense her self-assurance and sovereignty.[20] The same is true of the actual Hellenistic variations on the Cnidia theme, like the Capua (see Ill. 14), probably from the first century, as we have just seen: she may indeed be preoccupied with the reflection of her looks, but the shield after all belongs to the god of war, whom she has in her thrall, to judge by the way she feels free to borrow his armor. With a late second-century work like the Melian Aphrodite we may go one step further. The Melian Aphrodite (Ill. 31) is an example of what art historians call "eclecticism." Bieber summarizes the rationale behind the statue's realistic body and the idealistic Classical style of the hair and head when she remarks that the Aphrodite of Melos is typical of late Hellenistic art in that it "strove to impart new life into traditional types by combining retrospective traits with new realism and movement. It certainly is an eclectic work."[21] This is precisely analogous to the strategies employed by the third-century poets like Apollonius and Theocritus who place her directly in the tradition while bringing to the fore new realistic elements in the behavior they ascribe to her.

A similar rationale is discernible in the Slipper Slapper group (see Ill. 2) of between 110 and 100 B.C. The group, from the clubhouse of the Berytan Poseidoniastes on Delos, features Pan, Eros, and an Aphrodite whose pose is commonly accepted as being in the tradition of the Cnidia,[22] except that this time it is the goddess's left hand which covers her crotch; one presumes that this is to free up her right-handed delivery of the slap with the slipper.

Pan's clearly unwelcome advances and Eros' laughing push against one of his horns are ostensibly comic elements which lend the group its contentious, erotic, playful quality, thus extending to its extreme the frivolity of the Hellenistic Aphrodite-types inspired by the Cnidia. But this group perhaps also represents a timely warning that the meaning of statues like it was not exclusively light, because there is good reason for thinking that the Delian group may actually allude to a local Berytan cult of Aphrodite and Pan. This would fit in with the inscription, which specifies that it is a religious dedication.[23] All this only confirms the suspicion, nourished by the evidence of the poetic texts, as we have repeatedly seen, that with these pieces we are operating on at least two levels, one of superficial frivolity and a second, momentarily masked by the first, of a more serious reality.

Suffering is another serious reality addressed in Hellenistic poetry and art. In no other period does the presentation of physical pain and the evocation of pathos arising from it reach a higher pitch than in the Hellenistic. Spine-chilling images in visual art include the prospect of excruciating torture, as, for example, in the Marsyas group (see Ills. 7a–b); writhing agony, as on the Pergamon frieze; trauma-induced unconsciousness and death by stages, as in the Suicidal Gaul group (see Ill. 19b); distressingly reduced circumstances, as I shall argue the Drunken Old Woman has experienced (Ill. 34). All find parallels in the age's poetry: Apollonius' description of Mopsus' fatal snakebite (*Argonautica* 4.1518–36) and of Phineus fainting with hunger (2.197–205); Callimachus' remarkably detailed accounts of Leto's labor pains during Apollo's birth (*Hymn to Delos* 205–14) and of the impoverished but noble Hecale's dwelling and environment (*Hecale, Frr.* 29–32, 35–39, 58, 65, 66, 74.24–28 Hollis), passages which we shall examine in detail. But by what techniques do artist and poet produce the emotional effect of pathos out of this material?

In addressing these vital issues in Hellenistic poetry and art, I have chosen my examples very much *exempli gratia*. This is especially the case with those from art: they do not by any means exhaust the repertoire of Hellenistic sculpture and painting that could be adduced. An example that immediately springs to mind in addition to those just mentioned is the Farnese Bull (see Ill. 12) of arguably around 160–150 B.C. (though we have seen that scholars now think in terms of a down-dating to 42 B.C.).[24] Here Dirce is trampled to death while Amphion and Zethus determinedly concentrate on attaching her to the bull, paying no attention whatsoever to her agonized gestures of entreaty.[25]

The Suicidal Gaul group (see Ills. 19a–b) of around 220 B.C. brilliantly illustrates the two general processes at work in sculpture: composition in the round, so that we relate to the Gallic chieftain and his wife as if they were part of our personal space, and the realism with which their plight is depicted. The chieftain has, of course, not yet thrust his sword right down into his chest; his pain is at this moment emotional. It is when we walk around the group and see his all but dead wife held upright only by her husband's grip on her upper left arm that we are confronted by the image of the last moment of life, when the pain is almost irrelevant. Her right arm and upper torso sink involuntarily to the ground; her hair hangs down clear of her forehead as her head falls onto her chest, though her neck muscles are still able to support her head slightly;[26] her facial muscles and mouth are now relaxed, heavy even. Her eyes seem to register very little any more, as the last vestige of consciousness fades.

It is the group's invitation to be viewed from all angles (at no one angle, for example, can the faces of both figures be fully taken in), which permits this contrast of states of pain and death. In the one case death's pain is still to be endured; in the other, the death throes have already been endured almost to the end. "Being in the presence" of the Gaul and his wife, who are moreover both represented with the most painstaking clinical and anthropological realism, makes us experience their pain as if at first hand. Thus involved, we also inevitably sense the overwhelming pathos of their plight. Placing the subject before our eyes so that we seem to move in the presence of the protagonists is the visual-art equivalent of literary *enargeia.*

Such "sculptural *enargeia*" is a powerful factor in producing the pathos of other works of art. In Hugo Meyer's reconstruction of the "white" Marsyas group (see Ill. 7a), we can walk around the Scythian as he whets his knife for the flaying and observe his barbarically cruel upward stare at his victim, his uncouth squatting stance, and facial features like the tufts of hair around his chin and cheeks and his dramatically recessive forehead.[27] From these details of anthropological realism (which put the Marsyas group in the tradition of the Suicidal and dying Small Gauls [Ills. 18 and

19a–b])[28] we can project just what kind of mentality will without the slightest remorse inflict hideous pain on the wretched Marsyas. And this is not to mention Marsyas' own agonized grimace at the prospect of the pain in store for him, or the terrifyingly vulnerable exposed state of his body hanging naked from wrists bound to the tree above his head. The Hellenistic sculptor's intense concern to convey the silen's pain is brought out strikingly when we compare the group with a Classical image like Myson's red-figure amphora of about 490 B.C.,[29] where an impassive and dignified Croesus is seated on his pyre, which is being lit by his obedient servant.[30]

The second procedure by which the Suicidal Gaul group would have evoked special pathos in a Hellenistic viewer concerns the iconographical tradition which it cites and within which it works while departing from it in ways which render its pathos even more effective. The group is conceived in the tradition of the victory monument and designed to serve as such. Leaving aside the recently discredited view that it is the first Greek victory monument that we know of to omit the victors and concentrate exclusively on the vanquished, the fact remains that the Suicidal Gaul group is innovative in the degree to which it evinces the suffering of a conquered foe. This fact in itself testifies to a redefinition of ethical perspectives.[31] There is a high plausibility to the suggestion upheld by Stewart that the sculptor had in mind the passage in Aristotle's *Nicomachean Ethics* (1115b24–16a16) where Aristotle describes the Celts as rash, overpassionate, and blind to the Mean, and immediately thereafter comments on those who seek suicide as an easy way out. The Pergamene viewer would have seen in the warrior a zenith of barbaric defiance at the very moment of its extinction, and would have read behind the moment the greater glory of Attalus' victory. That said, Stewart is prepared to accept the universally perceived pathos of the group, which Pollitt also helpfully discusses, pointing to the sadness of the pose and expression of the Gaul's wife as her life ebbs.[32]

It is the extent of the evocation of pathos in a heroic context that is a *novum* on victory monuments. The form and framework are heroic; the theme stresses human suffering unprecedentedly and pathetically associated with a familial relationship, that of man and wife. We contrast all this with the Aegina warriors dying as if in isolation, with what looks like an Archaic smile;[33] their facial expression is no different from that of the striding warrior.[34] The Pergamene group is thus marked as belonging within the tradition of victory monuments, but the incorporation of unfamiliar motifs underlines the distance from the iconographical tradition, and attention is simultaneously drawn to the innovatory elements and emotional effects.

Concentration on the suffering of victims can in fact be discerned in an earlier group from the Classical period, the pedimental group from the Horti Sallustiani depicting the killing of the children of Niobe by Apollo and Artemis (see Ill. 26).[35] There the pathos of the stumbling and fleeing girls and the one preserved wounded boy is accorded powerful expression, within the celebration of divine power, though it is worth noting that the rather expressionless faces of the mortally wounded contrast with the agony of Hellenistic faces like that of Marsyas.[36] Interestingly, there are thematic similarities between the two groups, for sympathy is evoked for the innocent victims of an act of hubris, in one case against a deity, in the other against a human king, however much emphasis is placed on the superiority of the victorious parties. Emphasizing the suffering of victims was, therefore, not new in Greek art, but it was something new in a victory monument. The procedure is evidenced elsewhere in Hellenistic art: for example, in the Dying Gauls and in the Alexander mosaic, where the dying Persian's expression of despair is reflected in his shield (see Ill. 13). The latter case may point to the strategy's use in Hellenistic painting as well.

Very different in subject matter and function, but strikingly analogous in its means of evoking pathos, is a statue produced outside Pergamon though in all likelihood at roughly the same period. I refer to the Drunken Old Woman (Ill. 34), a votive offering to Dionysus which, as Paul Zanker plausibly argues, was commissioned for display at the Lagynophoria at Alexandria instituted by Ptolemy IV Philopator.[37] Walking around her emaciated figure, we can build up a case history of the poor woman. The sculptor has included many details which reveal that she was formerly a hetaera, and in fact a "big earner" (*megalomisthos*). He "cites" motifs from the fifth-century Attic "rich" style, in particular in the detail of the elegantly folding hems of her dress, to signify the expensiveness of her clothing. Otherwise, we may point to her earrings, the two rings on her left hand, the headcloth

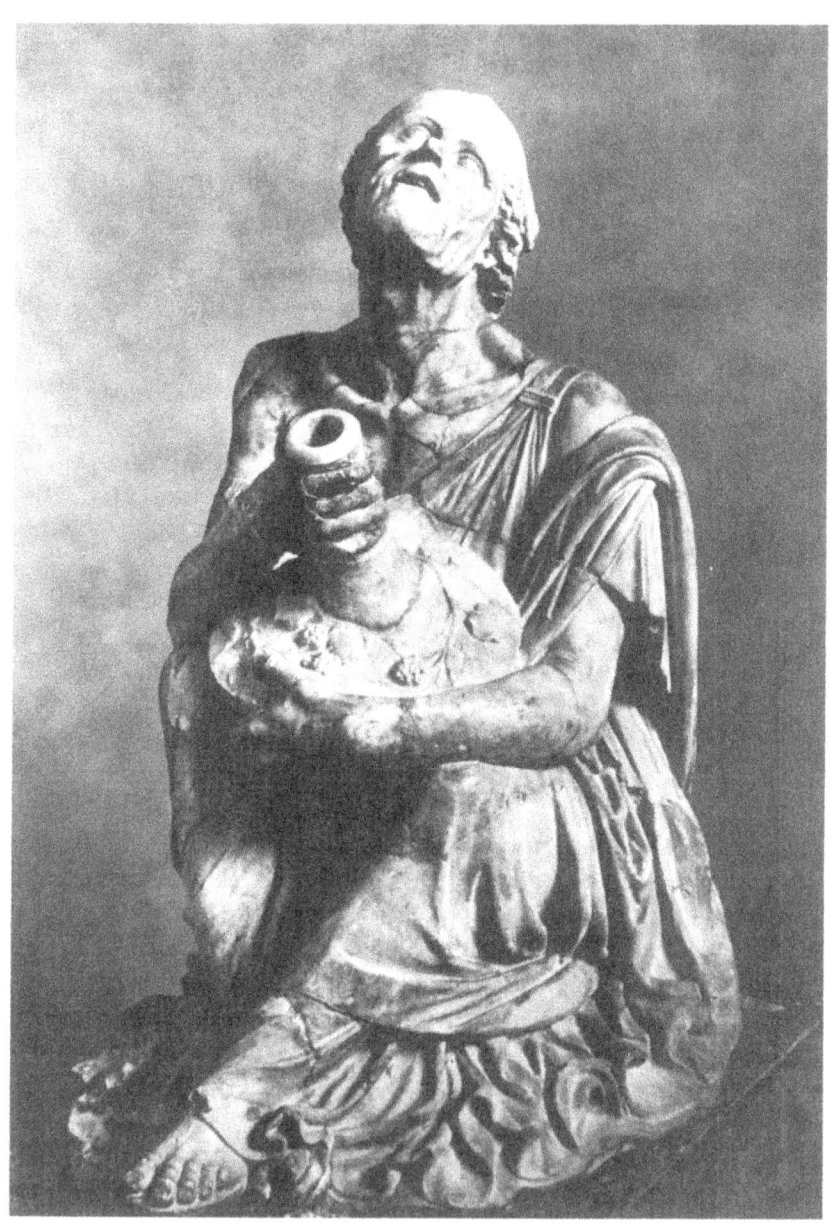

34a. Drunken Old Woman. Glyptothek, Munich. DAI negative number 55.81

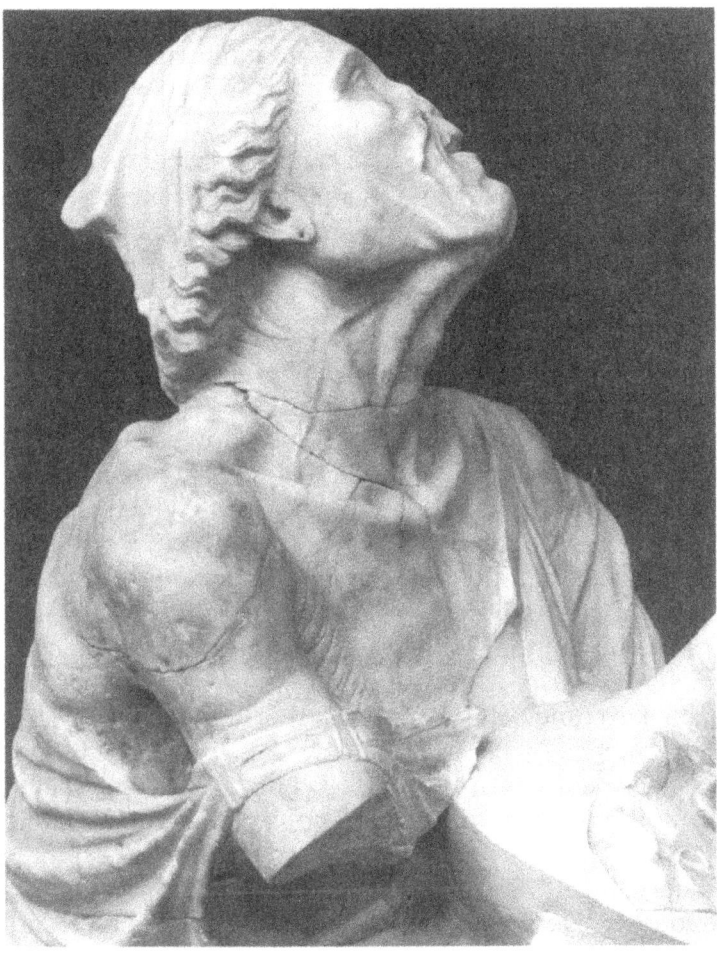

34b. Detail of upper right torso and head. Staatliche Antiken-
sammlungen und Glyptothek, Munich, inv. Gl 437

which was part of the accoutrement of well-dressed women and
which here covers the old hetaera's careful coiffure, and the *per-
onêtris* or *peronêma*, a tunic fastened with buckles which was worn
by the respectable women visiting the Adonis festival in Theo-
critus' fifteenth *Idyll* (21, 79). All this unobtrusively realistic detail
presents us with a picture of the woman's life and professional
success in the past. But now she has come down in the world, as
is evident from the clinical realism with which the physical decay
of her body is rendered. Apart from her old age, her missing teeth,

and the emaciation of her face and body, there is the remarkable motif of the shoulder strap of her dress falling off her right shoulder. This detail is another "citation," for it recalls the statues of Aphrodite on which the same thing happens, but whereas the detail on the statues of the goddess had an erotic appeal, on the Drunken Old Woman it merely serves to emphasize, in large part by contrast with the feature on the Aphrodite statues, the brutal facts: the emaciation of the old woman's shoulder and collar-bone areas, her sunken breasts, and the wrinkles below her armpit.

So much for the old woman's story as it can be pieced together as a result of her in-the-round presentation and the strategic and pitiless realism with which she is portrayed. We even have the additional element of gaze, for we can look down into her eyes as she throws her head back, however oblivious her own eyes are to ours in her inebriation. This is another feature which reduces the distance between her and us and adds to the directness of the pathos, perhaps paradoxically, given the uncomprehending nature of her gaze. But now we ask what such a figure is doing as a votive offering, in the setting of a sanctuary to Dionysus and in the likely context of a festival in the god's honor. As a hetaera fallen on hard times, she was outside the bounds of bourgeois society, as is mercilessly clear from New Comedy.[38] She might seem an affront rather than an offering to Dionysus. But there can really be no question of the statue's enormous pathos, which contrasts dramatically with the old hetaerae caricatured unsympathetically on Classical vases.[39] Once the Drunken Old Woman is seen in the context of the period's interest in the personal philosophies of "looking after oneself," we can easily appreciate that any moderately well-off Hellenistic citizen must have both sensed the pathos and been stopped short by the reflection that he or she might suffer a similar downturn in fortune.[40] The statue would thus have had an underlying seriousness which contrasted with earlier *Kleinkunst* depicting such marginal figures of society or the many later imitations of the Drunken Old Woman herself.[41] Any similarity to the Suicidal Gaul might seem unlikely indeed, but a similarity does exist in the way both groups evoke pathos by the realism of execution, presented from every viewing angle, and in the way they seem to break with the expectations traditionally entertained of their serious function, only to reaffirm that seriousness on a new, deeper emotional level.

The evocations of pain and pathos in Hellenistic poetry show techniques and strategies analogous to all of the art objects that we have been considering. Apollonius in particular shows a thoroughgoing preoccupation with depicting various states of consciousness and various stages of dying in order to increase pathos. A good example is his description of the blind Phineus as the Argonauts first see him, fainting with hunger as a result of the Harpies' loathsome food-filchings (*Argonautica* 2.197–205). Relevant details, which add up to a highly picturable study of physical suffering, include his reliance on a staff, his withered feet, his need to guide himself by feeling the walls, the tremor in his aged limbs, the emaciation, desiccation, and filthy state of his body, his dizziness (*karos porphyreos*) as the earth seems to spin beneath him, and his collapse and inability to speak in his faint-ness (*ablêchron kôma*). The two terms for dizziness, reworkings of Homeric phrases, gain their full significance only when it is real-ized that they are specifically modified to allude to the contem-porary specialist medical vocabulary describing *kataphora*, the giddiness experienced between the sleeping and waking states.[42] The terminology testifies to the realistic precision with which Apollonius was prepared to invest his descriptions of patholog-ical and mental states. Together, the details motivate the Arg-onauts' pity and desire to help. They also successfully create the sense of pathos in the reader through their *enargeia*, placing the subject before the reader's eyes. This is a procedure in some ways paralleled by the artist's invitation to walk around the Gallic chieftain's wife, for example, and thereby to feel as if one is wit-nessing the last conscious moments of her life.

Apollonius uses a similar approach in his account of the death of Mopsus by an asp-bite (4.1518–36). His ensuing numbness, swoon, sensation of cold, rotting flesh, and falling hair are viewed with horror by his comrades, Medea, and the servant girls, who in their pity quickly bury and mourn their friend. We are perhaps reminded of the motif on the Telephus frieze of the wound of Tele-phus which will not heal and which causes such a dramatic re-sponse in Telephus himself and in those who look on him, when, for example, he asks the Argive princes for healing. The pathos of the Mopsus scene is perhaps balanced by a degree of morbid fascination because of the extremely clinical nature of the list of symptoms. The account is in fact remarkably similar to Nicander's description of death by the asp in his treatise on snakebites (*Theriaca* 186–89), and the two poets may be drawing on a common medical source.[43] And here again there is a debt to medical terminology, for the asp is said to strike between the tibia and the calf muscle, and the word for "tibia," *kerkis,* appears to have been first used in this sense by Herophilus.[44] Moreover, when Mopsus is said to "feel his bloody wound" (*aphassen*), Apollonius is using the technical medical term for examining a wound by touch.[45] This cold, clinical manner of observation may in fact be said to intensify the evocation of physical suffering and the sense of pathos: it would have brought Hellenistic readers, especially if they were versed in contemporary medical research, into the presence of the dying man.

My last example of a Hellenistic poet's use of *enargeia* for the rendering of pain and the creation of pathos is a *tour de force*. This is Callimachus' account in the *Hymn to Delos* of the climactic moment when Leto finally gives birth to Apollo. After her desperate search for a haven in which to bring forth her child, Leto comes to rest by the River Inopus on Delos. She undoes her girdle and, wearied by her pain, leans backward with her shoulders supported by the trunk of a palm tree. Her whole body covered with sweat, she addresses her unborn baby and begs him to come forth (205–14). The realistic visual elements here certainly heighten the pathos of the scene.

Comparison with Callimachus' model, the *Homeric Hymn to Apollo,* illustrates the degree of his realism. In the Homeric hymn, the god's birth is mentioned briefly at lines 25–27, but is only treated at length ninety lines later (115–19). Eileithyia visits Delos, and Leto longs to give birth; she throws her arms around the palm tree, kneeling on the soft meadow, and the earth smiles beneath; Apollo springs forth into the light of day, and all the attendant goddesses shout for joy. The scene is pictorial enough, if miraculous in some of its detail, but the birth is an easy one, and Eileithyia is allowed to help. In Callimachus Leto is on her own. Significantly, moreover, Callimachus has altered Leto's position as she gives birth. It has been suggested that her sitting position, leaning back against the palm tree, is inspired by medical research.[46] Herophilus in his treatise *On Midwifery* talks of forward curvature of the spine as a cause of difficult delivery, and he would hardly have recommended the position of the Homeric

Leto, which would have resulted in a curved back. It is therefore likely that Callimachus has followed Herophilus in altering Leto's traditional pose and bringing it into line with accepted modern practice.

Callimachus has invested the scene with a dramatic force and pathos absent from his model. His choice of pictorial detail from actual childbirth, with its emphasis on pain, and particularly his alteration of Leto's pose to one realistically evocative of utter exhaustion, are the main means of achieving his effect. Again, the precise observation and the *enargeia* of a scene perform a function analogous to the detail and multi-view composition which play such an important role in sculptors' depiction of pain and creation of pathos. A possible anticipation of the Hellenistic interest in childbirth and its pain may have been the late fourth-century grave stelae commemorating women who have died in childbirth (a very unusual motif for Classical art).[47]

A poem of the greatest interest in this connection is the *Hecale* of Callimachus. Despite its fragmentary state, its editors, most recently Adrian Hollis,[48] have allowed us to see with convincing clarity that it developed the pathos of its titular hero's situation in all the ways that we have seen are common to Hellenistic poetry and art.[49] First, Hecale's person and present circumstances were clearly given graphic description. She is probably described as having "the ever-moving lips of an old woman" (*Fr.* 58 Hollis). She wears a rustic's broad-rimmed felt hat and carries a staff, "a support for her old age" (*Frr.* 65, 66 Hollis). The poverty of her hut and life comes through in the scene where she welcomes Theseus in from the rainstorm. She sits the hero down on her pauper's couch, over which she throws a scanty rug from her own bed, brings down from her loft firewood which she has put aside long ago to dry, and cuts it (*Frr.* 29–32 Hollis). The fragmentary details of the meal she serves him also bring out the humbleness of her resources, minutely detailed types of olives, wild vegetables, and coarse-floured bread-loaves "of the kind that women store up for herdsmen," which she now takes out of her breadbasket (*Frr.* 35–39 Hollis). We are given a vivid picture of Hecale's humble surroundings in the description of the awakening of the nearby village at dawn on the day on which Theseus returns to her hut. The poet sketches a genre-scene of lanterns being lit over the town, a water-carrier singing, wagons with squeaking axles waking up the houses near the roadside, and, possibly, people queuing up to fetch fire from the blacksmith (*Fr.* 74.24–28 Hollis). All this pictorialism helps us visualize and as it were enter into Hecale's pauper's world, and in itself powerfully contributes to the pathos of her lot, in much the same way that the sculptor of the Drunken Old Woman draws us into the presence of his poor derelict.

Also parallel to the Drunken Old Woman on the interpretation that I have adopted is the way the picture of Hecale's present impoverishment is balanced by an account of her past. Apparently in response to Theseus' asking why she, an old woman, dwells in such a lonely place, she perhaps begins by asking in turn why he wants to "awaken a sleeping tear" (*Fr.* 158 Hollis). At any rate, she certainly tells Theseus of her former life, possibly prefacing her story with the statement "my poverty is not hereditary, nor am I a pauper from my grandparents" (*Fr.* 41 Hollis). She mentions men who guarded her threshing-floor, which her oxen trod in a circle, an indication of her wealth, and describes the arrival of a man who must have been her husband, handsome and dressed in a rich cloak (*Fr.* 42 Hollis). She talks of her two sons, whom she reared in an abundantly rich household, with slaves, in all probability, to bathe them in warm baths (*Fr.* 48 Hollis). We find her lamenting the successive deaths of her husband, her elder son, and the younger, who was apparently killed by the robber Cercyon in his cruel wrestling contests (*Frr.* 47–49 Hollis). By depicting the fall in Hecale's fortunes in this way (and again pictorialism evidently played a significant part), Callimachus intensifies the pathos of her position.

Another potent means of achieving this effect lies in the way Callimachus makes Hecale cite traditional epic. Her welcome of Theseus recalls Eumaeus' reception of the disguised Odysseus in the *Odyssey* (14.48–79, 418–45); the foot-washing scene cites the encounter between Odysseus and Eurycleia (*Od.* 19.386–89, 467–70, 503–7). Thus the poet places his heroine in the company of the canonical tradition's exempla of sympathetic representatives of the lower social class. On the other hand, when she recounts her family's ruin, he makes her cite the noble personages of traditional epic, figures of intense suffering. Thus, when she says that her two sons grew up like towering aspens beside a river (*Fr.* 48.7–9 Hollis), we have a clear reminiscence of Thetis' words about Achilles, doomed to die, at *Iliad* 18.56–57: "he shot up like a sapling; I nursed him like a tree in the rising ground of an orchard." Similarly, when she wishes that she could pierce Cercyon's eyes with thorns while he is still alive and eat his raw flesh (*Frr.* 14–16 Hollis), we are meant to remember another grief-stricken mother, Hecuba, and her wish to eat Achilles' liver in revenge for the death of her son Hector at *Iliad* 24.212–13. And whereas that son says of himself that he recognizes that "the gods have called me deathward" (*Il.* 22.297), Hecale says of herself, in a most moving transfer of context, that she refused to die "when death had been calling for a long time," only to witness the death of the last member of her family (*Fr.* 49.2–3 Hollis). This citation of the tradition in order to deepen pathos is again paralleled in the Drunken Old Woman. As we have seen, the sculptor cites the "rich" fifth-century style in the treatment of the drapery of the old woman's cloak-hems as they lie on the ground, and the motif, beginning with Phidias, of the cloak falling off Aphrodite's shoulder. Even through this more "literary," less "direct" strategy, Callimachus brings us into the presence of Hecale and her suffering, and creates a personal emotional bond with the reader.

But this is not all. A second major strategy involves the type of genre-crossing whereby the personnel from the Greek literary forms traditionally considered "low" (like comedy) are introduced into a high form like epic. The formulation of the "separation of styles" is Aristotelian, but Aristotle was only encapsulating standard Greek literary feeling when he said that tragedy, and by association epic, represents "[in essence socially] superior people," comedy "[in essence socially] inferior people" (*Poetics* 48a16–18).[50] In the *Hecale*, Callimachus is violating the separation of styles for serious tonal effects, here among other things elevating a figure traditionally thought appropriate only in comedy and for comic effect to a level of moral nobility not even accorded her forebears, Eumaeus and Eurycleia. Theseus' celebration of the old woman's goodness when he awards her the posthumous honors of a shrine to Zeus Hecaleius and an Attic deme named after her is only the formal acknowledgment of the generosity she has already demonstrated so abundantly. When the "grand" genre of epic recognized the moral worth of a person who had, in conventional Greek aristocratic thinking, no standing to back up her claim to moral virtue, it was doing something typically Hellenistic in its novelty. Not that this entailed social activism; the novelty was in the aesthetic and moral shock tactic. And the shock tactic will have contributed integrally to the evocation of pathos.[51]

Is there any analogue to this in Hellenistic art? In both strategy and effect the Suicidal Gaul group is analogous to the *Hecale*. It stands firmly in an iconographical tradition of grand social and national significance, that of the victory monument, and yet it shocks by its fascination with the vanquished, their heroic and dramatic defiance in defeat, and their suffering. The suffering of the chieftain's wife in particular is a moment of undeniable pathos, but pathos must also have been sensed in the demise of a recognizably noble foe. In the poem and the sculpture group, therefore, we have the same strategy of surprise. Familiar human suffering, as well as suffering in a noble if desperate dying gesture, is embedded in a form that is marked as heroic. And the upset of traditional expectations of the form will have focused the attention of readers and viewers on the pathos of these daringly innovative Hellenistic works of art.

As an appropriate conclusion, we may take stock of our findings on genre-crossing and genre-marking or citing in Hellenistic poetry and art and try to offer a synoptic elaboration of them, in so far as they impinge on how visual images were meant to be viewed. Here again my strategy is to use the late Classical and Hellenistic attitudes to poetry, where the situation is comparatively well known and uncontroversial,[52] to suggest ways in which the period may have considered its artifacts in terms of genres amenable to crossing and marking.

By the time of Plato and Aristotle, the Greeks had divided their poetry into genres, as defined by the generic "rules" of formal features like meter, subject matter, narrative or dramatic mode, and occasion. We have already seen Plato's distinction between encomia, which were reserved for humans, and hymns, the preserve of the gods. For his part, Aristotle states at the very outset of the *Poetics* that the mimetic arts of poetry, epic, tragedy, comedy, and dithyramb, but also painting, sculpture, and dance, can be distinguished in three ways: medium, subject matter, and mode (*Poetics* 47a16–18). Then he proceeds to differentiate poetry alone on these criteria, ἐν οἷς τε καὶ ἃ καὶ ὡς ("in what media and forms, what objects and in what manner": *Poetics* 48a25). What analogous "rules" can be discerned in art, always bearing in mind the almost total silence on such matters in what we possess of written ancient Greek art criticism, and not expecting any 100 percent correspondence with what we know for poetry?

That the Greeks did think analogously about their art is made clear enough by the distinction between *andriantopoiia* and *agalmatopoiia* that we have already had occasion to notice. But we also have Aristotle's comments at *Poetics* 48a1–6 on the painters Polygnotus, Pauson, and Dionysius. I have concluded in an earlier study[53] that if we start from the likelihood that σπουδαῖος (*spoudaios*) and φαῦλος (*phaulos*) in the *Poetics* have a basically social reference, according to Aristotle Polygnotus depicted people of higher-than-ordinary social scale, Pauson depicted people inferior on the social scale, and Dionysius depicted subjects in the middle social bracket, "like you and me." Consequently, Aristotle thought that Polygnotus depicted the grand people represented in tragedy and epic, while Pauson painted the people lower on the social scale who are the proper subjects of the genre of comedy. In terms of subject matter, therefore, Polygnotus had an affinity to the grand poetic genres of epic and tragedy, while Pauson was akin to the poetic genre of comedy. This suggests that the ancient Greeks viewed painting at least to some extent as divisible into at least two genres.

For sculpture we have no such extant written information. Yet perhaps we can tease out some guidelines from literary theory and the known thinking about art classification. We would seem to be on safe enough ground in assuming that the sculptures of the severe style depicting gods, heroes, and men, along with its ephebes and victory monuments, were all felt to belong to a group which would have been thought of as "grand," in a "grand" medium representing "grand" subjects in a "grand" mode or style of execution. In Greek, an adjective denoting this grandeur might have been σπουδαῖος (*spoudaios*), which Aristotle used to characterize the subject matter and action of tragedy (*Poetics* 49b24); another adjective which suggests itself is σεμνός (*semnos*, "solemn," "stately," "majestic"), used for example by Aristotle at *Rhetoric* 3.8.4 1408b32–33 to describe the elevated hexameter meter. Be that as it may, such sculpture was felt to possess indissoluble associations of grandeur in the subsequent centuries. When, for example, marble or bronze sculpture representing deities or heroes started to take on "low" or "everyday" motifs,[54] the perception of "crossing" would have been more striking than it might at first appear to our eyes. As the "rules" became more entrenched and rigid (perhaps they had become more fixed than in the period of the severe style itself), their flouting would have been all the more pointed, and the effects all the more dramatic.

We have surveyed the process in the succeeding depictions of Aphrodite, from Phidias' restraint in the panel representing her on the Parthenon frieze, through her nudity in the Cnidian statue, to her ultimate *embourgeoisement* in the Slipper Slapper group, where she repels a suitor's unwelcome advances. The rift between expectations of how a deity should be presented and what the spectator is actually offered is enormous—but something that it takes an effort of our imagination to recreate. The same is true of the statues of Heracles, which move from the heroic grandeur of the Olympia metopes to the less dignified tone of the statues highlighting the hero's moments of exhaustion or relaxation. And how far the Terme Boxer has come down in the world, compared with his grand fifth-century forebears, in the emphasis on his physical exhaustion and pain. Finally, the victory monuments of the sixth and fifth centuries had certainly presented images of the suffering of a worthy, noble foe, but the Pergamene commissioners and sculptors of the Suicidal Gaul must have shocked their third-century contemporaries by including the suffering of a conquered enemy's wife and the motif of a marriage cut short by death, which brings the statue into the more recognizably familiar world of the *family*. The fact that classicizing statues continued to be produced is testimony to the fact that the "rules" were still felt to be in full vigor. Breaking them would have been seen as an intentional step, which might lead, however, and in the event did lead, to a more vital creativity. All this is entirely consonant with what we know happened in Hellenistic poetry. And a knowledge of the processes at work in the art of the period can help us appreciate more deeply the artists' visual strategies and the tones they meant to elicit thereby.

The theory that various types of fifth-century sculpture and painting had taken on grand associations also sheds new light on the Hellenistic artists' technique of genre-marking, the citation of iconographical traditions for unprecedented effects. The Boy with a Goose, for example, cites the tradition of the Classical ephebe only to go its emphatically non-grand way, household pet and all. The traditional Classical ephebe "genre" is also indispensable for the full effect of an eclectic work of art like the Vatican Spinario, which "cites" the ephebe "genre" in its carefully rendered Classical hairstyle. The citation of the visual detail helps emphasize the vast distance between the new statue and its origins, a shock tactic which modern viewers are naturally not acculturated to appreciate. And yet literary scholars have no difficulty nowadays in accessing the creative incongruity with which Callimachus' mousetrap cites the grander world of the *Iliad* and Achilles' "twofold dooms," which has the effect both of reminding the reader of the world the mousetrap "actually" inhabited and of contrasting Callimachus' reconstruction of that world with the way it appeared in Homer.[55] The continuing vitality of the "rules" of art thus made it possible for Hellenistic artists to direct their spectators' viewing and consequently to manipulate their intellectual and emotional responses. These are modes of viewing in Hellenistic art to which the modern eye should be alerted and trained by every means.

Notes

Bibliography

Index

Notes

Chapter 1. Aims, Approaches, and Samples

1. Webster (1964) 156-77.
2. B. H. Fowler (1989).
3. Onians (1979).
4. Stewart (1993b).
5. On visual theory see now Nelson (2000) 1-21 (with lit.), together with the earlier studies by e.g. Bérard and Durand (1989); Elsner (1995) esp. 1-48 passim; Elsner and Rubiés (1999); Elsner (2000); and Osborne (1994) 52-84, an analysis of the viewer's changing physical vantage points as key factors in guiding his interpretations of fifth-century architectural sculpture. For literature, Vasaly (1993) 20, 89-104, explores in exemplary fashion the rhetorical and philosophical treatises on visual description and sense perception current in Cicero's day in order to analyze his speeches' representation of his world.
6. See Gutzwiller (2002) 6-8, 10, commenting on the poem preserved at columns X 38-XI 5 of the new Posidippus papyrus in the edition of Bastianini and Gallazzi (2001). The essays in Bulloch et al. (1993) have become the standard work for discussion and literature on these matters in general.
7. Bibliography and discussion in G. Zanker (1987) 42-50; D. Fowler (1991); Graf (1995); for a brief history of some of the problems associated with ἔκφρασις, *ekphrasis*, from antiquity to the modern period, see Krieger (1995).
8. Nicolaus the Sophist, *Progymnasmata* 12, Spengel 3.491.15-493.19. See Palm (1965-66) 113-17; Graf (1995) 147-48; Schönberger (1995) 160 n. 6.
9. Cf. D. Fowler (1991) on the relationship of *ekphrasis* to narrative: it is a "rhetorical figure," which adds meaning to the narrative as a simile

does. But even for the Greek rhetors *ekphrasis* could involve narrative, though the distinction between description and narrative worried them, too. The earlier term ἐνάργεια, *enargeia,* denoting the stylistic quality of vivid pictorialism (on which see further below, pp. 9, 17, 25, 28–30), is far more flexible: narrative could be full of it without being what the rhetors called an *ekphrasis,* so the ancients would have had no problem in accepting the idea that a description might add meaning, rhetorically. As a term and concept to start from, *ekphrasis* thus again narrows the inquiry undesirably. Moreover, as Schönberger (1995) 160 n. 6 points out, even when Nicolaus mentions descriptions of works of art as *ekphraseis,* he regards *ekphrasis* generally as only a part of a larger context — that is, not as a separate genre.

10. Elsner (1995) 21–48. See also Schönberger (1995).

11. Graf (1995); Elsner (1995) 23–28.

12. Elsner (1995) 4.

13. See Elsner (1995) 36–38.

14. Elsner (1995) 29–32; Schönberger (1995) 165–70; the Byzantine ecphrasts try to read into the artist's mind, as recommended by Nicolaus and Aphthonius: Macrides and Magdalino (1988) 48–49.

15. On the date see most recently Chiron (1993) xiii–xl and Innes (1995) 312–21, who both favor a late second- or early first-century B.C. dating.

16. Graf (1995) 147; see Schönberger (1995) 171 on this phenomenon in Philostratus' *Imagines.*

17. Von Blanckenhagen (1975) 199.

18. Simon (1995) 134.

19. See further below, chapter 3, n. 26. On the other hand, those typically Hellenistic literary innovations, the "mimetic" hymns of Callimachus, can outstrip their traditional forebears in their direct presentation of the supernatural: see below, pp. 115–18. For the rivalry of literature with art in Philostratus, see Schönberger (1995), esp. 159, 167.

20. Elsner (1995) 28–39.

21. See especially Nicosia (1968) 15–42. Gutzwiller (1991) 91 with n. 38 (p. 239) has further lit. She concludes: "The goatherd's entire description is concerned with presenting the figures dramatically as if they had living form, not with delineating the cup as a work of art."

22. Dover (1971) 79; cf. the references cited by Gutzwiller (1991) 239 n. 38.

23. Arnott (1988) 12 draws my attention to the Flaxman-Storr vase in Liverpool, which was in fact designed as a realization of Theocritus' description; see also Arnott (1978) 129–34.

24. The audience is also invited to supply a link between the cup description and its frame in a way which makes Theocritus' practice far

more challenging than that of Moschus in the *Europa:* Manakidou (1993) 198. See further Gutzwiller (1991) 93 on the view of love here being "that of a male outsider himself immune to the temptations of love or perhaps not as susceptible as he once was."

25. The Derveni krater makes use of the *ABA* configuration, in country settings: ithyphallic Silenus bewitching two women into Dionysiac frenzy, the second woman being restrained by a sister; two maenads carrying a faun between them; dancing woman carrying a human child, confronted by an armed man (see Robertson [1972] for interpretation). Note also the casual pose of the reclining Dionysus, his leg on Ariadne's lap. For illustrations see most conveniently Barr-Sharrar (1982); full publication by Giouri (1978). For two *ABA* "conversation pieces" on a fourth-century Apulian Greek dish, see Gow (1952) pl. III. For a silver cup from Pompeii depicting a shepherd struggling with a ram, see Nicosia (1968) ill. 1, with pp. 31–35. See also the silverware in the Metropolitan Museum, which is datable to the later third century and is Sicilian in production; there we have, for example, Scylla hurling a rock and Demeter holding a cornucopia with Plutus on her lap: von Bothmer (1984) figs. 95 and 101. Adriani's Alexandrian bronze cup (Adriani [1959]) has two *ABA* groups: Athene, a seminude woman, and, above them, the bust of a man holding a shepherd's staff; and two seated males with one standing between them. Adriani (1959) esp. 40 uses the cup in *Idyll* 1 as a parallel to his Alexandrian cup, using the two to support his argument for a specifically Alexandrian taste for the "idillico-bucolico" in figurative art, now challenged e.g. by Stewart (1996a).

26. G. Zanker (1987) 155–227.

27. R. R. R. Smith (1991) 139, cited below, p. 134.

28. See further below, pp. 134–36.

29. Pollitt (1986) 138–39.

30. G. Zanker (1987) 70–71, 206–7.

31. G. Zanker (1987) 105 n. 56.

32. See Manakidou (1993) 155–56; Campbell (1994) on 135–41.

33. Cf. Onians (1979) 129; B. H. Fowler (1989) 150–55.

34. Pollitt (1986) 131. See below, pp. 151–52.

35. See the sensitive discussion by Pollitt (1986) 133–34.

36. Ridgway (1990) 328.

37. Pollitt (1986) 141–47; the quotations are from p. 142.

38. Laubscher (1982); Simon (1984), followed by Ridgway (1990) 335.

39. P. Zanker (1989) 50–55.

40. See G. Zanker (1987) 162.

41. P. Zanker (1989).

42. Arnott (1984); G. Zanker (1989) 102; for Hunter (1999) 144–51 (q.v. for some more recent discussions), Lycidas is part of the *Idyll's* explo-

ration "of 'bucolic' song." On the attitude of the pastorals in general to-
ward people low on the social scale, see G. Zanker (1987) 164–74.

43. Pollitt (1986) fig. 153, p. 142.

44. So, approximately, R. R. R. Smith (1991) 137–38.

45. Cf. Hebert (1989) 91–92, who calls fishermen the "Prototyp des ar-
men Teufels." Gutzwiller (1991) 94 believes that we cannot tell the Goat-
herd's attitude to the fisherman in Theocritus, but this seems to me to ig-
nore the element of admiration for the old man's youthful strength.

46. Pollitt (1986) 146.

47. I am not claiming that Theocritus is anything like a guide to orig-
inal perceptions of the grotesques, which are a class apart (for one thing,
they are miniatures, not like the lifesize fishermen etc.). See Stewart
(1997) 262 for a bibliography on the complex question of the statuettes'
functions, esp. Wrede (1988, 1991), who has put forward a good argu-
ment that the statuettes, and even some of the larger-scale works, might
be Dionysiac in their function.

48. Pollitt (1986) 144.

49. Von Hesberg (1986).

50. Pollitt (1986) 146. On Lysippus' Heracles see below, p. 93. For
Amycus and the Boxer see below, pp. 36–38.

51. The "maximalist" view is represented by Villard (1973) 167–85;
for skepticism about the extent of Alexandrian landscape painting see
Ling (1991) 142–49, with bibliography at 230. Yet the appearance of a
Primaporta-like *paradeisos* on Delos, published by Bulard (1926), esp.
146 and color pl. 23, suggests that this genre, at any rate, goes back to
c. 100 B.C.

52. G. Zanker (1987) 71–72; see further below, p. 51.

53. E.g. Hermogenes, *Progymnasmata* 10, Spengel 2.16.11–17.8; Theon,
Progymnasmata 11, Spengel 2.118.7–120.11; Aphthonius, *Progymnasmata*
12, Spengel 2.46.15–49.72.

54. XII 6 Bastianini-Gallazzi; see below, p. 175 n. 2.

55. G. Zanker (1981) 305–7, (1987) 39–54.

56. Adriani (1959), with Rolley (1986) 214 on the date. For landscape
in painting see Rouveret (1989) esp. 323–36.

57. Stewart (1996a) 239.

58. Webster (1964) esp. 88, 174; Ziegler (1966) 42–43. Nicosia (1968) is
more subtle, exploring an interplay of influences. Shapiro (1980) repre-
sents the view that Apollonius' manner "betrays an awareness of the
aesthetic principles of contemporary art" (284). Elvira (1977–78), who
agrees with Webster on Apollonius' "painterly eye," argues that Apollo-
nius can be used as a source for reconstructing some of the effects which
were admired in antiquity and were achieved in third-century painting

because his eye was conditioned by art. This is close to tautology, but I find particular difficulty with Elvira's approach because he fails to acknowledge poetic envisioning as an aim within poetry itself and because so many of Elvira's painterly passages are paralleled closely by earlier and contemporary poetry, which makes such passages more traditionally poetic than he thinks. B. H. Fowler (1989) 40–43, 83, 89 postulates inspirations from visual art and vice versa. Hebert (1987) is more reasonable: he tries to elucidate the lion-fight of *Id.* 25 from the inspiration of visual art in general, though see my reservations expressed at G. Zanker (1996) 411–12 n. 4.

Chapter 2. Full Presentation of the Image

1. Von Prittwitz und Gaffron (1999) (accepting a common identification of the maenad as a nymph). Cf. Stähli (1999) 75–89, who, however, denies a continuous interpretation to a similar group, the Satyr-Hermaphrodite group in Dresden (pp. 43–49).

2. On *enargeia* see G. Zanker (1981) and (1987) 39–54 (with lit.). The new Posidippus papyrus now attests to the use of the adjective ἐναργής (*enargês*) to describe the visual vividness that certain works of representational art can attain. After his chariot's victory at Delphi, Callicrates of Samos dedicated to the Theoi Adelphoi, Philadelphus and Arsinoe, "as a vivid image of those games a chariot and a charioteer of bronze," εἰκὼ ἐναργέα τῶν τότ᾽ [ἀγώνω]ν/ἄρ[μα καὶ ἡνί]οχον χάλκεον (XI 33–XII 7 Bastianini-Gallazzi). Moreover, this brings *enargeia* as a term denoting the visually vivid quality in poetry and art firmly into the early Hellenistic period, and further demonstrates the positive value placed on it.

3. G. Zanker (1981) 301.

4. Von Blanckenhagen (1975); H. Meyer (1987); von Hesberg (1988).

5. Ridgway (2000) 283–84 (with lit.). Actually, we do not even know that the omission was not a Roman one, the hanging Marsyas having been separated from an original Greek three-dimensional group and displayed free-standing. For the possibility that the "red" type itself is in fact Roman, see Weis (1982) and (1992) 66–73. And now Maderna-Lauter (1999) argues that the "red" Marsyas type goes back to an original of around 150 B.C. and was accompanied by the Scythian, but not Apollo: she regards the "white" type, in all its divergent details, as "harmonizing" first-century B.C. Roman copies of the "red" type, and detached from the Scythian. On her reconstruction, it was in the *"red"* group that the viewer had to supplement the deity.

6. Von Blanckenhagen (1975) 196.

7. H. Meyer (1987) 24.

8. Bing (1993) perceptively studies the gradual definition of the officiant in *Hymn* 2; see also Depew (1992) 328–29, (1993) 65–69.

9. For Amycus' forebear in Polyphemus at *Od.* 9.187–89, see Hunter (1996) 63 n. 63 (with lit.) and Sens (1997) on 44–52, 44, 84, 132–34. To see, with Hunter (1996) 61–63, a further model for Theocritus' transgressor against all the rules of *xenia* in the Heracles of the conclusion to *Argonautica* 1, who "destroys nature" when he fells a tree to make a new oar, is, however, taking intertextuality a little far.

10. Interestingly, cutting away from a boxing ring to the reaction of a spectator in the audience and then returning to the main action is a standard example of the device in film; see e.g. Katz (1980) 952.

11. See now Sens (1997) on 84.

12. Himmelmann (1989) 158–64, 174, followed by Ridgway (2000) 308.

13. On cauliflower ears in antiquity see Sens (1997) on 45.

14. With the version in Apollonius' *Argonautica* 2.67–97, where the king is killed, we have wandered impossibly far from the Terme athlete.

15. Sens (1997) on 44–52, 47 has argued that σφυρήλατος οἷα κολοσσός has a specific reference to an inscription on a statue of Zeus dedicated at Olympia by one of the Cypselids: εἰ μὴ ἐγὼ χρύσεος σφυρήλατός εἰμι κολοσσός, ἐξώλης εἴη Κυψελιδᾶν γενεά (Anon. 92 *FGE*). This would mean that Amycus is compared to a particular archaic statue, and that the simile cannot be used to support the view that Theocritus is inspired by a particular Hellenistic statue like the Terme Boxer (as is done by Nicosia [1968] 55–65).

16. In Heubeck and Hoekstra (1989) on 188–89.

17. At G. Zanker (1987) 109 n. 126 I argued against Gow's comment at Gow (1952) on 112 that "the picture of Amycus being reduced by sweating from a giant to a pygmy is ridiculous." I suggested that Gow's paraphrase is an overstatement (as is his translation: "from a giant in a little while he became small"), that Gow ignores the medical coloring of συνίζανον, which, as he himself notes, is used by the medical writers to describe constriction of the blood vessels, and that "the phenomenon can be seen in any situation where there is strenuous physical labour." Now Sens (1997) on 83–134 and 112–14 remarks that the motif of profuse sweating "is here exaggerated to the point of absurdity: there is humour in the image of Amycus literally shrinking while Polydeuces grows in size and improves in appearance"; the "sense of athletic realism" in the narrative is thus "undercut." Such thinking does not seem to be grounded on any very precise consideration of the facts, which can be examined under three headings. First the physiological: though struc-

tural mass (height, lean body mass, limb length, etc.) obviously will not change, after violent physical exertion an 80 kg athlete will commonly lose 2 to 3 kg in fluid, and in extreme cases a loss of 5 kg is entirely conceivable; an athlete can therefore indeed become smaller. Secondly, the psychological: when an athlete has, like Amycus, taken a severe beating, ensuing exhaustion and lack of coordination can lead to the loosening of postural muscles, so that stature can be lessened, and, conversely, the winner seems to increase in stature. In modern sports-psychology training, athletes are in fact explicitly taught to maintain posture while under stress, so as not to present a weaker image, and thus an advantage, to the opponent. Finally, there is the level of perception. Sportswriters and commentators often respond to these physiological and psychological indicators in words comparable to Theocritus': winning athletes are said to have "grown another leg," become "bulletproof," or developed "a second set of lungs," and correspondingly depreciatory terms can be heard to describe the losers. In short, there seems no reason at all to conclude that Theocritus in his description of Amycus is breaking with the "athletic realism" of the rest of the narrative. I am grateful to Paul Carpinter, director of the University of Canterbury Sport and Recreation Centre, for sharing his expertise in this matter.

18. On the likelihood that this move was illegal in ancient boxing see Sens (1997) on 119–21.

19. For the reworkings of Homer in *Id.* 22 see, in addition to the works cited above, n. 9, Sens's more detailed treatments in his articles: Sens (1992) on Theocritus' use of Homer in the Lynceus episode; (1994) on the proem and the priority of Apollonius 2.1–97 to Theocritus' Polydeuces narrative; and (1996), the Lynceus episode once more. See also Laursen (1992) with specific treatment of Homer and the Polydeuces episode at pp. 77–87, though obviously I cannot agree with the conclusion that in the boxing match "movements involving reference to left and right seem to fill the picture to the confusion of the reader" (p. 83). On the novelties in Theocritus' use of the narrator-figure, see in general Damon (1995).

20. In Heubeck and Hoekstra (1989) on 105–566.

21. Stewart (1990) 178.

22. Havelock (1995) 58–63.

23. *NH* 36.20–21.

24. Stewart (1990) 280; Havelock (1995) 61.

25. *Amores* 13–14.

26. Stewart (1997) 102–5, with quotation at p. 104.

27. See Havelock (1995) 60; cf. *LIMC* 2 (1984) 49–50 (Delivorrias); *LIMC* 8 (1997) s.v. Venus, cat. no. 110 (Schmidt) for lit.

28. Late third-century: Stewart (1990) 207 (who implies a dating of

ca. 230–200 B.C.), hesitantly Pollitt (1986) 134; mid-second-century: Krahmer (1923–24 and 1927), discussed by Pollitt (1986) 268, and R. R. R. Smith (1991) 135; "of the Roman period": Ridgway (1990) 313–18, 320–21.

29. Ridgway (1971), (1981), (1983).

30. But in later art, as with Eros and the Centaur (see Ill. 3) or the Slipper Slapper group (see Ill. 2), the groups are "einansichtig" and tend toward allegory: P. Zanker (1998) 10, 48, 77, 95–102.

31. For discussion, drawings, and pictures see Gow (1952) pls. xiv–xv; Köhnken (1965) 90–93; Nicosia (1968) 51–55 with pl. II; LIMC 1 (1981) s.v. Amykos 5 (Beckel) (with lit.); LIMC 2 (1984) s.v. Argonautai 10 (Blatter) (with lit.); Brendel (1995) 354–57.

32. Fantuzzi (1985) 142–44; Reed (1997) 2–3 now puts Bion's floruit "sometime between the mid second and mid first century B.C., probably in the earlier part of this period."

33. See especially *Od.* 19.109–14; *Oedipus Tyrannus* 14–57; Theocritus 16.88–97, with the remarks of Griffiths (1979) 41–42.

34. *Fr.* 257.13, 15, 21–31 *SH.*

35. Parsons (1977) 15.

36. The audience reactions in Homer, especially at the games for Patroclus and the games in Phaeacia, are more in line with Apollonius' practice than Theocritus'. In the funeral games Homer merely tells how the onlookers were amazed at Odysseus' prowess in the wrestling match (*Il.* 23.728), shouted encouragement at him in the foot race (766–67), laughed when Ajax fell in the ox dung (784), were amazed at the sight of Diomedes and Ajax facing up in the duel for the first blood (815), feared for Ajax and asked for the contest to be stopped (822–23), laughed at Epeius' efforts in the shotput (840), shouted at Polypoetes' winning throw (847), and shouted or were awed as the archery contest progressed (869, 881). In the Phaeacian games the only audience response is the Phaeacians' awed silence when Odysseus challenges them to better his huge discus throw, but they are obviously in fact involved in a way true onlookers are not (*Od.* 8.234). This throws into even greater relief Theocritus' achievement in filling in his picture of Amycus and Polydeuces' encounter. That said, the simile describing Aeëtes' dismay is worth further comment. Its closest Homeric predecessor is at *Il.* 17.53–58, where the fall of Euphorbus is compared with an olive sapling which a man has carefully watered in some deserted spot but which is flattened by gusts of wind. Apollonius has foregrounded the reaction of the gardener, which in Homer is secondary to the image of the destruction of a beautiful living thing. At least in this respect, therefore, the Hellenistic poet directs his model to purposes characteristic of his age.

37. Bieber (1961) 181–82; Pollitt (1986) 205; von Hesberg (1988) 347; Heres (1997) 97–98, who comments on the manner in which the servants

establish a tone: "Its [the scene's] particular mood is due to the contrast between the mourners in the upper part and the men busily working in the lower zone of the picture, with the detailed rendering of the carpenter's tools."

38. See Stewart (1990) pls. 477–79, 515.

39. E.g. the calyx crater by Asteas in the John Paul Getty Museum, discussed and illustrated by Jentoft-Nilsen (1983), figs. 1 and 3.

40. Von Hesberg (1986) 24.

41. Manakidou (1993) 192–95 has useful remarks on the way the passive observers of Io's progress are replaced in the scene with *Europa* and Zeus by the sea cortège of the Nereids, Poseidon, and Tritons, by the reader, and, during her speech, by Europa herself, who informs the reader's perceptions. On the sea cortège cf. Barringer (1995) and the Ahenobarbus relief in Munich and Paris with the sea thiasos, illustrated in P. Zanker (1988) 12–14, fig. 10, with full discussion by Lattimore (1976) 16–18.

42. See G. Zanker (1987) 71–72.

43. Pollitt (1986) 205–8. This is not to deny the fact that landscape painting existed before the Nilotic mosaics, but these latter seem to have surpassed their ancestors in their interest in the detailed depiction of natural scenery for its own sake. An idea of the comparatively general and ancillary depiction of landscape in fifth-century art can be gleaned from Hecuba's speech in Euripides' *Trojan Women* 686–93, where she explains that although she has never set foot on a ship, she has learnt about storms at sea from pictures. That paintings of the sea must have been familiar from the fifth century onward is demonstrated by Aristotle's passing comment (on a property of water) that "painters paint their rivers in a pale color, but the sea in blue" (*Problems* 23.6 932a31–32). Among proto-landscapes are the paintings of Polygnotus, who is said to have introduced landscape into narrative in the fifth century; see Stansbury-O'Donnell (1999) 83–86.

44. Pollitt (1986) 191–92; cf. Scheibler (1994) 120, 126.

45. See esp. Stähler (1966).

46. Phinney (1967); Elvira (1977–78); B. H. Fowler (1989) 29.

47. There are the sixth-century olive-tree pediment on the Acropolis (where the details are incised, not in relief, and are therefore "painterly") and the rocks on the Parthenon frieze, but landscape elements are extremely rare on reliefs from the Archaic period, as Wegener (1985) 4–10 and cat. 1–7 and Carroll-Spillecke (1985) show. For the notoriously limited presentation of landscape in Archaic vases and painting, see Hurwit (1991).

48. Onians (1979) 51.

49. Ridgway (1990) 15.

50. Pausanias 6.2.6; Pliny, *NH* 34.51 places his floruit at 296–293 B.C.; illustrations of copies of the statue in Bieber (1961) fig. 102 and Stewart (1990) pls. 626–28.

51. Ridgway (1990) 233–35, esp. 234; lit. at 243–44 n. 24. She disputes the association of the rock with Mount Silpios, maintained by e.g. Stewart (1990) 201.

52. R. R. R. Smith (1991) 76 assumes that the group was displayed in the open air, but there seems to be no doubt that the cult statue was covered: see Dohrn (1960) 40.

53. Bieber (1961) 134, Pollitt (1986) 117–18, Ridgway (1999) 519 (briefly; cf. the even more cautious results at [2000] 273–77), and Stewart (2001b) have now with varying degrees of conviction brought the date of the group down to 42 B.C., arguing that it was commissioned by the Rhodians to honor Antony and Octavian after Philippi. On this group see further below, pp. 152–53.

54. See Meyboom (1995) 44–50, 101–7, with lit. at 282 n. 5, noting especially Steinmeyer-Schareika (1978) 102–8.

55. Bieber (1961) 152–55.

56. Pollitt (1986) 185–209.

57. Above, p. 24.

58. Von Hesberg (1986).

59. The excesses of late nineteenth-century scholars like Brunn (1879; reprint 1906), who argued that all Theocritus' bucolic *Idylls* were derived from visual art, and who thus assumed the widespread popularity of country themes in visual art, have been checked by Nicosia (1968) 10, who shows that Theocritus and art, far from showing a single direction of influence, actually interpenetrate, with Theocritus, for example, establishing themes for art, like Polyphemus and Galatea.

60. On the different modes of narrative and the modern debate about them, see Shapiro (1994) 7–10, with bibliography at pp. 184–85, and Stansbury-O'Donnell (1999) esp. 1–17, 118–57. Shapiro would call the Telephus frieze "cyclic," and shows that the narrative style has its origins in the late Archaic period — e.g. on metopes like those of the Athenian Treasury at Delphi (see also Stansbury-O'Donnell [1999] 145–49); cf. the narrative of the Trojan war on the Siphnian Treasury (Stewart [1990] pls. 187–98).

61. For further examples see G. Zanker (1987) 57–59, 60, 65–68, 73–74, 88, 97–98.

62. Below, pp. 88–99.

63. G. Zanker (1987) 69.

64. Feeney (1991) 70.

65. Simon (1995) 135. Of course, Simon's construction faces a challenge of a more practical sort if we accept Havelock's recent dating in

which the Capua comes *after* the Melian Aphrodite: Havelock (1995) 95–98; so also Furtwängler (1964) 387 (the reprint of the 1895 English translation). It should also be noted that Apollonius' Aphrodite and the Capua are inverse images of one another. If we are meant to indulge in a mental picture of Aphrodite's breast in Apollonius' description, it must be her left one, since her tunic has fallen onto her left forearm, and we must therefore imagine that we are looking at her left side. The Capua demands that we view the goddess from her right.

66. *Hymn* 5.17. I have never understood the offense taken at the training mileage the goddess clocks up before the judgment: the obvious thought is surely that even after a hefty training session the goddess literally "comes up roses": "her body had a glow like a morning rose or a pomegranate seed" (27–28).

67. See above, n. 65.

68. Ridgway (1990) 89–90.

69. Havelock (1981) 250.

70. Shapiro (1980) 279, 281–82. On the associations of eroticism in women's personal mirrors, see most recently Stewart (1996c) and Frontisi-Ducroux and Vernant (1997) (with lit.).

71. Museo Nazionale Naples, Inv. no. 9380; LIMC 6 (1992) s. v. Narkissos 48 (Rafn).

72. One contrasts the formal perfection in such matters displayed in Burne-Jones's *Mirror of Venus*, in the Museu Calouste Gulbenkian, Lisbon. From the walls of Pompeii we have the still-life paintings which capture the reflection and refraction effects of water and glass: P. Zanker (1998) 89, with ill. 50.

73. Onians (1979) 45, however, points out that the size of the image of the face is scientifically correct, being about half the size of the face itself.

74. On this simile see Reitz (1996) 110–15.

75. E.g. Phinney (1967) 147; Elvira (1977–78) 41–42.

76. *NH* 35.138. On reflection and luster in Hellenistic painting (Latin *splendor*), see e.g. Gombrich (1976) 3–18 and Rouveret (1989) 39–49, 246–47, 265 n. 99 (with lit.).

77. *NH* 35.143.

78. See Reitz (1996) 15–19.

79. See Reitz (1996) 57–62.

80. Discussed by Reitz (1996) 67–74.

81. See Onians (1979) 45; A. M. Smith (1996) 15–16 with nn. 51 and 54.

82. See Fraser (1972) 1.386–88, 396.

83. Fraser (1972) 1.309, 399.

84. A. M. Smith (1996) 16 with n. 54.

85. See e.g. Boardman (1989) ills. 223, 232, 362, and Trendall (1989) il-

lustrations 14, 65, 101, 150, 159, 178, 192–93, 214–15, 216–17, 229–30, 261, 262, 263, 316, 328, 329–30, 370, 422.

86. Pollitt (1986) 59–78.

87. P. Zanker (1995a) 146–97, esp. 166–71, with quotations at p. 186.

88. *Alexander* 4.1–7, *De Alexandri Magni Fortuna aut Virtute* 2.2.3 (*Moralia* 335A) = Stewart (1993a) T9 and 10, with extended discussions at 31–33, 37, 72–78, 164.

89. Gow-Page (1965) on Asclepiades 43, *HE* 2.147.

90. P. Zanker (1995a) 154.

91. Bing (1988); P. Zanker (1995a) 146–71.

92. Pollitt (1986) 62; on the shift see P. Zanker (1995a) 155–56.

93. See Sens (2002). Other poems in the collection illustrate Posidippus' admiration for detailed, accurate art in miniature. This admiration is evident in the poem on Theodorus' self-portrait with its miniature chariot in the sculptor's left hand and a file in his right, discussed above, p. 6, but also in the series on engravings on gemstones, like the piece celebrating the artisan's skill in capturing—in miniature—the horse Pegasus at the precise moment when his bridle has just been taken off but he is still trembling at the bit (ἔτι τρομέοντα χαλινοῖς, II 33–38 Bastianini-Gallazzi). Another expresses amazement that the engraver did not damage his eyes when he incised the chariot device on a snake-stone seal—he must have had the eyesight of Lynceus (II 39–III 7 Bastianini-Gallazzi).

94. Pollitt (1986) 64–70; P. Zanker (1995a) 73–89.

95. Kerkhecker (1999) 39–40, 42–44, discusses the ingenious suggestion that Callimachus deliberately leaves it an open question whether the diagram illustrates Pythagoras' theorem or the rule that a triangle inscribed inside a semicircle and having the diameter as one side is always a right-angled triangle. The latter was ascribed in antiquity either to Thales or to Pythagoras: in the end, it all comes back to Apollo.

96. See Pfeiffer (1949) ad loc.; Kerkhecker (1999) 41, citing at n. 193 P. Zanker (1995a) 108–13, and General Index s.v. "Beard: philosopher's beard or intellectual beard"; Acosta-Hughes (2002) 150. On Aratus as the philosopher fingering his beard on coins, see Franke (1990) and Kovacs (n.d.) no. 31.

97. It is noteworthy that Ovid, ever on the alert for significant visual detail, should have twice borrowed from Callimachus the motif of thoughtful beard-stroking: see *Met.* 15.655–57 and *Fasti* 1.259.

98. Fantuzzi in Fantuzzi and Hunter (2002) suggests that behind his use of the proverb Callimachus' intention is also to hint that he is following Asclepiades' steps in decoding visual love-symptoms as one love-poet imitating another.

99. P. Zanker (1998) 50–63, esp. 59–60. Though a personification

rather than a portrait of love's longing, Scopas' Pothos does capture, through gesture and facial expression ("mouth half open [an expression of longing]": LIMC 7 503 s.v. Pothos I [Bazant]), the internal movement of an emotion; see Stewart (1997) 108–10.

100. See on this matter e.g. Barkhuizen (1979); G. Zanker (1987) 198–201; Holmberg (1998) with lit.

Chapter 3. Reader or Viewer Supplementation

1. Von Blanckenhagen (1975); H. Meyer (1987); von Hesberg (1988).

2. On the other hand, H. Meyer (1987) 25 (see also von Blanckenhagen [1975] 199) is wrong to take these terms as meaning "Bildwerke, die einen ergänzenden Betrachter voraussetzen": he seems to be proceeding from *Inst. Or.* 6.2.29, where Quintilian is referring to orators — not artists — who can move our emotions by their vivid descriptions, by making us see and feel we exist among things which are not in our view or presence; but this is not the kind of supplementation which Meyer is exploring.

3. Stewart (1997) 89–92, with ills. On the late Classical warrior stelae see Ridgway (1971) 343; at Ridgway (1983) 194–97 she discusses votive reliefs from the same period which project spatially. Von Blanckenhagen (1975) 195–96 suggests as a parallel to Theon's painting the first-century Borghese Warrior (Havelock [1981] fig. 98), for whom he thinks we must supply an opponent in our mind's eye, but the Borghese Warrior seems to belong directly to the tradition of the Archaic and Classical statues.

4. Von Blanckenhagen (1975) 196.

5. H. Meyer (1987) 24.

6. Bieber (1961) 145–46; von Blanckenhagen (1975) 196–97; Ridgway (1990) 330–32 with pls. 168–70.

7. Von Blanckenhagen (1975) 197; Ridgway (1971) 352.

8. H. Meyer (1987) 24; see above, pp. 30–33 for problems now seen in Meyer's scheme. Even if wrong, it still illustrates the strategy we are discussing, as does Maderna-Lauter's suggestion (1999).

9. See Bieber (1961) 21–22; the contrast is exploited even more fully by the third-century Pergamene artist's group of Marsyas, the Scythian, and Apollo, described by Bieber (1961) 110–11.

10. Stewart (1993b) 143. See even more recently Knell (1995) esp. 45–81, who in an excellent reconstruction of the topography shows how the statue's original leftward glance and dramatic left aspect were directed to the west portico, while her frontal aspect and the prow on which she alights were aligned so as to face viewers standing in the lower-lying theater, the votive building, the shrine of the Cabiri, the Arsinoeion, and the Anaktoron, thus comprehensively commanding the view from and directly facing the major locations of the entire sanctuary, with the

exception of the hieron and the Great Altar. Knell is followed by Ridg-
way (2000) 154. Ira S. Mark is undertaking a study of this statue and its
setting.

11. R. R. R. Smith (1991) 102, though the exact location is still open to
question, which in particular means that we cannot reconstruct the con-
ditions under which the Suicidal Gaul was viewed; see below, p. 106.

12. R. R. R. Smith (1991) 102; Stewart (1990) 205.

13. Stewart (1990) pls. 671–74, with discussion at 205–7.

14. Von Blanckenhagen (1975) 194.

15. R. R. R. Smith (1991) 101.

16. Cf. e.g. Hölscher (1985), on whom see below, chapter 6, n. 31; see
also Schalles (1985) 79 n. 491, 102–3 on the group's assumed lack of op-
ponents.

17. Summary: Stewart (1990) 205–6; Stewart and Korres (forthcom-
ing). Cf. Marszal (2000) esp. 207–9, 220–22, who, on the basis of the life-
size human heel and horse hoofprint on the capping block, removes the
oversized Suicidal Gaul from the long base.

18. *Fr.* 543 Campbell. On the other hand, Auge's downcast look is
quite like Demeter's in the tomb of Persephone at Vergina, which also
adumbrates the trouble to come from the kidnapping, though the pro-
lepsis is not meant to fill in a stage in a narrative sequence as on the Tele-
phus frieze.

19. D. Meyer (1993), with quotation at p. 174.

20. This is at least a corrective to the view of Krieger (1995) 47, who
assigns epigram a role secondary to the art objects which ecphrastic
epigrams describe; he ignores the achievement of Hellenistic epigram
entirely.

21. Goldhill (1994) 198, 204, 206; Onians (1979) 110.

22. Goldhill (1994) 206.

23. Goldhill (1994) 223.

24. Dover (1971) 210.

25. Griffiths (1979) 118. Burton (1995) 134–54 now "proposes ways in
which aspects of the hymn most commonly perceived as ineptitudes are
instead conscious refinements contributing to the overall effectiveness
of a strikingly unconventional hymn" (p. 135).

26. Goldhill's identification of *ekphrasis* with the description of works
of art leads him to deplore the way in which criticism of *ekphrasis* has, as
he sees it, somehow got stuck in a rhetorical rut, bogged down in the
rhetorical polarity of description versus narration. But this is tilting at
windmills. As we have seen, the ancient writers on *ekphrasis* from Her-
mogenes onward were primarily interested in description in general,
not merely description of works of art; the history of the catachresis is
sketched by Thiel (1993) 10–16; cf. D. Fowler (1991) nn. 1 and 2; Graf
(1995) 155; Webb (1999); G. Zanker (2003). And Hermogenes' *Progym-*

nasmata demands that *ekphraseis* tell the events leading up to and sub-
sequent upon the subject being described, as Elsner (1995) 23–24 re-
minds us; see also Palm (1965-66) 108–17, which Goldhill apparently
does not know. Goldhill has thus superimposed the difficulties he per-
ceives in the general theory of *ekphrasis* onto the specialized field of de-
scription of works of art. Moreover, as I have described it above, pp. 9,
17, 25, 28–30, the concept of *enargeia* handles the problem of narrative
and description without any strain—not that *enargeia* is an Aristotelian
term, as Goldhill (1994) 208 would have us believe: see my discussion of
the question at G. Zanker (1981) 307-8 n. 40. Finally, Goldhill's samples
are aggressively selective, as the apologetic descriptions of them quoted
above suggest. He has selected exclusively what have long been known
as "interpretative" epigrams on works of art. Such epigrams feature a
minimal descriptive element, concentrating instead on interpreting—in
terms of the meaning of iconographical detail or, say, psychological ele-
ments—the art objects with which they deal: see Palm (1965-66) esp.
149-53 and Fantuzzi in Fantuzzi and Hunter (2002) 437-48, who has a
particularly thorough historical contextualization of this type of epi-
gram. And now we have the new Posidippus papyrus with its poem on
Theodorus' portrait of himself filing a miniature chariot (X 38–XI 5 Bas-
tianini-Gallazzi, discussed above, p. 6). On this poem Bastianini and
Gallazzi (2001) 193 observe, "Posidippo, *senza descrivere la scultura nel
suo complesso*, si sofferma esclusivamente sulla perfezione dei dettagli
visibili nella pur piccolissima quadriga" (italics mine). Yet there is no
"discourse" with the reader whatsoever in, to take one example among
many, Posidippus' epigram explaining to a questioner the allegorical
significance of Lysippus' Kairos (19 *HE*). The majority of epigrams on
objets d'art are concerned with appraisal of their lifelike quality, in
which case the descriptive element is in general, once again, quite slight.
A good example of this is the series in the *Palatine Anthology* on Myron's
Cow (*AP* 9.713-44, 793-98), and now, on the same statue, the new
epigram by Posidippus (X 34-37 Basianini-Gallazzi). Some poems, of
course, do aim at an ocular representation, like Anyte of Tegea's piece on
a painting or relief of a goat near a temple (13 *HE*), Leonidas of Taren-
tum's on a statue of Anacreon in drunken disarray (31 *HE*), or Meleager's
vividly dramatic description of a painting of Niobe being killed for her
insolence (128 *HE*; see further G. Zanker [1987] 94-96). These are decid-
edly in the minority, however. Goldhill has thereby projected the picture
through too narrow a hole, and the true image has been inverted. See
also my remarks in G. Zanker (2003).

    27. Manakidou (1993) 198.

    28. Simon (1995) 134; see above, p. 9.

    29. G. Zanker (1979) 55-56, (1987) 201-2; Clauss (1993) 120-29; Man-
akidou (1993) 102-42, esp. 133-36; cf. Hunter (1993) 52-58; De Forest

(1994) 96, 144–48; even Shapiro (1980) e.g. 271, 282, who argues that the description of Jason's cloak evinces an interest as much in matters of contemporary visual aesthetics as in the thematics of the *Argonautica*, is prepared to admit a simultaneous thematic function for the description.

30. Cf. Hunter (1993) 14; Jackson (1999).

31. Preisshofen (1979); Gelzer (1985); Goldhill (1994) 221–22. Cunningham (1971) 128 reminds us of the detachment Herodas can exercise through making his characters talk art criticism.

32. See Cunningham (1971) on 20–26 for the position of the separate groups.

33. If that is what the sacrificial implement is: see Cunningham (1971) ad loc.

34. See especially Mastromarco (1984).

35. Gow (1952) on 84–85. On the significance of Adonis in *Id.* 15 see the important recent study by Reed (2000).

36. Above, pp. 39–41.

37. Fuller discussion at G. Zanker (1987) 47–48, 73–74. Important earlier discussions, especially of the scene of Hylas at the spring, include Händel (1954) 27–33 and Köhnken (1965) 58–67. See more recently Clauss (1993) 176–211, whose focus is, however, on Heracles' status as a hero; his conclusions agree with mine at G. Zanker (1987) 201–2 (with lit.).

38. I.e. narrative contextualization, discussed by Elsner (1995) 23–24.

39. Fuhrer (1992) 71–75, 121–25, (1993) 85–86, followed by Bing (1995) 123.

40. See Hollis (1990) 215 and on *Fr.* 69.1.

41. G. Zanker (1977), (1987) 209–14.

42. The technique is related to the general device of the *Abbruchsformel*, which need not be visual in appeal; an example is the passage in the Acontius and Cydippe fragment where Callimachus specifies what Acontius would not have wanted in exchange for his first night of married life with Cydippe; this procedure seems to have been adopted in order to avoid expatiating directly on Acontius' ecstasy, a well-trodden path in any reader's life: as the poet puts it, "Anyone not ignorant of the difficult god of love would bear witness to my assessment" (*Fr.* 75.44–49 Pfeiffer).

43. See Stewart (1996b) 39–45 (with comparisons with the narrative style of Apollonius' *Argonautica*); for the artistic antecedents of the frieze, see 45–48.

44. I have discussed this piece at greater length in G. Zanker (1996).

45. For a discussion of other reconstructions of the last section see G. Zanker (1996) 418–19.

46. A little later, after this "painting," the Farmhand describes the

plain in additional detail: the plain is entirely Augeas', as it rises through cornfields and orchards right up to Acrorea with its springs (29–31). Moreover, the mention of vats at line 28 prepares neatly for Heracles and Phyleus' departure from Augeas' farm on a path from the stables through a vineyard, at line 157. The poem in general presents a remarkable spatial and temporal precision and coherence. This can be seen in the Farmhand's account of the geography of Augeas' sheep pastures: the River Helisous (9) is five miles south of the township of Elis; the River Alpheus (10) about twenty; Buprasium (11) is on a main road some fifteen miles north. The separate properties are credibly located, with just enough distance involved to make Augeas' realm impressive.

47. Above, pp. 51–55.

48. The graphic elements here "corroborate" the poem's ethical theme of Heracles as Soter. The last two lines of the poem have Heracles concluding, "My friend, this was the means of the destruction of the Nemean beast, which up till then had created much misery for cattle and humans" (280–81). This highlights the theme clearly and reminds the reader that it was the ordinary people who benefited from Heracles' labor. It appears also, however, in Heracles' mention of the inhabitants of the town of Bembina near Nemea. These lowlanders suffered especially from the lion's depredations: "The lion caused merciless devastation like a river in spate" (201–2), and Heracles was left entirely on his own as he hunted the beast, since the countryfolk had deserted their fields and were keeping to their homes through fear (218–20). And Phyleus, while questioning Heracles as they leave Augeas' farm, refers to the lion as "an evil curse upon country-dwellers" (168). In the inspection of Augeas' herds we have an eminently picturable exemplification of the hard work of field laborers, except that these workers are in comparative safety: Augeas' herds are said to be untouched by diseases "which destroy the work of herdsmen" (121–22). How much more terrible the suffering of the victims of the Nemean lion! And Heracles' heroism has removed a hazard from the lives of people just like Augeas' farmhands. Thus pictorialism plays a significant role in a unificatory theme of the poem. Cf. Gutzwiller (1981) 31, 34, who considers the real aim of the poem to be the "confrontation between the pastoral and the heroic," Heracles being "a stranger to pastoral life." But, as Duchemin (1963) 312–15 shows, Heracles traditionally had strong pastoral associations, notably in epic, and readers must have brought their knowledge of this to their appreciation of the poem.

49. Good examples include Laocoön in the famous group (Pollitt [1986] 121, fig. 124), especially his left shoulder and upper arm, and the Borghese Warrior (Havelock [1981] fig. 98, discussed on pp. 126–27). The motif of muscles standing out in the neck region occurs at Theocritus,

Idyll 1.43 (discussed above, p. 13), in the description of the old fisherman depicted on the rustic cup.

50. Bieber (1961) 35–36; Ridgway (1971) 355.

51. Stewart (1990) 190. Ridgway (1981) 25–26 explores the tempting possibility that the statue, with its fruit, had as its setting a "sacred or private garden."

52. Polygnotus: Pausanias 10.26.3 (Reinach [1921] no. 107a), Pausanias 9.4.1 (Reinach [1921] no. 123); Timanthes: Reinach (1921) nos. 305–9.

53. See G. Zanker (1987) 88–89, 176–81 for a more extended treatment of the poem's pictorial and everyday elements.

54. For discussion and bibliography see G. Zanker (1987) 179–81 and Hunter (1996) 11–13, 27. The relevance of the *Idyll* especially to the Ptolemies' Egyptian preservation of themselves is most recently explored by Stephens (2003) 123–46 (who incidentally doubts at pp. 125–27 any significance to Philadelphus and Arsinoe behind the reference to Hebe).

55. See further below, chapter 5, esp. pp. 130–39.

56. Pollitt (1986) 118 with lit.

57. E.g. Bieber (1961) 78–79; Pollitt (1986) 118; R. R. R. Smith (1991) 104–5. Green (2000) 184–85 now suggests that the Pasquino group shows Ajax's recovery of the body of Achilles after he was ambushed by Paris and Deiphobus at the precinct of Thymbraean Apollo where he had arranged to discuss terms of marriage to Polyxena (for this version of Achilles' death, which Green argues must have been known to early Greek epic, see e.g. Philostratus, *Her.* 19.11, *Vit. Apollon.* 4.16, schol. on Euripides, *Hec.* 41, Servius on *Aen.* 3.322, Hyginus 110; cf. *Little Iliad, Fr.* 32); but his mode of defining the actors and action is the same as for the Menelaus–Patroclus interpretation.

58. Lit. and discussion in Stewart (1993b) 153–58.

59. See Stewart (1993b) 146–53.

60. Brilliant (1984) 41–42, quoted and followed by Stewart (1996b) 47 (q.v. for recent lit.). In general, see also e.g. Pollitt (1986) 200–205, 255–56.

61. Brilliant (1984) 54–59; in general Sadurska (1964); Pollitt (1986) 200–205; Rouveret (1989) 354–63.

62. Brilliant (1984) 57–58.

63. Stewart (1996b) 47–48.

64. Pollitt (1986) 53–54.

65. Bieber (1961) pl. 497. See in general e.g. Onians (1979) 104–5; Pollitt (1986) 15–16; von Hesberg (1988) 333–34.

66. Discussed by e.g. Massing (1990), Scheibler (1994) 43–45.

67. *Fr.* 1.17–21 Powell.

68. See the study of the passage by Kokolakis (1976) esp. 137–39.

69. Kerkhecker (1999) 134–36. Acosta-Hughes (2002) 263–64 doubts that the lines in question (23–29) really constitute allegory: they use "standard erotic metaphors," and the effect is to "showcase the poet's

allusive facility." At pp. 191–204, on the other hand, he subscribes to the interpretation of *Iambus* 4 as "in some sense allegorical," arguing that "the allegorical nature of the dispute lies in its representation of a debate between different aesthetics, quite probably literary stylistics." But, again, the visual component in the dispute of the laurel and the olive is confined (possibly) to the laurel's unflattering description of the olive at lines 22–23.

70. *Fr.* 114.8–17 Pfeiffer.

71. See von Hesberg (1988) 312–20 for the archaeological background.

72. Cf. Antipater of Sidon 22 *HE*, discussed by Onians (1979) 110 and Goldhill (1994) 201–2.

73. See Onians (1979) 99–105, Rouveret (1989) 351–53, and Stewart (1996a) 241–43 for the evidence associating allegory in visual art with Alexandria in particular.

Chapter 4. Reader or Viewer Integration

1. Von Hesberg (1988).

2. Pollitt (1986) 128–29; P. Zanker (1998) n. 56.

3. Cunningham (1971) 134 ad loc.

4. Not the Boy Strangling a Goose of Pliny *NH* 34.84: here we have a χηναλώπηξ (*chênalôpex*), an Egyptian goose.

5. P. 40.

6. P. Zanker (1998) 68.

7. Gaze is a theme of the statues standing before the women: immediately preceding we have Cynno's remark on the soulful and longing gaze of the girl looking up at the apple (27–29).

8. Himmelmann (1989) 158–64, 174 (with lit.), followed by Ridgway (2000) 308.

9. See Himmelmann (1989) 150–51 for the possibilities.

10. Above, pp. 75–80.

11. See e.g. Pollitt (1986) 89–90 and Stewart (1990) 206 against locating the groups on the round base at Pergamon. It should be noted, however, that Hellenistic art uniformly prefers quite high bases, 1.5 m or more: see most recently I. Schmidt (1995).

12. Stewart and Korres (forthcoming), against e.g. Palma (1981).

13. Pollitt (1986) 90–93 captures the vivid drama of the scene admirably.

14. On the allusions and three-dimensionalization, see the discussion of the Small Gauls in Ridgway (1990) 284–304, esp. 291, 298, 300, 303.

15. Stewart (1993b) 137–53, esp. 141–43.

16. R. R. R. Smith (1991) 78.

17. Pseudo-Lucian, *Amores* 13.

18. Havelock (1995) esp. 27–37.

19. Havelock (1995) 31, 122.

20. Moreover, at Xenophon, *Mem.* 3.11 Theodote chooses to reveal her courtesan's beauty to Socrates and his friends, so her "nonchalance" is, despite Havelock (1995) 30, hardly comparable with Athene's response or, I suggest, to the Cnidia's.

21. Havelock (1995) 74–76, followed by Ridgway (1997) 263–65. Cf. e.g. Corso (1992), who argues for a dating around 300 B.C. and attributes her to Praxiteles' son Cephisodotus; Moreno (1994) 108–10, 664; Andreae (1998) 47–50, who attributes the Capitoline Aphrodite to Cephisodotus and Timarchus.

22. Ridgway (1990) 355.

23. Havelock (1981) 124.

24. Ridgway (1990) 230–32 dates her to after 200 B.C.; Havelock (1995) 80–83 implies a similar dating. Cf. P. Zanker (1998) 73–74 with caption to ill. 41, who places her in the mid-third century; so also Moreno (1994) 221 (who retains the ascription to Doedalsas) and Andreae (1998) 61–66 (also accepting Doedalsas).

25. Ridgway (1981) considers the possibility that she originally looked at her reflection in the water of a pool in a sanctuary or an agora. Roman copyists supplemented the object of her gaze with a statue of Cupid by her right buttock: Stewart (1990) pl. 719, (1997) 222.

26. Stewart (1997) 222–23. See von Blanckenhagen (1975) 193–94 on our restoration of her context among maidservants, a supplementation inspired by late Classical representations of her; but it is dubious that the goddess is trying to hide her charm specifically from us.

27. For further discussion of viewer-incorporation see most recently P. Zanker (1998) 10, 48–49, 97–102, 107–10, who draws the useful comparison with later Hellenistic "Einansichtigkeit," featured e.g. in the Delian Pan and Aphrodite group (Ill. 2), or in the Centaur tormented by Eros (Ill. 3), which, together with the under-lifesize execution and its citation of earlier statues, involves a process of distancing which leads to a more objective reflection, indeed to allegorical interpretation.

28. Above, pp. 80–82.

29. This masterstroke is missing from Callimachus' exquisite model, Asclepiades' 18 *HE*, quoted and discussed above, p. 70.

30. Ridgway (1971) 351.

31. Accepting Gow and Page's ἁμὲ: Gow and Page (1965) ad loc.

32. Roughly speaking, the positions of Legrand (1901), Cahen (1929), and Cameron (1995) 63–67 respectively; see Cameron (1995) 63–67 for an account of the literature.

33. G. Zanker (1987) 62.

34. Depew (1993) 77.

35. So Farrington (1953) 199–200.

36. Fraser (1972) 1.114, 322, 427–28. Vitruvius, *De Arch.* 9.9.2 states that it was Ctesibius of Alexandria who discovered the strength of air pressure and was the first to use it to drive machines.

37. Schurmann (1991) 224–25.

38. Schurmann (1991) 226–27.

39. Schurmann (1991) 224–25.

40. The vessel is celebrated in the epigram of Hedylus (4 *HE*); discussion in Rice (1983) 63.

41. Rice (1983) 62–65.

42. Von Hesberg (1987) 66; Schurmann (1991) 242–46.

43. Von Hesberg (1987) 52. Among other Hellenistic automata, Lysippus' Zeus at Tarentum could be moved by hand (Pollitt [1986] 49); see for further instances and literature Rice (1983) 62–65; Schurmann (1991) 239–42 (Demetrius of Phaleron's snail), 246–49 (Herodes Atticus' ship). More generally, von Hesberg (1987) 57–58 sees Apollonius as inspired by gadgetry in his depiction of Aeëtes' palace and Talos, and Theocritus as similarly inspired in his description of Amycus.

44. Plutarch, *Sulla* 11. Von Hesberg (1999) 73 remarks, "Clearly, the moment of the king's crowning was meant to create a miraculous tableau, in which the fixation of the figures would acquire a rather abstract character."

45. Gordon (1979); in general, Schurmann (1991) 249–51.

46. Stewart (1990) 178. See further Stewart (1997) 97–107. For a modern contextualization of the cultural and sexual significance of the Cnidia in the late Classical period see Salomon (1997).

47. Ridgway (1990) 355.

48. The Crouching Aphrodite (see Ill. 25) does not respond to us, but it is significant that she inspired the middle Hellenistic painting which depicted Artemis surprised by Actaeon: von Blanckenhagen (1975) 194.

49. On modern theories of "gaze" versus "glance" as proposed by Sartre, Lacan, Mulvey, and Gay, see Stewart (1997) 13–14. On surprise in early Hellenistic statues of Aphrodite, see P. Zanker (1998) 73–75. At pp. 77–78 Zanker also discusses the "directed gazes" of early Hellenistic art, adducing the Aphrodite of the Beautiful Buttocks (Ill. 27) and the Sleeping Hermaphrodite (Ill. 28), on which see below, pp. 121–22.

50. R. R. R. Smith (1991) 81 warns us that "we are dealing with a society in which men controlled almost all aspects of art production and in which statues were oriented primarily to male viewers. . . . what [Hellenistic women] might want to see expressed in male and female statues . . . was not a consideration in their creation."

51. See Pollitt (1986) 149; LIMC 5 (1990) s.v. Hermaphroditos (Ajoot-

ian) 276; Ajootian (1997) 231–33; R. R. R. Smith (1991) 131–32; and Stewart (1997) 228–30 for the viewer's progress.

52. Ajootian in LIMC 5 (1990) s.v. Hermaphroditos, 276; Ajootian (1997) 231 (with lit.).

53. Ajootian in LIMC 5 (1990) s.v. Hermaphroditos, 280, with cat. nos. 65–67, and Ajootian (1997) 233–35. Others take the group at face value: P. Zanker (1998) 80 suggests that the Sleeping Hermaphrodite's state of arousal makes him seem to turn from the viewer's gaze in shame; Stewart (1997) 231–32 would have it that the viewer/voyeur is turned into a (surprised) potential rape victim.

54. The association is made by Onians (1979) 49, under the rubric of "sexual inconsistency." From Pompeii, moreover, we have the painting of the transvestite Achilles, with Odysseus' expression of amazement at discovering "the best of the Achaeans" disguised as a woman among the daughters of Lycomedes (Havelock [1981] pl. IX). The famous Pompeii painting of Heracles and Omphale (Havelock [1981] pl. XII), with Heracles wearing her cloak and slippers, is perhaps different, if one subscribes to the view of P. Zanker (1998) 55–56, with ill. 30, p. 57. He argues that Heracles' *tryphê* would have been evaluated in a positive way, for "Festesfreude, Trunkenheit und Liebesglück bilden eine untrennbare Einheit," and "Seine Knechtschaft bei Omphale wird hier als Beweis für seine Genußfähigkeit gefeiert." The burlesque, comic treatment in literature by e.g. Ovid at *Fasti* 2.303–58, where Heracles' cross-dressing misleads the unfortunate Faunus into attempting to rape him instead of Omphale (thus providing Ovid with a Greek aetion for why Faunus and his ministers the Luperci do without clothing), might make us pause before accepting that the motif was seen in an entirely positive light. We should bear in mind, however, that Omphale and Heracles' exchange of clothing is part of their merry-making on the eve of a festival of Bacchus the discoverer of wine, and that it takes the place of the couple's lovemaking, for they wish to remain pure for the festival.

Chapter 5. An Eye for the New

1. The association is made by Onians (1979) 128, followed by B. H. Fowler (1989) 150–53. Less convincing perhaps is his association (at p. 125, followed by Fowler ibid.) of the poem with the thorn-pulling episode of *Id.* 4, where there is no evidence of an erotic context.

2. Ajootian (1996) admits that the ascription has never been seriously challenged, but suggests that it should be reconsidered in the light of motifs it shares with early Augustan compositions, in particular the so-called Ildefonso group.

3. Shapiro (1984).

4. Levi (1941) 224–25 explores the meaning of dwarves in the original publication of the ithyphallic dwarf in the later Imperial mosaic pavement at Antioch. Dasen (1993) does not take her study of dwarves past the Classical period.

5. Levi (1941) 228–29.

6. Giuliani (1987) 716–21; P. Zanker (1998) 28; on the "pan-Alexandrian" aspect of the motif see Stewart (1996a).

7. Ridgway (1971) 351; Hebert (1989).

8. P. Zanker (1989) 62–69.

9. See e.g. Pollitt (1986) 1–16; Nicosia (1968) 97–99, for the growing interest in the countryside; H. Meyer (1987) 25 on "Einfigurgruppen" like the "red" Marsyas as a result of the Hellenistic experience of Tyche, "Fortune," in the destruction of the poleis and the Persian kingdom and in the changing fortunes occasioned by the struggles of the Diadochi.

10. Bing (1988); cf. Cameron (1995) 24–103, esp. 32–33.

11. See especially Habicht (1997) on polis life in Athens after Alexander, with p. 366 n. 1 for literature on the other Hellenistic poleis.

12. P. Zanker (1995a), (1998) 14, 103–6.

13. P. Zanker (1993) 87–89.

14. P. Zanker (1995b) 260–61.

15. P. Zanker (1998) esp. 13–15, 81–85, 103–6. See also now Stähli (1999) 233–300.

16. P. Zanker (1998) 87–89.

17. P. Zanker (1989) 56–62, (1998) 17–22.

18. On Theocritus' strategic use of Aphrodite and love to make the royal family accessible to the lives and tastes of Alexandria's Greek and Macedonian citizenry, see esp. Griffiths (1979) 65–66, 71–82, 104–6, 116–28.

19. Stewart (1993b) 153–58 and (1997) 216–19 for lit. and discussion; see above, p. 97.

20. Von Hesberg (1996) esp. 91–96.

21. Koenen (1977) 79–96; see G. Zanker (1989) and Stephens (2003) 7 n. 14 for reservations concerning Koenen's use of Egyptian material in a Greek poem.

22. Examples at Griffiths (1979) 53–58, 66–67, 70, 83, 91–98, 104–6; G. Zanker (1987) 179–81; Hunter (1996) 11–1.3, 27.

23. Fraser (1972) 1.18–19.

24. G. Zanker (1989) 96.

25. See now Stähli (1999) 235–55. The audience for these displays of wealth will, moreover, have been mainly Greco-Macedonian—people who will have had an interest in the Hellenic origins and nature of the benefactions. The statuary depicting the Ptolemies and their queens similarly followed a strict policy of segregation under the first three

royal families, with Greek styles and materials for Greek viewership, Egyptian for Egyptian, though the traditions merge after Raphia: Pollitt (1986) 250–63; G. Zanker (1989); R. R. R. Smith (1991) 210–11; cf. Bieber (1961) 89–95, who fails to distinguish between the periods when she claims that the Ptolemies adapted themselves to ancient civilizations more than other Hellenistic monarchs (so also e.g. Onians [1979] 69–71; Spivey [1996] 188–205; cf. Stephens (2003) esp. 7 n. 14).

26. On genre-crossing see esp. Legrand (1898) 413–36; Kroll (1924) 202–24; Rossi (1971); Schwinge (1981); G. Zanker (1987) 7–8, 133–227; and Cameron (1995) 146–64.

27. G. Zanker (1987) 164–65. On the other hand, at pp. 167–68 I argued, with statistics, that Theocritus tried to make the hexameters of his "low-life" pieces convey the feel of "everyday" conversation by admitting a high incidence of the definite article; I further argued that Theocritus thereby set off his "low-life mimes" from the other branches of his poetry, where the incidence of the definite article is low, in accordance with traditional epic practice. I restated my position at G. Zanker (1998) 231 n. 11 (q.v. for further discussion and intervening lit.). And now the idea appears, as if some new thing, in Hunter (1996) 39–40.

28. G. Zanker (1998).

29. P. Zanker (1998). See now also Stähli (1999) 126–32.

30. Kerkhecker (1997).

31. G. Zanker (1987) 53 n. 53, 83, followed by Stanzel (1995) 142; cf. Nicosia (1968) 79–94; Onians (1979) 128; Pollitt (1986) 133–34.

32. Pollitt (1986) 133–34; Bieber (1961) 148; P. Zanker (1974) 73.

33. P. Zanker (1974) 71–74; cf. R. R. R. Smith (1991) on ill. 171, who places it in the third century.

34. R. R. R. Smith (1991) 139.

35. Bieber (1961) figs. 633–35.

36. Bieber (1961) 14–15; Boardman (1995) 52–53; Ridgway (1997) 259–60; P. Zanker (1998) 14–15.

37. See above, p. 192 n. 2. The Hermes with Baby Dionysus would be an obvious example of experimentation with unheroic themes and the grand style, but its attribution to Praxiteles has been disproved by Ajootian (1996) 103–10, who, however, concludes by saying: "While we can be reasonably certain that the Hermes is not a fourth-century work, the question still remains: does it copy a sculpture by Praxiteles?"

38. Bieber (1961) 111, 114. See Ajootian (1996) 113–16 on the problems involved in relating extant Erotes to Praxiteles' originals.

39. Bieber (1961) 136–56; cf. P. Zanker (1998) 11–12.

40. Bieber (1961) 95.

41. R. R. R. Smith (1991) 137.

42. P. Zanker (1974) 74–75.

43. Pollitt (1986) 175.
44. Pollitt (1986) 167.
45. Bieber (1961) 159–60.
46. Cunningham (1971) on 4.20–26.
47. *Progression of Animals* 710b12–17; cf. *Parts of Animals* 686b8–12.
48. Pollitt (1986) 141–47.
49. On the pathos of this group see below, pp. 153–55.
50. But see above, p. 175 n. 5 on Maderna-Lauter's (1999) association of the Scythian with the "red" Marsyas type. For a photograph of the Scythian see Stewart (1990) pl. 749.
51. Von Blanckenhagen (1975) 196; H. Meyer (1987) 24.
52. See in general Himmelmann (1971).
53. On eclecticism's enrichment of viewing, see in general P. Zanker (1998) 8, 23–25, 39, 48–49, 65–67, 101–2.
54. Stewart (1993a) 195 and, generally, 15–102, 191–209. See also Svenson (1995) 12 and Bergmann (1998) 16–39.
55. Further strictures against comparable experimentation are enunciated at *Laws* 656c–57b, 660b, 669b–70e.
56. Text in Powell (1925) 173–74.
57. Fraser (1972) 1.216, 666.
58. See esp. Meincke (1965) 89–94; Griffiths (1979) 71–82.
59. See Mineur (1984) 163–82; Bing (1988) 128–39.
60. Rolley (1994) 22.
61. Plutarch, *On Isis and Osiris* 24.360d; see Stewart (1993a) 10–11, 37, 197–98.
62. And yet his own statue of Alexander holding a lance involved an essay in genre-mixing, for it was a phenomenal-realist response to the categorical-idealist representation of heroes formulated in the Classical period by works such as Polyclitus' Doryphorus; see Stewart (1990) 189 and (1995), though perhaps there is less reason for pessimism than he expresses at (1995) 249 about evidence for the literary concept of genres: see the material I assembled at G. Zanker (1987) 133–54. In a way, the statue represents a statement on what Lysippus proposed as the limits of genre-mixing in this area, and, for all his artistic innovativeness, he is surprisingly close to Plato's conservatism here.
63. See Stewart (1990) 51–52; Pekáry (1978) esp. 729.
64. Svenson (1995) 71–73, 209–10 with cat. no. 43 (pl. 32); Bergmann (1998) 13, 26, 29–30, 32, 60–61, 114.

Chapter 6. Viewing Pleasure and Pain

1. P. Zanker (1998).
2. Neumer-Pfau (1982); Havelock (1995).

3. Pliny, *NH* 36.20–21. Not even Havelock (1995) challenges this story, despite her thesis that the Cnidia was originally not perceived pruriently as displaying modesty or shame, but rather as simply stating the goddess's sovereign power. At one point, Havelock accepts that Praxiteles designed the Cnidia with the specific requirements of Aphrodite's cult at Cnidus in mind, also tailoring it to an eastern canon of the goddess: Havelock (1995) 28–29. But even if the Cnidians found her nudity "familiar and acceptable," this acceptance would have been localized and not shared by all Greeks of the period; the story of the Coans' reaction shows that.

4. Havelock (1995) 95–98.

5. R. R. R. Smith (1991) 81.

6. Ridgway (1990) 98. Later significant variations on the theme include the mid- or late third-century Capitoline Aphrodite (Ill. 24) (dated by Havelock [1995] 74–76 to after 100 B.C.), right hand rising up to cover breasts, left over pubes; the Crouching Aphrodite (Ill. 25; Ridgway [1990: 230–32], 356 dates her to after 200 B.C.; she is followed by Havelock [1995] 80–83), whom R. R. R. Smith (1991) 80 regards as no longer conceivable as a cult statue; and the Melian Aphrodite (Ill. 31) of ca. 100 B.C. (Havelock [1995] 93–98). The Aphrodite Kallipygos (Ill. 27) is now firmly classified by Havelock (1995) 98–101 as late Hellenistic.

7. Theocritus, *Id.* 15.128–30; Boardman (1995) fig. 285.

8. Züchner (1942) 5–27, esp. 19–22 (Klappspiegel 22, 23, 24), 100–101 (Bronzerelief 1); Schwarzmaier (1997) s.v. Aphrodite, sitzend, esp. 279–80 (cat. no. 114), 290 (cat. no. 135), 318–19 (cat. no. 206), 319–20 (cat. no. 209) (with lit.).

9. Havelock (1995) esp. 103–11.

10. G. Zanker (1987) 204–7.

11. R. R. R. Smith (1991) 79–83.

12. Havelock (1995) 69–101.

13. Simon (1995) 135; on Jason's cloak cf. Hunter (1993) 52–59, Manakidou (1993) 102–42, 143–56; on Zeus's ball, Thiel (1993) 90–105. On art's influence on poetry's description of the erotic moment, see e.g. Spivey (1996) 186, who claims that the Cnidia lies behind the poetic descriptions of erotic beauty as found in *Chaereas and Callirhoe* 2.2.2. Elvira (1977–78) 40 argues that the veiled female faces in Apollonius' *Argonautica* are inspired by contemporary painting. The motif in poetry of Aphrodite pampering herself may also have been trained by paintings like Apelles' Aphrodite Anadyomene, especially given Apelles' connections with Alexandria. Callimachus' Athene bathing may have been shaped by the vases depicting Actaeon and Artemis (von Blanckenhagen [1975] 194 with nn. 3–5, who at p. 193 with n. 2 also sees late Classical forerunners of the Crouching Aphrodite, again principally on vases, which might

have influenced the poetic evocations of Aphrodite as well). B. H. Fowler (1989) 137–55 examines eroticism in poetry and art to establish the "Hellenistic aesthetic" rather than to detect influences.

14. See Lennox (1980); G. Zanker (1987) 205–6; Campbell (1994) on 36–37.

15. G. Zanker (1987) 206.

16. Above, pp. 16–19.

17. Lines 105–10. For the possibility of Anchises' blinding see Gow (1952) on 106–7.

18. *Od.* 8.334–43.

19. *Il.* 5.428–30; cf. Diomedes at lines 348–51 and Athene at 418–25.

20. This is emphasized by Havelock (1995) esp. 16–37.

21. Bieber (1961) 159–60.

22. See now Havelock (1995) 55–58, 104–9.

23. Details in Ridgway (2000) 147–49.

24. *LIMC* 3 (1986) s.v. Dirke 7, with 642–43 (Heger). The recent lowering of the date by scholars is detailed above, chapter 2, n. 53. The group's influence can be gauged by the Pompeian paintings in ills. 12–16 of the LIMC entry.

25. A similar procedure can be seen in the "white" Marsyas group: his executioner is horrifically unmoved by Marsyas' terror (see below). We feel the pathos of the two victims, though they are both evildoers.

26. This detail contradicts the common opinion that the woman is already dead, as does the fact that her left foot is on the tips of its toes in an effort to restore her balance: see e.g. Bieber (1961) 80 and Stewart (1997) 220; cf. e.g. Pollitt (1986) 86–89.

27. See above, pp. 30–33 with n. 5 for other reconstructions of the group.

28. Pollitt (1986) 118.

29. Simon (1976) pl. 133, with discussion at p. 107.

30. The depiction of physical suffering in a frieze format, which can offer only a limited viewing angle, is to be found at every step on the Pergamon Gigantomachy. One example which may stand for many: the giant being bitten on the lower back of his head by Artemis' dog and trying to ward off the animal's attack by driving a finger of his right hand into its left eye, thus revealing the matted hair in his right armpit.

31. While retaining the traditional view that the victors were not depicted in the Suicidal Gaul group, Hölscher (1985) sees the concentration on the Gaul and other defeated enemies, historical and (like Marsyas) mythical, as the product of the Hellenistic feeling that sovereigns and gods were elevated so far beyond human suffering that Tyche filled the gap and held sway there. Though this conjecture is no longer supported by the notion that the Suicidal Gaul was free-standing, it is

still defensible given the extant evidence of the concentration on the victims' suffering. Hölscher further sees the pathos of these groups as paralleled in the "tragic" history of Duris and Phylarchus (pp. 130, 134), but the present chapter may help widen the net to include Hellenistic poetry as well.

32. Stewart (1990) 206; Pollitt (1986) 13, 86–89. Schalles (1985) 80–100, in an approach similar to Stewart's, sees the group as exemplifying the lack of Greek μετριότης (*metriotês*, "moderation"). Interestingly, Stewart (1997) 220 has more recently emphasized the chieftain's barbarity and played down any sympathy the Pergamene viewer would have felt for him and his wife. But calling the Celts' heads "satyrlike" and their physiques "un-Greek" seems to me to ignore the sense of engagement evidenced by the anthropological realism expended on the rendering of Celtic physiognomy. Especially given the depiction of the wife's submission and suffering to the point of death, it would appear a little extreme to minimize the Pergamene viewer's empathy for the figures, and in fact Stewart still sees pathos as one element in the group's conception. Finally, if the group's subject were so utterly beyond the pale, wild, cowardly, and monstrous, why the oversize and monumental form and execution? Stewart must postulate very grand Pergamene cavalrymen indeed in order to introduce a dignified encomiastic element into the scene as he paints it.

33. Stewart (1990) pls. 245–48.

34. Stewart (1990) 144.

35. Boardman (1985) 175–77, pls. 133.1, 133.2, and 133.3 = LIMC 6 (1992) s.v. Niobidai cat. nos. 21a, b, c (Geominy); Geominy (ibid.) 918 dates the Horti Sallustiani Niobids to 440 B.C.

36. See especially Boardman (1985) pl. 133.1 (= LIMC 6 [1992] s.v. Niobidai cat. no. 21a [Geominy]), the staggering girl trying to extract an arrow from her back, whose face seems to register the pain only minimally. Cf. the Florentine Niobids (LIMC 6 [1992] cat. no. 23 [Geominy]), where the same is observable: see for example LIMC 6 (1992) cat. no. 23k[1] (Geominy), a cowering girl, with a gesture of fear and a relatively untroubled facial expression. Geominy at LIMC 6 (1992) 926–27 inclines one to a fourth-century dating. Hölscher (1985) 130–31 argues for a late Hellenistic dating on stylistic grounds, but the lack of pathos in the faces of the Florentine Niobids comes as a surprise in late Hellenistic sculpture: there is none of Laocoön's agony here.

37. P. Zanker (1989) 50–55. Cf. Ridgway (1990) 337, who summarily follows Simon (1984) in taking the old woman as possibly being some sort of priestess of Dionysus and not just an old derelict who has seen better days; Zanker's monograph (1989) appeared too late for her to consider. She similarly regards the Old Market Woman in New York as a

participant at a Dionysiac festival, rather than as peddling her wares, and considers that she conformed with the positive response to "old age and ravaged faces": Ridgway (1990) 333, 338. This thinking is present in von Hesberg (1986); see above, p. 24.

38. P. Zanker (1989) esp. 22–39.

39. A good example of this stock figure of ridicule can be found in Fantham (1994) 119, with comment at p. 118.

40. So P. Zanker (1989) 62–69. The statue also contrasts with pieces on similar themes in the Hellenistic period, like the old woman, probably not a hetaera, in a sordidly inebriated state, who figures on a bronze bottle (Bieber [1961] fig. 586). The Drunken Old Woman of the Lagynophoria may therefore have been unique in the Hellenistic age as well.

41. P. Zanker (1989) 43–48, 74–77.

42. Erbse (1953) 186–87; Fraser (1972) 634; Rengakos (1994) 29, 42.

43. See Gow and Scholfield (1953) on *Theriaca* 187–89.

44. Erbse (1953) 189 n. 5; Fraser (1972) 634; Rengakos (1994) 136.

45. Erbse (1953) 188.

46. Most (1981) 188–96.

47. Boardman (1995) 116 with ill. 129. On the childbirth stelae and related vases (taken up by some of the painted stelae from Demetrias), see now Gray and Stewart (2000) 248–74.

48. Hollis (1990).

49. See G. Zanker (1987) 209–14 for a discussion of the poem's realism, which is obviously related to its evocation of pain and pathos. Further substantiation for the interpretation of all the fragments discussed in what follows are found in Hollis (1990).

50. G. Zanker (1987) 133–54, with 139–45; see G. Zanker (2000) for the social reference.

51. Cf. the funerary epigrams on fishermen etc.: e.g. Callimachus 34, 48, 49 *HE*, Hedylus 10 *HE*, Leonidas 20 *HE*, Theocritus 11 *HE*.

52. See e.g. Rossi (1971); G. Zanker (1987) 7–14, 133–227; Depew and Obbink (2000).

53. G. Zanker (2000).

54. I have discussed these terms at length at G. Zanker (1987) 7–14, 133–227.

55. *Il.* 9.411 (διχθαδίας κῆρας), Callimachus *Fr.* 239. 32 *SH* (διχθαδίους φονέας): see for discussion G. Zanker (1998) 227–28.

Bibliography

Acosta-Hughes, B. 2002. *Polyeideia: The* Iambi *of Callimachus and the Archaic Iambic Tradition. Hellenistic Culture and Society* 35. Berkeley, Los Angeles, London.

Adriani, A. 1959. *Divagazioni intorno ad una coppa paesistica del museo di Alessandria.* Rome.

Ajootian, A. 1996. "Praxiteles." In O. Palagia and J. J. Pollitt (eds.), *Personal Styles in Greek Sculpture. Yale Classical Studies* 30. Cambridge. Pp. 91–129.

———. 1997. "The Only Happy Couple: Hermaphrodites and Gender." In A. O. Koloski-Ostrow and C. L. Lyons (eds.), *Naked Truths: Women, Sexuality and Gender in Classical Art and Archaeology.* London. Pp. 220–42.

Andreae, B. 1998. *Schönheit des Realismus: Auftraggeber, Schöpfer, Betrachter hellenistischer Plastik. Kulturgeschichte der antiken Welt* 77. Mainz/Rhein.

Arnott, W. G. 1978. "The Theocritus Cup in Liverpool." *Quaderni urbinati di cultura classica* 29:129–34.

———. 1984. "Lycidas and Double Perspectives: A Discussion of Theocritus' Seventh Idyll," *Estudios clásicos* 87:333–46.

———. 1988. Review of G. Zanker, *Realism in Alexandrian Poetry: A Literature and Its Audience* (London, 1987). *Liverpool Classical Monthly* 13.1:11–13.

Barkhuizen, J. H. 1979. "The Psychological Characterization of Medea in Apollonius of Rhodes, *Argonautica* 3, 744–824." *Acta classica* 22:33–48.

Barr-Sharrar, B. 1982. "Dionysos and the Derveni Krater." *Archaeology* 35.6:13–19.

Barringer, J. M. 1995. *Divine Escorts: Nereids in Archaic and Classical Greek Art.* Ann Arbor.

Bastianini, G., and Gallazzi, C., with the collaboration of C. Austin. 2001. *Posidippo di Pella: Epigrammi (P. Mil. Vogl. VIII 309). Papiri dell' Università degli Studi di Milano 8.* Milan.

Bérard, C., and Durand, J. L. 1989. "Entering the Imagery." In C. Bérard et al., *A City of Images: Iconography and Society in Ancient Greece.* Princeton. Pp. 23–37.

Bergmann, M. 1998. *Die Strahlen der Herrscher: Theomorphes Herrscherbild und politische Symbolik im Hellenismus und in der römischen Kaiserzeit.* Mainz.

Bieber, M. 1961. *The Sculpture of the Hellenistic Age.* 2d ed. New York.

Bing, P. 1988. "Theocritus' Epigrams on the Statues of Ancient Poets." *Antike und Abendland* 34:117–23.

———. 1989. *The Well-Read Muse: Past and Present in Callimachus and the Hellenistic Poets. Hypomnemata* 90. Göttingen.

———. 1993. "Impersonation of Voice in Callimachus' *Hymn to Apollo.*" *Transactions of the American Philological Association* 123:181–98.

———. 1995. "Ergänzungsspiel in the Epigrams of Callimachus." *Antike und Abendland* 41:115–31.

von Blanckenhagen, P. H. 1975. "Der ergänzende Betrachter: Bemerkungen zu einem Aspekt hellenistischer Kunst." In *Wandlungen: Studien zur antiken und neueren Kunst, Ernst Homann-Wedeking gewidmet.* Waldsassen. Pp. 193–201.

Boardman, J. 1985. *Greek Sculpture: The Classical Period: A Handbook.* London.

———. 1989. *Athenian Red Figure Vases: The Classical Period: A Handbook.* London.

———. 1995. *Greek Sculpture: The Late Classical Period and Sculpture in Colonies and Overseas: A Handbook.* London.

Boehm, G., and Pfotenhauer, H. (eds.). 1995. *Beschreibungskunst-Kunstbeschreibung: Ekphrasis von der Antike bis zur Gegenwart.* Munich.

von Bothmer, D. 1984. "A Greek and Roman Treasury." *Bulletin of the Metropolitan Museum of Art*, summer: 1–72.

Brendel, O. J. 1995. *Etruscan Art.* 2d ed. with an additional bibliography by F. R. S. Ridgway. New Haven and London.

Brilliant, R. 1984. *Visual Narratives: Storytelling in Etruscan and Roman Art.* Ithaca and London.

Brunn, H. 1879. "Die griechischen Bukoliker und die bildende Kunst." *Sitzungsberichte der Bayerischen Akademie der Wissenschaften, Philosophisch-Philologisch-Historische Klasse* 2:1–20 (= *Kleine Schriften*, vol. 3 [Leipzig, 1906]. Pp. 217–28).

Bulard, M. 1926. *Description des revêtements peints à sujets religieux. Exploration archéologique de Délos* 9, ensemble no. 25:133–49.

Bulloch, A. W., Gruen, E. S., Long, A. A., and Stewart, A. F. (eds.). 1993. *Images and Ideologies: Self-Definition in the Hellenistic World. Hellenistic Culture and Society* 12. Berkeley, Los Angeles, London.

Burton, J. B. 1995. *Theocritus' Urban Mimes: Mobility, Gender, and Patronage. Hellenistic Culture and Society* 12. Berkeley, Los Angeles, London.

Cahen, É. 1929. *Callimaque et son oeuvre poétique.* Paris.

Cameron, A. 1995. *Callimachus and His Critics.* Princeton.

Campbell, D. A. 1991. *Greek Lyric.* Vol. 3. Cambridge, Mass., and London.

Campbell, M., 1994. *A Commentary on Apollonius Rhodius Argonautica III 1–471. Mnemosyne* Suppl. 141. Leiden, New York, Cologne.

Carroll-Spillecke, M. 1985. *Landscape Depictions in Greek Relief Sculpture: Development and Conventionalization.* Frankfurt.

Chiron, P. 1993. *Démétrios: Du style.* Paris.

Clauss, J. J. 1993. *The Best of the Argonauts: The Redefinition of the Epic Hero in Book 1 of Apollonius'* Argonautica. *Hellenistic Culture and Society* 10. Berkeley, Los Angeles, London.

Corso, A., 1992. "L'Afrodite Capitolina e l'arte di Cefisodoto il giovane." *Quaderni ticinesi di numismatica e antichità classiche* 21:131–49.

Cunningham, I. C. 1971. *Herodas: Mimiamboi.* Oxford.

Damon, C. 1995. "Narrative and Mimesis in the *Idylls* of Theocritus." *Quaderni urbinati di cultura classica* 51:101–23.

Dasen, V. 1993. *Dwarfs in Ancient Egypt and Greece.* Oxford.

DeForest, M. M. 1994. *Apollonius'* Argonautica: *A Callimachean Epic. Mnemosyne* Suppl. 142. Leiden.

Depew, M. 1992. "ἰαμβεῖον καλεῖται νῦν: Genre, Occasion, and Imitation in Callimachus, frr. 191 and 203 Pf." *Transactions of the American Philological Association* 122:313–30.

———. 1993. "Mimesis and Aetiology in the *Hymns* of Callimachus." In M. A. Harder, R. F. Regtuit, and G. C. Wakker (eds.), *Callimachus. Hellenistica Groningana* 1. Groningen. Pp. 57–77.

Depew, M., and Obbink, D. (eds.). 2000. *Matrices of Genre: Authors, Canons, and Society.* Cambridge, Mass., and London.

Dohrn, T. 1960. *Die Tyche von Antiochia.* Berlin.

Dover, K. J. 1971. *Theocritus: Select Poems.* Basingstoke and London.

Duchemin, J. 1963. "A propos de l'Héraclès Tueur de Lion." In *Miscellanea di studi alessandrini in memoria di Augusto Rostagni.* Turin. Pp. 311–21.

Elsner, J. 1995. *Art and the Roman Viewer: The Transformation of Art from the Pagan World to Christianity.* Cambridge.

———. 2000. "Between Mimesis and Divine Power: Visuality in the Greco-Roman World." In R. Nelson (ed.), *Visuality before and beyond the Renaissance: Seeing as Others Saw.* Cambridge. Pp. 45–69.

Elsner, J., and Rubiés, J.-P. 1999. "Introduction." In J. Elsner and J.-P.

Rubiés (eds.), *Voyages and Visions: Towards a Cultural History of Travel.* London. Pp. 1–56.

Elvira, M. A. 1977–78. "Apolonio de Rodas y la pintura del primer helenismo." *Archivo Español de Arqueología* 50–51:33–46.

Erbse, H. 1953. "Homerscholien und hellenistische Glossare bei Apollonios Rhodios." *Hermes* 81:163–96.

Fantham, E. 1994. *Women in the Classical World: Image and Text.* With H. P. Foley, N. B. Kampen, S. B. Pomeroy, and H. A. Shapiro. New York and Oxford.

Fantuzzi, M. 1985. *Bionis Smyrnaei Adonidis Epitaphium. Arca* 18. Liverpool.

Fantuzzi, M. and Hunter, R. L. 2002. *Muse e modelli: la poesia ellenistica da Alessandro Magno ad Augusto.* Roma-Bari.

Farrington, B. 1953. *Greek Science: Its Meaning for Us.* Harmondsworth.

Feeney, D. P. 1991. *The Gods in Epic.* Oxford.

Fowler, B. H. 1989. *The Hellenistic Aesthetic.* Madison, Wisconsin.

Fowler, D. P. 1991. "Narrate and Describe: The Problem of Ekphrasis." *Journal of Roman Studies* 81:25–35.

Franke, P. 1990. "'τῶν Ἀκαδημιακῶν στραγγαλίδων κοπίς': Zu einem Münzbildnis des Stoikers Chrysippus." In K.-O. Apel (ed.), *Zur Rekonstruktion der praktischen Philosophie: Gedenkschrift für Karl-Heinz Ilting.* Stuttgart/Bad Cannstatt. Pp. 77–88.

Fraser, P. M. 1972. *Ptolemaic Alexandria.* Oxford.

Frontisi-Ducroux, F., and Vernant, J. P. 1997. *Dans l'oeil du miroir.* Paris.

Fuhrer, T. 1992. *Die Auseinandersetzung mit den Chorlyrikern in den Epinikien des Kallimachos. Schweizerische Beiträge zur Altertumswissenschaft* 23. Basel/Kassel.

———. 1993. "Callimachus' Epinician Poems." In M. A. Harder, R. F. Regtuit, and G. C. Wakker (eds.), *Callimachus. Hellenistica Groningana* 1. Groningen. Pp. 79–97.

Furtwängler, A. 1964. *Masterpieces of Greek Sculpture.* Ed. A. N. Oikonomedes. Chicago.

Gelzer, T. 1985. "Mimus und Kunsttheorie bei Herondas, Mimiambus 4." In C. Schäublin (ed.), *Catalepton: Festschrift für Bernhard Wyss zum 80. Geburtstag.* Basel. Pp. 96–116.

Giouri, E. 1978. Ὁ κρατήρας τοῦ Δερβενίου. Βιβλ. τῆς ἐν Ἀθήναις Ἀρχαιολογικῆς Ἐταιρείας. 89. Athens.

Giuliani, L. 1987. "Die seligen Krüppel: Zur Deutung von Missgestalten in der hellenistischen Kleinkunst." *Archäologischer Anzeiger:* 701–21.

Goldhill, S. 1994. "The Naive and Knowing Eye: Ecphrasis and the Culture of Viewing in the Hellenistic World." In S. Goldhill and R. Osborne (eds.), *Art and Text in Ancient Greek Culture.* Cambridge. Pp. 197–223.

Gombrich, E. H. 1976. *The Heritage of Apelles: Studies in the Art of the Renaissance.* Oxford.

Gordon, R. L. 1979. "The Real and the Imaginary: Production and Religion in the Graeco-Roman World." *Art History* 2:5–34.

Gow, A. S. F. 1952. *Theocritus.* Cambridge.

Gow, A. S. F., and Page, D. L. 1965. *The Greek Anthology: Hellenistic Epigrams.* Cambridge.

Gow, A. S. F., and Scholfield, A. F. 1953. *Nicander: The Poems and Poetical Fragments.* Cambridge.

Graf, F. 1995. "Ekphrasis: Die Entstehung der Gattung in der Antike." In G. Boehm and H. Pfotenhauer (eds.), *Beschreibungskunst-Kunstbeschreibung: Ekphrasis von der Antike bis zur Gegenwart.* Munich. Pp. 143–55.

Gray, C., and Stewart, A. F. 2000. "Confronting the Other: Childbirth, Old Age, and Death on an Attic Tombstone at Harvard." In B. Cohen (ed.), *Not the Classical Ideal: Athens and the Construction of the Other in Greek Art.* Leiden. Pp. 248–74.

Green, P. E. 2000. "Pergamon and Sperlonga: A Historian's Reaction." In N. T. de Grummond and B. S. Ridgway (eds.), *From Pergamon to Sperlonga: Sculpture and Context. Hellenistic Culture and Society* 34. Berkeley, Los Angeles, London. Pp. 166–90.

Griffiths, F. T. 1979. *Theocritus at Court. Mnemosyne* Suppl. 55. Leiden.

Gutzwiller, K. 1981. *Studies in the Hellenistic Epyllion. Beiträge zur klassischen Philologie* 114. Königstein/Ts.

———. 1991. *Theocritus' Pastoral Analogies: The Formation of a Genre.* Madison, Wisconsin.

———. 2002. "A New Hellenistic Poetry Book: P. Mil. Vogl. VIII 309." At www.apaclassics.org/Publications/Posidippus. January 2002.

Habicht, C. 1997. *Athens from Alexander to Antony.* Trans. D. L. Schneider. Cambridge, Mass., and London.

Händel, P. 1954. *Beobachtungen zur epischen Technik des Apollonios Rhodios. Zetemata* 8. Munich.

Havelock, C. M. 1981. *Hellenistic Art: The Art of the Classical World from the Death of Alexander the Great to the Battle of Actium.* 2d ed. New York and London.

———. 1995. *The Aphrodite of Knidos and Her Successors: A Historical Review of the Female Nude in Greek Art.* Ann Arbor.

Hebert, B. 1987. "Der Löwenkampf des Herakles: Über das Verhältnis von Literatur und bildender Kunst im 25. Idyll des Theokrit." *Grazer Beiträge* 14:151–65.

———. 1989. *Schriftquellen zur hellenistischen Kunst: Plastik, Malerei und Kunsthandwerk der Griechen vom vierten bis zum zweiten Jahrhundert. Grazer Beiträge* Supplementband 4. Graz-Horn.

Heres, H. 1997. "The Myth of Telephos in Pergamon." In R. Dreyfus and
    E. Schraudolph (eds.), *Pergamon: The Telephos Frieze from the Great Al-
    tar.* Vol. 2. San Francisco. Pp. 83–108.
von Hesberg, H. 1986. "Das Münchner Bauernrelief: Bukolische Utopie
    oder Allegorie individuellen Glücks?" *Münchner Jahrbuch der bilden-
    den Kunst,* ser. 3, 37:7–32.
———. 1987. "Mechanische Kunstwerke und ihre Bedeutung für die
    höfische Kunst des frühen Hellenismus." *Marburger Winckelmann-
    Programm:* 47–72.
———. 1988. "Bildsyntax und Erzählweise in der hellenistischen
    Flächenkunst." *Jahrbuch des Deutschen Archäologischen Instituts* 103:
    309–65.
———. 1996. "Privatheit und Öffentlichkeit der frühhellenistischen
    Hofarchitektur." In W. Hoepfner and G. Brands (eds.), *Basileia: Die
    Paläste der hellenistischen Könige.* Mainz. Pp. 84–96.
———. 1999. "The King on Stage." In B. Bergmann and C. Kondoleon
    (eds.), *The Art of Ancient Spectacle. Centre for Advanced Study in the Vi-
    sual Arts Symposium Papers* 34. New Haven and London. Pp. 65–75.
Heubeck, A., and Hoekstra, A. 1989. *A Commentary on Homer's Odyssey,
    Volume II: Books IX–XI.* Oxford.
Himmelmann, N. 1971. *Archäologisches zum Problem der griechischen
    Sklaverei. Akademie der Wissenschaften und der Literatur, Mainz: Abhand-
    lungen der Geistes- und Sozialwissenschaftlichen Klasse* 13. Wiesbaden.
———. 1989. *Herrscher und Athlet: Die Bronzen vom Quirinal.* Milan.
Hollis, A. S. 1990. *Callimachus: Hecale.* Oxford.
Hölscher, T. 1985. "Die Geschlagenen und Ausgelieferten in der Kunst
    des Hellenismus." *Antike Kunst* 28:120–36, with pls. 30.1–30.5.
Holmberg, I. E. 1998. "Μῆτις and Gender in Apollonius Rhodius' *Ar-
    gonautica.*" *Transactions of the American Philological Association* 128:
    135–59.
Hunter, R. L. 1993. *The Argonautica of Apollonius: Literary Studies.* Cam-
    bridge.
———. 1996. *Theocritus and the Archaeology of Greek Poetry.* Cambridge.
———. 1999. *Theocritus: A Selection.* Cambridge.
Hurwit, J. M. 1991. "The Representation of Nature in Early Greek Art."
    In D. Buitron-Oliver (ed.), *New Perspectives in Early Greek Art. Centre
    for Advanced Study in the Visual Arts Symposium Papers* 16. New Haven
    and London. Pp. 33–62.
Innes, D.C. 1995. *Demetrius: On Style.* In *Aristotle, Longinus, Demetrius;
    Aristotle: Poetics* (ed. S. Halliwell), *Longinus: On the Sublime* (ed. W. H.
    Fyfe; rev. D. Lucas), *Demetrius: On Style* (ed. D.C. Innes; based on
    W. Rhys Roberts). Cambridge, Mass. Pp. 311–525.

Jackson, S. 1999. "Apollonius' *Argonautica:* The Theseus / Ariadne Desertion." *Rheinisches Museum* 142:152–57.

Jentoft-Nilsen, M. 1983. "A Krater by Asteas." In *Occasional Papers on Antiquities* 1: *Greek Vases in the J. Paul Getty Museum.* Malibu. Pp. 139–48.

Katz, E. 1980. *The International Film Encyclopedia.* London and Basingstoke.

Kerkhecker, A. 1997. "Μουσέων ἐν ταλάρῳ—Dichter und Dichtung am Ptolemäerhof." *Antike und Abendland* 43:124–44.

———. 1999. *Callimachus' Book of Iambi.* Oxford.

Knell, H. 1995. *Die Nike von Samothrake: Typus, Form, Bedeutung und Wirkungsgeschichte eines rhodischen Sieges-Anathems im Kabirenheiligtum von Samothrake.* Darmstadt.

Köhnken, A. 1965. *Apollonios Rhodios und Theokrit: Die Hylas- und die Amykosgeschichten beider Dichter und die Frage der Priorität. Hypomnemata* 12. Göttingen.

Koenen, L. 1977. *Eine agonistische Inschrift aus Ägypten und frühptolemäische Königsfeste. Beiträge zur klassischen Philologie* 56. Meisenheim / Glan.

Kokolakis, M. M. 1976. "'Ριανὸς ὁ Κρής, ἐπικὸς τοῦ 30υ π.Χ. αἰῶνος." In M. M. Kokolakis, Φιλολογικὰ μελετήματα εἰς τὴν ἀρχαῖαν ἑλλενικὴν γραμματείαν. Athens. Pp. 129–62.

Kovacs, F. L. n.d. *Ancient Coins and Antiquities* 29. San Mateo.

Krahmer, G. 1923–24. "Stilphasen der hellenistischen Plastik." *Mitteilungen des Deutschen Archaeologischen Instituts, Römische Abteilung* 38–39:138–89.

———. 1927. "Die einansichtige Gruppe und die späthellenistische Kunst." *Nachrichten der Gesellschaft der Wissenschaften zu Göttingen, Philologisch-Historische Klasse:* 53–91.

Krieger, M. 1995. "Das Problem der Ekphrasis: Wort und Bild, Raum und Zeit—und das literarische Werk." In G. Boehm and H. Pfotenhauer (eds.), *Beschreibungskunst-Kunstbeschreibung: Ekphrasis von der Antike bis zur Gegenwart.* Munich. Pp. 41–57.

Kroll, W. 1924. *Studien zum Verständnis der römischen Literatur.* Stuttgart.

Lattimore, S. 1976. *The Marine Thiasos in Greek Sculpture. Monumenta Archaeologica* 3. Los Angeles.

Laubscher, H.-P. 1982. *Fischer und Landleute: Studien zur hellenistischen Genreplastik.* Mainz.

Laursen, S. 1992. "Theocritus' Hymn to the Dioscuri: Unity and Intention." *Classica et mediaevalia* 43:71–95.

Legrand, Ph. E. 1898. *Étude sur Théocrite.* Paris.

———. 1901. "Problèmes alexandrins, I: Pourquoi furent composés les *Hymnes* de Callimaque?" *Revue des études grecques* 3:281–312.

Lennox, P. G. 1980. "Apollonius, Argonautica 3,1ff. and Homer." *Hermes* 108:45–73.

Levi, D. 1941. "The Evil Eye and the Lucky Hunchback." In R. Stilwell (ed.), *Antioch-on-the-Orontes III: The Excavations 1937–1939*. Princeton. Pp. 220–32.

Lexicon Iconographicum Mythologiae Classicae. 1981–99. 8 vols., with 2 index vols. Zurich.

Ling, R. 1991. *Roman Painting*. Cambridge.

Lloyd-Jones, H., and Parsons, P. J. 1983. *Supplementum Hellenisticum*. Berlin and New York.

Macrides, R., and Magdalino, P. 1988. "The Architecture of Ekphrasis: Construction and Context of Paul the Silentiary's Poem on Haghia Sophia." *Byzantine and Modern Greek Studies* 12:47–82.

Maderna-Lauter, C. 1999. "Überlegungen zum 'roten' und zum 'weißen' Marsyas." In *Gedenkschrift für Andreas Linfert: Hellenistische Gruppen*. Mainz. Pp. 115–40.

Manakidou, F. 1993. *Beschreibung von Kunstwerken in der hellenistischen Dichtung: Ein Beitrag zur hellenistischen Poetik. Beiträge zur Altertumskunde* 36. Stuttgart.

Marszal, J. R. 1998. "Tradition and Innovation in Early Pergamene Sculpture." In O. Palagia and W. Coulson (eds.), *Regional Schools in Hellenistic Sculpture*. Oxford. Pp. 117–27.

———. 2000. "Ubiquitous Barbarians: Representations of the Gauls at Pergamon and Elsewhere." In N. T. de Grummond and B. S. Ridgway (eds.), *From Pergamon to Sperlonga: Sculpture and Context. Hellenistic Culture and Society* 34. Berkeley, Los Angeles, London. Pp. 191–234.

Massing, J.-M. 1990. *Du texte à l'image: La Calomnie d'Apelle et son iconographie*. Strasbourg.

Mastromarco, G. 1984. *The Public of Herondas. London Studies in Classical Philology* 11. Amsterdam.

Meincke, W. 1965. *Untersuchungen zu den enkomiastischen Gedichten Theokrits*. Diss. Kiel.

Meyboom, P. G. P. 1995. *The Nile Mosaic of Palestrina: Early Evidence of Egyptian Religion in Italy. Études préliminaires aux religions orientales dans l'empire romain* 121. Leiden, New York, Köln.

Meyer, D. 1993. "Die Einbeziehung des Lesers in den Epigrammen des Kallimachos." In M. A. Harder, R. F. Regtuit, and G. C. Wakker (eds.), *Callimachus. Hellenistica Groningana* 1. Groningen. Pp. 161–75.

Meyer, H. 1987. *Der weiße und der rote Marsyas: Eine kopienkritische Untersuchung. Münchner Archäologische Studien* 2. Munich.

Mineur, W. H. 1984. *Callimachus: Hymn to Delos. Mnemosyne* Suppl. 83. Leiden.

Moreno, P. 1994. *Scultura ellenistica*. Rome.

Most, G. W. 1981. "Callimachus and Herophilus." *Hermes* 109:188–96.

Nelson, R. S. (ed.). 2000. *Visuality before and beyond the Renaissance: Seeing as Others Saw*. Cambridge.

Neumer-Pfau, W. 1982. *Studien zur Ikonographie und gesellschaftlichen Funktion hellenistischer Aphrodite-Statuen*. Bonn.

Nicosia, S. 1968. *Teocrito e l'arte figurata*. Palermo.

Onians, J. 1979. *Art and Thought in the Hellenistic Age: The Greek World View 350–50 B.C.* London.

Osborne, R. 1994. "Framing the Centaur: Reading Fifth-century Architectural Sculpture." In S. Goldhill and R. Osborne (eds.), *Art and Text in Ancient Greek Sculpture*. Cambridge. Pp. 52–84.

Page, D. L. 1981. *Further Greek Epigrams: Epigrams before A.D. 50 from the Greek Anthology and Other Sources, Not Included in 'Hellenistic Epigrams' or 'The Garland of Philip.'* Cambridge.

Palm, J. 1965–66. "Bemerkungen zur Ekphrase in der griechischen Literatur." *Kungl. Humanistiska Vetenskapssamfundet i Uppsala*: 108–211.

Palma, B. 1981. "Il Piccolo donario pergameno." *Xenia* 1:45–84.

Parsons, P. J. 1977. "Callimachus: Victoria Berenices." *Zeitschrift für Papyrologie und Epigraphik* 25:1–50.

Pekáry, T. 1978. "Statuen in kleinasiatischen Inschriften." *Studien zur Religion und Kultur Kleinasiens: Festschr. F. K. Dörner. Études préliminaires aux religions orientales dans l'empire romain* 66. Vol. 2. Leiden. Pp. 727–44.

Pfeiffer, R. 1949–51. *Callimachus*. Oxford.

Phinney, E. 1967. "Hellenistic Painting and the Poetic Style of Apollonius." *Classical Journal* 62:145–49.

Pollitt, J. J. 1986. *Art in the Hellenistic Age*. Cambridge.

Powell, J. U. 1925. *Collectanea Alexandrina: Reliquiae minores Poetarum Graecorum Aetatis Ptolemaicae 323–146 A.C. Epicorum, Elegiacorum, Lyricorum, Ethicorum*. Oxford.

Preisshofen, F. 1979. "Kunsttheorie und Kunstbetrachtung." In H. Flashar (ed.), *Le classicisme à Rome aux Iers siècles avant et après J. C. Entretiens sur l'antiquité classique* 25. Vandoeuvres-Geneva. Pp. 263–82.

von Prittwitz und Gaffron, H.-H. 1999. "Die andere Seite der Einansichtigkeit." In *Gedenkschrift für Andreas Linfert: Hellenistische Gruppen*. Mainz. Pp. 181–86.

Reed, J. D. 1997. *Bion of Smyrna: The Fragments and the Adonis. Cambridge Classical Texts and Commentaries* 33. Cambridge.

———. 2000. "Arsinoe's Adonis and the Poetics of Ptolemaic Imperialism." *Transactions of the American Philological Association* 130:319–51.

Reinach, A. 1921. *Textes grecs et latins relatifs a l'histoire de la peinture ancienne*. Paris.

Reitz, C. 1996. *Zur Gleichnistechnik des Apollonios von Rhodos. Studien zur klassischen Philologie* 99. Frankfurt/Main.

Rengakos, A. 1994. *Apollonios Rhodios und die antike Homererklärung. Zetemata* 92. Munich.

Rice, E. E. 1983. *The Grand Procession of Ptolemy Philadelphus.* Oxford.

Ridgway, B. S. 1971. "The Setting of Greek Sculpture." *Hesperia* 40: 336–56.

———. 1981. "Greek Antecedents of Garden Sculpture." In E. B. Mac-Dougall and W. F. Jashemski (eds.), *Ancient Roman Gardens. Dumbarton Oaks Colloquium on the History of Landscape Architecture.* Washington, D.C. Pp. 7–28.

———. 1983. "Painterly and Pictorial in Greek Relief Sculpture." In W. G. Moon (ed.), *Ancient Greek Art and Iconography.* Madison, Wisconsin. Pp. 193–208.

———. 1990. *Hellenistic Sculpture I: The Styles of ca. 331–200 B.C.* Madison, Wisconsin.

———. 1997. *Fourth-Century Styles in Greek Sculpture.* Madison, Wisconsin.

———. 1999. Review of Ch. Kunze, *Der Farnesische Stier und die Dirkegruppe des Apollonios und Tauriskos* (*Jahrbuch des Deutschen Archäologischen Instituts* Ergänzungsheft 30 [Berlin 1998]). *Journal of Roman Archaeology* 12:512–20.

———. 2000. *Hellenistic Sculpture II: The Styles of ca. 200–100 B.C.* Madison, Wisconsin.

Robertson, M. 1972. "Monocrepis." *Greek, Roman and Byzantine Studies* 13:39–48.

Rolley, C. 1986. *Greek Bronzes.* Trans. R. Howell. London.

———. 1994. *La sculpture grecque I: Des origines au milieu du Ve siècle.* Paris.

Rossi, L. E. 1971. "I generi letterari e le loro leggi scritte e non scritte nelle letterature classiche." *Bulletin of the Institute of Classical Studies of the University of London* 18:69–94.

Rouveret, A. 1989. *Histoire et imaginaire de la peinture ancienne (Ve siècle av. J.-C.–Ier siècle ap. J.-C.). Bibliothèque des Écoles Françaises d'Athènes et de Rome* 274. Rome.

Sadurska, A. 1964. *Les Tables Iliaques.* Warsaw.

Salomon, N. 1997. "Making a World of Difference: Gender, Asymmetry, and the Greek Nude." In A. O. Koloski-Ostrow and C. L. Lyons (eds.), *Naked Truths: Women, Sexuality and Gender in Classical Art and Archaeology.* London. Pp. 197–219.

Schalles, H.-J. 1985. *Untersuchungen zur Kulturpolitik der pergamenischen Herrscher im dritten Jahrhundert vor Christus.* Tübingen.

Scheibler, I. 1994. *Griechische Malerei der Antike.* Munich.

Schmidt, I. 1995. *Hellenistische Statuenbasen.* Frankfurt am Main.

Schmidt, W. 1899. *Herons von Alexandria Druckwerke und Automaten-theater.* Leipzig.

Schönberger, O. 1995. "Die 'Bilder' des Philostratos." In G. Boehm and H. Pfotenhauer (eds.), *Beschreibungskunst-Kunstbeschreibung: Ekphrasis von der Antike bis zur Gegenwart.* Munich. Pp. 157–76.

Schurmann, A. 1991. *Griechische Mechanik und antike Gesellschaft. Studien zur staatlichen Förderung einer technischen Wissenschaft* 27. Stuttgart.

Schwarzmaier, A. 1997. *Griechische Klappspiegel: Untersuchungen zu Typologie und Stil. Mitteilungen des Deutschen Archäologischen Instituts, Athenische Abteilung* Beiheft 18. Berlin.

Schwinge, E.-R. 1981. "Griechische Poesie und die Lehre von der Gattungstrinität in der Moderne." *Antike und Abendland* 27:130–62.

Sens, A. 1992. "Theocritus, Homer and the Dioscuri: *Idyll* 22.137–223." *Transactions of the American Philological Association* 122:335–50.

———. 1994. "Hellenistic Reference in the Proem of Theocritus, *Idyll* 22." *Classical Quarterly* 44:66–74.

———. 1996. "A Man of Many Words: Lynceus as Speaker in Theoc. 22." In M. A. Harder, R. F. Regtuit, and G. C. Wakker (eds.), *Theocritus. Hellenistica Groningana* 2. Groningen. Pp. 187–204.

———. 1997. *Theocritus: Dioscuri (Idyll 22). Hypomnemata* 114. Göttingen.

———. 2002. "The New Posidippus, Asclepiades, and Hecataeus' Philitas-Statue." At www.apaclassics.org/Publications/Posidippus. January 2002.

Shapiro, H. A. 1980. "Jason's Cloak." *Transactions of the American Philological Association* 110:263–86.

———. 1984. "Notes on Greek Dwarfs." *American Journal of Archaeology* 88:391–92.

———. 1994. *Myth into Art: Poet and Painter in Classical Greece.* London and New York.

Simon, E. 1976. *Die griechischen Vasen.* Munich.

———. 1984. Review of H.-P. Laubscher, *Fischer und Landleute: Studien zur hellenistischen Genreplastik* (Mainz, 1982). *Göttingsche Gelehrte Anzeige* 236:31–36.

———. 1995. "Der Schild des Achilleus." In G. Boehm and H. Pfotenhauer (eds.), *Beschreibungskunst-Kunstbeschreibung: Ekphrasis von der Antike bis zur Gegenwart.* Munich. Pp. 123–41.

Smith, A. M. 1996. *Ptolemy's Theory of Visual Perception: An English Translation of the Optics. Transactions of the American Philosophical Society* 86: pt. 2. Philadelphia.

Smith, R. R. R. 1991. *Hellenistic Sculpture: A Handbook.* London.

Spengel, L. 1853–56. *Rhetores Graeci.* 3 vols. Leipzig.

Spivey, N. 1996. *Understanding Greek Sculpture: Ancient Meanings, Modern Readings*. London.

Stähler, K. 1966. *Das Unklassische im Telephosfries*. Münster.

Stähli, A. 1999. *Die Verweigerung der Lüste: Erotische Gruppen in der antiken Plastik*. Berlin.

Stansbury-O'Donnell, M. D. 1999. *Pictorial Narrative in Ancient Greek Art*. Cambridge.

Stanzel, K.-H. 1995. *Liebende Hirten: Theokrits Bukolik und die alexandrinische Poesie*. Beiträge zur Altertumswissenschaft 60. Stuttgart and Leipzig.

Steinmeyer-Schareika, A. 1978. *Das Nilmosaik von Palestrina und eine ptolemäische Expedition nach Äthiopien*. Bonn.

Stephens, S. A. 2003. *Seeing Double: Intercultural Poetics in Ptolemaic Alexandria*. Hellenistic Culture and Society 41. Berkeley, Los Angeles, London.

Stewart, A. F. 1977. *Skopas of Paros*. Park Ridge, N.J.

———. 1990. *Greek Sculpture: An Exploration*. New Haven and London.

———. 1993a. *Faces of Power: Alexander's Image and Hellenistic Politics*. Hellenistic Culture and Society 11. Berkeley, Los Angeles, London.

———. 1993b. "Narration and Allusion in the Hellenistic Baroque." In P. J. Holliday (ed.), *Narrative and Event in Ancient Art*. Cambridge. Pp. 130–74.

———. 1995. "Notes on the Reception of the Polykleitan Style: Diomedes to Alexander." In W. G. Moon (ed.), *Polykleitos, the Doryphoros, and Tradition*. Madison, Wisconsin. Pp. 246–61.

———. 1996a. "The Alexandrian Style: A Mirage?" In M. True and K. Hammer (eds.), *Alexandria and Alexandrianism*. Malibu. Pp. 231–46.

———. 1996b. "A Hero's Quest: Narrative and the Telephos Frieze." In R. Dreyfus and E. Schraudolph (eds.), *Pergamon: The Telephos Frieze from the Great Altar*. Vol. 1. San Francisco. Pp. 39–52.

———. 1996c. "Reflections." In N. B. Kampen (ed.), *Sexuality in Ancient Art: Near East, Egypt, Greece, and Italy*. Cambridge. Pp. 136–54.

———. 1997. *Art, Desire, and the Body in Ancient Greece*. Cambridge.

———. 2001. Review of Ch. Kunze, *Der Farnesische Stier und die Dirkegruppe des Apollonios und Tauriskos* (*Jahrbuch des Deutschen Archäologischen Instituts* Ergänzungsheft 30 [Berlin, 1998]). *Gnomon* 73:468–70.

Stewart, A. F., with Korres, M. (forthcoming). *Little Barbarians: A Tale of Ten Statues*.

Svenson, D. 1995. *Darstellungen hellenistischer Könige mit Götterattributen*. Archäologische Studien 10. Frankfurt.

Thiel, K. 1993. *Erzählung und Beschreibung in den Argonautika des Apollonius Rhodius: Ein Beitrag zur Poetik des hellenistischen Epos*. Palingenesia 45. Stuttgart.

Trendall A. D. 1989. *Red Figure Vases of South Italy and Sicily: A Handbook.* London.

Usher, S. 1974. *Dionysius of Halicarnassus: The Critical Essays.* Vol. 1. Cambridge, Mass.

Vasaly, A. 1993. *Representations: Images of the World in Ciceronian Oratory.* Berkeley, Los Angeles, Oxford.

Villard, F. 1973. "Painting." In J. Charbonneaux, R. Martin, and F. Villard, *Hellenistic Art 330–50 BC.* Trans. P. Green. London. Pp. 167–85.

Webb, R. 1999. "*Ekphrasis* Ancient and Modern: The Invention of a Genre." *Word and Image* 15: 7–18.

Webster, T. B. L. 1964. *Hellenistic Poetry and Art.* London.

Wegener, S. 1985. *Funktion und Bedeutung landschaftlicher Elemente in der griechischen Reliefkunst archaischer bis hellenistischer Zeit.* Frankfurt.

Weis, A. 1982. "The Motif of the Adligatus and Tree: A Study in the Sources of Pre-Roman Iconography." *American Journal of Archaeology* 86:28–41.

———. 1992. *The Hanging Marsyas and Its Copies: Roman Innovations in a Hellenistic Sculptural Tradition.* Rome.

Wrede, H. 1988. "Die tanzenden Musikanten von Mahdia und der alexandrinische Götter- und Herrscherkult." *Römische Mitteilungen* 95:97–114.

———. 1991. "Matronen im Kult des Dionysos: Zur hellenistischen 'Genreplastik.'" *Römische Mitteilungen* 98:163–88.

Zanker, G. 1977. "Callimachus' Hecale: A New Kind of Epic Hero?" *Antichthon* 11:68–77.

———. 1979. "The Love Theme in Apollonius Rhodius' Argonautica." *Wiener Studien* n.s. 13:52–75.

———. 1981. "Enargeia in the Ancient Criticism of Poetry." *Rheinisches Museum* 124:297–311.

———. 1987. *Realism in Alexandrian Poetry: A Literature and Its Audience.* London.

———. 1989. "Current Trends in the Study of Hellenic Myth in Early Third-Century Alexandrian Poetry: The Case of Theocritus." *Antike und Abendland* 35:83–103.

———. 1996. "Pictorial Description as a Supplement for Narrative: The Labour of Augeas' Stables in *Heracles Leontophonos.*" *American Journal of Philology* 117:411–23.

———. 1998. "The Concept and Use of Genre-Marking in Hellenistic Epic and Fine Art." In M. A. Harder, R. F. Regtuit, and G. C. Wakker (eds.), *Genre in Hellenistic Poetry. Hellenistica Groningana* 3. Groningen. Pp. 225–38.

———. 2000. "Aristotle's *Poetics* and the Painters." *American Journal of Philology* 121:225–35.

———. 2003. "New Light on the Literary Category of 'Ekphrastic Epigram' in Antiquity: The New Posidippus (col. X 7–XI 19 P. Mil. Vogl. VIII 309)." *Zeitschrift für Papyrologie und Epigraphik* 143: 1–4.

Zanker, P. 1974. *Klassizistische Statuen: Studien zur Veränderung des Kunstgeschmacks in der römischen Zeit*. Mainz.

———. 1988. *The Power of Images in the Age of Augustus*. Trans. H. A. Shapiro. Ann Arbor.

———. 1989. *Die Trunkene Alte: Das Lachen der Verhöhnten*. Frankfurt.

———. 1993. "The Hellenistic Grave Stelai from Smyrna: Identity and Self-Image in the Polis." In A. W. Bulloch, E. S. Gruen, A. A. Long, and A. F. Stewart (eds.), 1993. *Images and Ideologies: Self-Definition in the Hellenistic World*. Berkeley, Los Angeles, London. Pp. 212–31.

———. 1995a. *The Mask of Socrates: The Image of the Intellectual in Antiquity*. Trans. H. A. Shapiro. Berkeley, Los Angeles, Oxford.

———. 1995b. "Brüche im Bürgerbild? Zur bürgerlichen Selbstdarstellung in den hellenistischen Städten." In M. Wörrle and P. Zanker (eds.), *Stadtbild und Bürgerbild im Hellenismus*. Vestigia 47. Munich. Pp. 251–73.

———. 1998. *Eine Kunst für die Sinne: Zur hellenistischen Bilderwelt des Dionysos und der Aphrodite*. Berlin.

Ziegler, K. 1966. *Das hellenistische Epos: Ein vergessenes Kapitel griechischer Dichtung*. 2d ed. Leipzig.

Züchner, W. 1942. *Griechische Klappspiegel. Jahrbuch des Deutschen Archäologischen Instituts* Ergänzungsheft 14. Berlin.

Index

WISCONSIN STUDIES IN CLASSICS

General Editors
Richard Daniel De Puma and Patricia A. Rosenmeyer

E. A. THOMPSON
Romans and Barbarians: The Decline of the Western Empire

JENNIFER TOLBERT ROBERTS
Accountability in Athenian Government

H. I. MARROU
GEORGE LAMB, translator
A History of Education in Antiquity (Histoire de l'Education dans l'Antiquité)

ERIKA SIMON
Festivals of Attica: An Archaeological Commentary

PIERRE GRIMAL
G. MICHAEL WOLOCH, editor and translator
Roman Cities: Les villes romaines, together with *A Descriptive Catalogue of Roman Cities* by G. Michael Woloch

WARREN G. MOON, editor
Ancient Greek Art and Iconography

KATHERINE DOHAN MORROW
Greek Footwear and the Dating of Sculpture

JOHN KEVIN NEWMAN
The Classical Epic Tradition

JEANNY VORYS CANBY, EDITH PORADA, BRUNILDE SISMONDO RIDGWAY, and TAMARA STECH, editors
Ancient Anatolia: Aspects of Change and Cultural Development

ANN NORRIS MICHELINI
Euripides and the Tragic Tradition

JUDITH LYNN SEBESTA and LARISSA BONFANTE, editors
The World of Roman Costume

JENNIFER LARSON
Greek Heroine Cults

WARREN G. MOON, editor
Polykleitos, the Doryphoros, and Tradition

PAUL PLASS
The Game of Death in Ancient Rome: Arena Sport and Political Suicide

MARGARET S. DROWER
Flinders Petrie: A Life in Archaeology

SUSAN B. MATHESON
Polygnotos and Vase Painting in Classical Athens

JENIFER NEILS, editor
Worshipping Athena: Panathenaia and Parthenon

PAMELA WEBB
Hellenistic Architectural Sculpture: Figural Motifs in Western Anatolia and the Aegean Islands

BRUNILDE SISMONDO RIDGWAY
Fourth-Century Styles in Greek Sculpture

LUCY GOODISON and CHRISTINE MORRIS, editors
Ancient Goddesses: The Myths and the Evidence

JO-MARIE CLAASSEN
Displaced Persons: The Literature of Exile from Cicero to Boethius

BRUNILDE SISMONDO RIDGWAY
Hellenistic Sculpture II: The Styles of ca. 200–100 B.C.

PAT GETZ-GENTLE
Personal Styles in Early Cycladic Sculpture

CATULLUS
DAVID MULROY, translator and commentator
The Complete Poetry of Catullus

BRUNILDE SISMONDO RIDGWAY
Hellenistic Sculpture III: The Styles of ca. 100–31 B.C.

ANGELIKI KOSMOPOULOU
The Iconography of Sculptured Statue Bases in the Archaic and Classical Periods

GRAHAM ZANKER
Modes of Viewing in Hellenistic Poetry and Art